THE FAITHFUL LAWYER

FLOURISHING FROM LAW STUDY TO PRACTICE

By Nelson P. Miller

Bridge Publishing Group LLC
Getzville, New York
2012

The Faithful Lawyer: Flourishing
From Law Study to Practice

Published and distributed in all formats exclusively by:
Bridge Publishing Group LLC
39 Concetta Court
Getzville, New York 14068
United States of America
Phone: 800.758.3010
Email: mail@bridgepg.com
Website: http://www.bridgepg.com

Library of Congress Control Number: 2011938659
ISBN: 978-1-935220-40-4

Please note: *Special discounts are available for bulk orders. Please contact Bridge Publishing Group LLC for more information.*

Table of Contents

Preface

As professionals, we speak a transactional language, while not always recognizing how distinct that transactional language is. For many people who are not lawyers, faith is all that matters. Law? Leave that to the lawyers! Yet because lawyers grow accustomed to reading and speaking a transactional language bereft of overt faith references, I tried to write the text of this faith guide more like a lawyer would write, using a lawyer's language. I want the text to be readable to the lawyer's professional eye. It is difficult to translate all faith concepts completely into the language of the law, but my idea was to avoid putting off law students or lawyers who may be unaccustomed to the language of faith with which many Americans are quite comfortable and familiar.

Yet to accomplish my end of linking the lawyer's life with the forms and life of faith, I filled the footnotes with references to and quotations of faith text. My idea was to demonstrate how closely law study and practice are to faith instruction and practice. I footnoted the guide heavily, for which I apologize. Yet I hope that the footnotes illustrate for the reader how rich sacred text can be and how richly faith text can connect with law studies and practice. Most of the faith footnotes' connections to the professional text should be obvious from the content of the quoted passages. A few of the footnotes require that the reader know the passage's context. My apologies if I have assumed too much faith knowledge on the reader's part. I have learned to read faith text without the professional's jaundiced eye, appreciating faith readings, while recognizing that not all law students and lawyers do. I hope that the text is readable in its mostly professional language, as much as I hope that you see the value of the faith writings the footnotes quote and reference.

My hope is that you find the value of this guide in the interplay between the prosaic text and its faith footnotes. All quotations are of the Bible's New International Version. This guide is not a commentary on that faith text. Indeed, that faith text will always be a commentary on us as law students and lawyers. It reveals the condition of a lawyer's soul. Instead, the text of this guide and its footnotes are meditations on that faith text from the standpoint of a lawyer. The italicized vignettes that precede each of the 24 meditations are reflections on a law career, meant to illustrate the workings of faith on the moral principle of that section. The vignettes are true accounts to the best of my recollection. I hope that you see from the vignettes that faith can be both personal and professional.

Acknowledgments

Faith is an academic property, nurtured through encouraging fellowship within schools, colleges, and universities. I acknowledge the support of brothers and sisters in faith within my academic community including Judges Thomas Brennan, Robert Holmes Bell, Daniel Zemaitis, Joseph Scoville, and William Kelly, Deans John Nussbaumer, Charles Toy, Charles Cercone, Tracey Brame, Amy Timmer, and Cynthia Ward, Professors John Brennan, Martha Moore, Paul Sorensen, William Wagner, Marjorie Gell, John Kane, Heather Garretson, Florise Neville-Ewell, Chris Johnson, Jim Hicks, and David Tarrien, and staff members Joan Rosema-David, Dawn Beachnau, Mike Foreback, Scot Koetje, and Aletha Honsowitz. I especially acknowledge the law students whose faith has encouraged and informed the students, faculty, and staff of my law school.

Faith is also a vocational property, tested through interaction with faithful members of one's trade or profession. I acknowledge the support of brothers and sisters of faith within my law-practice community including Doug Toering, Skip Pylman, Larry Mulligan, Ron Foster, Carole Bos, Ann Bachle-Fifer, Paul Ledford, Renee Stamper, Judge Calvin Bosman, and Kevin Megley, and practitioner graduates of my campus Anna Rapa, Mike Lichterman, John Zevalking, and Ben Symko.

Faith is also a product of education, nurtured through informed instruction within communities of faith. I acknowledge the instruction of Holy Trinity Church of God in Christ and its pastor Bishop Nathaniel Wells, Harvest Bible Chapel and its Pastor Ken Gentzler, and First Presbyterian Church and its former pastor Reverend Rick Snyder, among several other churches and their pastors and faithful instructors from whom and with whom I have learned lessons of faith.

Faith is also a product of family, for which I acknowledge the support of my beloved wife Anne, treasured daughter Sarah, parents-in-law Vern and Virginia, sister-in-law Sara, and brothers-in-law John and Jim, and in memory my maternal grandmother Terry and paternal grandfather Hans Miller. May we each find families of faith with whom to share our journey.

Introduction

LAW AS AN EXPRESSION OF FAITH

The premise of *The Faithful Lawyer* is that law students and lawyers best study and practice law as expressions of faith, drawing on the rich resources of faith.[1] Faith implies basing one's thoughts and actions, indeed one's life, on things firm,[2] powerful,[3] articulated,[4] omniscient,[5] and universal to human experience, beyond those things which we ourselves create. Faith is a commitment to examine human experience for the rich evidence of moral life.[6] Lawyers are acute observers of the consequences of personal and corporate behavior. Using those skills of observation, we can see that the causes and consequences of human behavior work within moral fields.[7] Faith has articulated those moral fields in a literature so rich as to far outpace anything law itself has offered.[8] Faith has also demonstrated the truths within

---

[1] REVELATION 3:18 ("I counsel you to buy from me gold refined in the fire, so you can become rich... ."); *see also* 2 CORINTHIANS 9:11 ("You will be made rich in every way so that you can be generous on every occasion... .").

[2] 1 PETER 5:10 ("God ... will himself ... make you strong, firm and steadfast").

[3] EPHESIANS 1:18-19 ("that you may know ... his incomparably great power").

[4] EPHESIANS 3:8-9 ("make plain to everyone the administration of this mystery").

[5] JOHN 16:30 ("you know all things"); *see also* JOB 38:4 (" 'Where were you when I laid the earth's foundations?' ").

[6] 1 CORINTHIANS 11:28 ("A man ought to examine himself ... .").

[7] EZEKIEL 44:12 ("they must bear the consequences of their sin").

[8] ECCLESIASTES 12:12 ("Of making many books there is no end... .").

1

its moral fields in varied and powerful personal experiences and community histories.[9] Those histories provide inexhaustible inspiration and models for law students and lawyers of faith.[10] Faith delights law students and lawyers,[11] just as much as it enlivens others.[12] Faith matters as much to the law student and lawyer as faith matters to others, to whom faith may matter most.

So, why should we not draw on faith in law studies and law practice? Drawing on faith presents a challenge for law students and lawyers, as much or more than it does in the study and practice of other professions. Ever since Nietzsche repeated that very old trick of declaring God dead,[13] and Holmes, the Realists, and the Crits believed him, law has struggled to articulate the transcendent basis that the Declaration of Independence so clearly claimed for it, the one to which Abraham Lincoln referred in his Gettysburg Address. Witness Judge Richard Posner, law's most prolific scholar but also a thoroughly anti-moral one. Yet the project of deriving for law and its practice the shared set of transcendent meanings from which it receives its dignity remains a highly worthwhile one.[14] Concluding that God is dead (that there is nothing transcendent or especially anthropic about the universe's origin and purpose) does not mean that everyone chooses their own morality. It would mean instead that there is

---

[9] JEREMIAH 30:20 ("their community will be established before me").

[10] PROVERBS 5:1 ("listen well to my words of inspiration"); HEBREWS 11:13 ("All these people were still living by faith when they died."); 1 THESSALONIANS 1:3 ("endurance inspired by hope").

[11] PSALM 1:2 ("But his delight is in the law of the Lord, and on his law he meditates day and night.").

[12] EZEKIEL 37:4-5 (" 'Dry bones, hear the word of the Lord! This is what the Sovereign Lord says to these bones: I will make breath enter you, and you will come to life.' ").

[13] PSALM 14:1 ("The fool says in his heart, 'There is no God.' "); MATTHEW 22:32 ("He is not the God of the dead but of the living."); see also GENESIS 3:4 (" 'You will not surely die,' the serpent said to the woman. 'For God knows that when you eat of it your eyes will be opened, and you will be like God, knowing good and evil.' ").

[14] DEUTERONOMY 6:20 (" 'What is the meaning of the stipulations, decrees and laws the Lord our God has commanded you?' "); JOB 28:13 ("Man does not comprehend its worth; it cannot be found in the land of the living.").

no choice, and so no freedom nor liberty nor conscience.[15] We readily know these things, especially consciousness and choice, to exist and just as readily recognize them to be essential to the most human aspects of life, as secularists are now discovering.[16]

You might have realized already, as I realize again each day, that it can help to have a guide when pursuing faith through an academy and profession not particularly articulate about it.[17] This guide is to help law student and lawyer connect law studies and practice to faith to be able to give pursuit of a law career its greatest meaning.[18] This Introduction begins that effort by outlining each of the guide's five chapters, showing briefly how the guide organizes each chapter around shared sets of transcendent meanings. The Introduction names morality, faith, redemption, and transformation as the first of those transcendent meanings, laying the groundwork for other meanings in each of the book's five ensuing chapters. Those five chapters begin with law studies, progress to law knowledge and skills, move on to law identity, and end in law practice, in the manner that lawyers tend to develop. In that manner the guide takes you through the development of a lawyer, articulating moral fields through which the law student and lawyer must pass to discover and embrace a transcendent law practice, meaning one that blesses the lawyer and lawyer's family and friends[19] while effectively supporting and serving the flourishing of others.[20]

---

[15] ROMANS 8:21 ("The creation itself will be liberated... ."); 2 CORINTHIANS 3:17 ("Where the Spirit of the Lord is, there is freedom."); GALATIANS 5:1 ("It is for freedom that Christ has set us free."); JAMES 1:23 ("the perfect law that gives freedom").

[16] ECCLESIASTES 3:11 ("He has also set eternity in the hearts of men.").

[17] NUMBERS 10:31-32 ("But Moses said, 'Please do not leave us. You know where we should camp in the desert, and you can be our eyes. If you come with us, we will share with you whatever good things the Lord gives us.' ").

[18] PSALM 73:24 ("You guide me with your counsel... .").

[19] GENESIS 49:26 ("Your father's blessings are greater than the blessings of the ancient mountains, than the bounty of the age-old hills."); ROMANS 4:6 ("the blessedness of the man to whom God credits righteousness apart from works").

[20] 1 PETER 5:2 ("Be shepherds of God's flock that is under your care, serving as overseers—not because you must, but because you are willing... .").

Take the last of this guide's moral propositions, charity, as the prime example[21] of the undeniable nature of these meanings that transcend law practice. In law practice, lawyers think of charity primarily as providing pro-bono service to the indigent. Now, we know that as a moral field within law practice, charity exists. That is, we know that some lawyers do pro bono, while others do not. We can study pro bono, as many have, and from its empirical study deduce certain of its beneficial properties to both the pro-bono client and charitable lawyer. Even if no lawyers did pro bono, we would know that pro bono exists, although we would think much less of lawyers if none were doing pro bono. Charity may not exist in law practices to a sufficient degree, but it certainly does exist. Choices whether to do well for others exist independent of our choosing. Because we so readily sense our choices and their consequences,[22] we also readily find within the broader field of human endeavor the proof of an objective morality,[23] just as other generations of lawyers have before us. We live in an inescapably moral world—thank goodness. Consider the following chapter-by-chapter outline of some other faith-imbued morals that guide a faithful lawyer's career, after this further introduction under the heading of morality itself.

Morality

The lawyer had practiced for a decade, long enough to hear just about every attitude that people generally have about lawyers, including all of the lawyer jokes. The lawyer respected what he did and felt that his wife and daughter did, too, even if others including his parents and some of his friends did not. Anyway, after a decade of practice, he did not think about it very much. Law

---

[21] 1 JOHN 4:8 ("God is love").

[22] JOSHUA 24:15 ("[C]hoose for yourselves this day whom you will serve... . But as for me and my household, we will serve the Lord."); ISAIAH 7:15 ("reject the wrong and choose the right").

[23] ROMANS 3:5 ("our unrighteousness brings out God's righteousness more clearly"); PHILIPPIANS 1:22 ("Yet what shall I choose? I do not know!"); 2 TIMOTHY 3:9 ("their folly will be clear to everyone"); JAMES 1:21 ("get rid of all moral filth and the evil that is so prevalent and humbly accept the word planted in you, which can save you.").

practice was law practice. He did what he could to help others, and anyone who thought otherwise—well, let that be their problem.

In retrospect, it was probably just that sense of having settled in to what the lawyer hoped would be a long if underappreciated career that made what happened next such a surprise. The lawyer and his wife had begun attending Friday evening services at an African-American Pentecostal church in a desperately poor community, ridden by drug crime, that the pastor called the "armpit" of the region. Just why the lawyer and his wife had picked this church was hard to say and did not really matter. What seemed to matter was that both the lawyer and his wife had found new opportunities within this vibrant but quite poor faith community to serve others. There were no other lawyers in the congregation, that was for sure, nor were there any doctors, accountants, or other professionals.

The lawyer and his wife had arrived a few minutes early this particular evening, either that or the evening service was going to start habitually late. The service had not yet started. The music director was putting the youth choir through its rehearsal, the choir singing the refrain over and over as the lawyer's weary mind drifted over work-related events of the past week. Then it hit him. The lawyer heard for the first time the refrain that the youth choir was singing, over and over as it practiced: "You are my lawyer, thank you, Jesus."

The lawyer shook his head as if to clear the misimpression. "Warrior, they must be singing warrior," the lawyer thought with a slight chuckle at what he assumed had surely been an amusing Freudian aberration. "Yeah," the lawyer thought again, "that would be the day, wouldn't it, that anyone associates in song a lawyer with anything other than mockery?" The lawyer listened again for the refrain to return, this time anticipating the proper allusion "warrior." The lawyer knew with complete confidence that Jesus was the strongest and bravest individual ever to have graced the earth, truly the great Warrior. The lawyer leaned forward in the old pew to catch the proper refrain.

Yet no, there it was again: the youth were clearly singing "lawyer," not "warrior." The song sung, even by the youth choir, with such reverence equated an incomparable Savior with a lawyer. The teenagers swayed back and forth, closed their eyes, raised their voices, and sang it repeatedly, "You are my lawyer, thank you, Jesus." The lawyer knew that law could be a noble profession, when it functions at its best. He knew how important law was to so many. Yet he had never even considered the possibility that there was something reverential in the lawyer's role, certainly not so much as to lend itself to divinity. The reference so surprised the lawyer that he had the sense of letting his jaw drop open, although it was only a sense, the lawyer long ago having learned the professional art of concealing when something occurred that the lawyer had not in any respect anticipated.

It took the lawyer a little while to settle on the meaning of the event, probably a few weeks of mulling it here and there, without giving the event any primacy but still needing to place it in some professional context. In the end, the lawyer decided that the song changed nothing of what the lawyer thought of himself. He had no particular fantasy of being anything particularly special as a lawyer. The lawyer certainly knew that there was nothing special about him. He was, at most, a decent if still obviously flawed husband, father, and lawyer. The song was not at all about the lawyer or even about what the lawyer did, within or outside of this faith community, for the needy or for others. Whatever messages the song conveyed to the lawyer were not personal but corporate and vocational, the lawyer decided.

The song helped the lawyer appreciate the nature of the faith community in which he heard the song. This rare community of faith had the unusual ability to see its own great need for justice. That ability was a tribute to the effective work of its insightful and responsible pastor. It was not that the congregation was poor, although it was in economic terms. It was that the congregation was rich in its moral life, that it could see its transgressions, which gave it the capacity to see its need for a very special kind of redemptive justice. The lawyer was sufficiently wise to know that we all share that same need for justice, at least the kind of redemptive justice this congregation sought through a moral Savior. Yet only in some communities (like this one) is it acceptable to admit it, even to sing imploringly about it, to the point of calling upon the great Lawyer.

In the end, the lawyer decided that it was too bad that more communities did not admit the same need, especially that the profession did not often seem to see itself and its members as in need of a moral and redemptive justice. The legal profession certainly had similar needs to this poor community. It needed a clear sense of its failings and a clear call for where it would find relief from those failings. Yet most of all, the song gave the lawyer a much greater sense of the possibilities of the role of a lawyer that he wanted to share with other lawyers. The song meant that there was something broader, deeper, richer, and more profound about the law as a vocation, even if the law profession did not seem to evoke much respect from others. You need only find respect in the *right quarters, the lawyer concluded, and the right meaning with it. This faith community had quite unintentionally but providentially given that rare gift to the lawyer.*

The study of law challenges law students,[24] and the practice of law challenges lawyers, enough that both need help.[25] I know those challenges first-hand as a former practitioner and present law-campus dean. Law studies are simply not easy, nor should they be.[26] Some law students do seem to find law school to be readily manageable. Most probably find it more challenging than they thought.[27] Some find it overwhelming in a way that requires them to leave law school or identify, develop, and draw on new resources. The same evaluation is true for law practice. Some practitioners find practice readily manageable. At one time or another, most probably find it more challenging than they thought. Some find it overwhelming, requiring them to leave or find new help.[28]

Law students and lawyers do not always recognize their challenges as involving issues of faith. That oversight may be part of the problem that the law profession has in addressing the challenges that law studies and law practice present. We misinterpret the challenges of law studies and law practice to be primarily intellectual, psychological, emotional, economic, social, and technological, when overcoming those challenges requires something deeper-rooted in faith.[29] Faith matters to both law studies and law practice, that is, to forming a complete and effective professional identity through which to practice law.[30] Faith matters in overcoming the challenges of law studies and

---

[24] ECCLESIASTES 12:12 ("much study wearies the body").

[25] TITUS 3:13 ("Do everything you can to help Zenas the lawyer and Apollos on their way and see that they have everything they need.").

[26] 2 TIMOTHY 2:15 ("Do your best to present yourself ... a workman who ... correctly handles the word of truth.").

[27] JEREMIAH 12:5 ("If you stumble in safe country, how will you manage in the thickets ... ?").

[28] JOHN 10:12 ("The hired hand is not the shepherd who owns the sheep. So when he sees the wolf coming, he abandons the sheep and runs away.").

[29] LUKE 8:48 (" 'your faith has healed you' ").

[30] ISAIAH 29:18 ("In that day the deaf will hear the words of the scroll, and out of gloom and darkness the eyes of the blind will see.").

practice, giving meaning to the work, and being effective in its service.[31] Law students and lawyers should recognize how faith affects how we learn law and using that learning engage in law practice. Chapter 1 articulates how law students and lawyers need belief, obedience, honesty, and trust for effective law studies. Those four moral fields help to define the faith required by law studies, just as their antitheses doubt, disobedience, dishonesty, and distrust would inhibit the law studies necessary for a successful law practice and career.

Just as law studies require faith, so is law itself built on foundations of faith, meaning on shared transcendent qualities.[32] Lawyers must possess a broad and active knowledge base, and not simply about positive law but about human nature and shared commitments, if their knowledge is to serve clients well.[33] It is the mark of a lawyer to know law. A master lawyer knows much law in detail and breadth, in a way that acts on the social issues that law practice presents. Law schools devote the curriculum, particularly the first-year curriculum, to helping students build that rich knowledge base. The concepts taught in doctrinal courses like torts, contracts, crimes, property, and constitutions reflect articles of faith. Law and theology have always had close connections, coming from like source.[34] Legal concepts are fundamentally moral concepts rooted in traditional faith. To miss that connection is to miss a great opportunity to improve and give meaning to law studies and law practice. Chapter 2 explores how doctrinal law courses and their associated legal fields reflect foundations of faith laid in love, covenant, provision, and consent. Those four moral fields begin to define the faith that helps us embrace the deep truths of law knowledge, just as their antitheses hate, breach, want, and coercion would inhibit law knowledge.

---

[31] MATTHEW 11:5 ("The blind receive sight, the lame walk, those who have leprosy are cured, the deaf hear, the dead are raised, and the good news is preached to the poor.").

[32] MATTHEW 5:18 (" 'I tell you the truth, until heaven and earth disappear, not the smallest letter, not the least stroke of a pen, will by any means disappear from the Law until everything is accomplished.' ").

[33] PHILIPPIANS 1:9 ("that your love may abound more and more in knowledge and depth of insight").

[34] JAMES 4:12 ("There is only one Lawgiver and Judge... .").

Law students and lawyers also require specific professional skills.[35] Professional skills, like doctrinal knowledge, have foundations in faith.[36] Law is a service profession. A lawyer with knowledge but no skill is utterly ineffective. Clients expect and deserve that the lawyer apply law knowledge to client circumstance. Law knowledge is action logic, social and strategic in nature. The kinds of skills that lawyers exercise are peculiarly moral skills, rooted in faith concepts. Lawyer skill involves reason, relationship, counsel, and discernment.[37] Those skills are articles of faith, having their faith expression and equivalents. Indeed, those skills reflect fundamental moral concepts. You would find those terms as commonly in a sermon as in a law school skills course. Chapter 3 explores how those four moral fields begin to define lawyer skill, just as their antitheses arbitrariness, isolation, ignorance, and foolishness would inhibit lawyer skill. It takes faith to serve effectively as a lawyer, just as it takes faith to embrace the deep truths of law knowledge.

Lawyers also require professional identity grounded in faith. Professional identity arises out of the moral fields of calling, character, fitness, and responsibility. Lawyers develop a sense of their calling, that they have a purpose beyond themselves in providing legal service.[38] By persevering through their own and their clients' troubles, lawyers also develop professional character, enabling them to project hope.[39] Lawyers must also be fit for law practice, ready to conform not to aimless or detrimental patterns but to conduct rules the profession imposes to determine and maintain fitness.[40] In effect, the rules list a complete set of professional responsibilities. Together, a lawyer's calling, charac-

---

[35] PROVERBS 22:29 ("Do you see a man skilled in his work? He will serve before kings... .").

[36] EXODUS 35:31 ("He has filled them with skill to do all kinds of work... .").

[37] PROVERBS 28:11 ("A rich man may be wise in his own eyes, but a poor man who has discernment sees through him.").

[38] 2 PETER 1:10 ("be all the more eager to make your calling and election sure").

[39] ROMANS 5:4 ("suffering produces perseverance; perseverance, character; and character, hope").

[40] ROMANS 12:2 ("Do not conform any longer to the pattern of this world but be transformed by the renewing of your mind.").

ter, fitness, and responsibility form the lawyer's professional identity in moral terms. Law firms hire lawyers and clients retain lawyers for their identity as much as for their law knowledge and lawyer skill. Chapter 4 explores how these four moral fields help lawyers build professional identity, just as their antitheses aimlessness, corruption, unfitness, and irresponsibility would inhibit lawyer identity. It takes faith to be a great lawyer, just as it takes faith to serve effectively as a lawyer and embrace the deep truths of law knowledge.

It is not enough that we have faith during law studies, build our knowledge of law on its connection to faith, let faith inform our law skills, and then become faithful lawyers in our professional identity. For the greatest benefit, lawyers should also practice law using the forms and conventions of faith. Moral fields defining the faith aspects of law practice include service, stewardship, diligence, and charity. Above all, law practice requires a devotion to service like that which is borne of faith.[41] It also requires stewardship of finances and other resources,[42] and diligence in one's service.[43] Finally, it requires charity in legal services, meaning pro-bono service. Faith informs the practice of law as much as its study, foundations, and skills, and the identity that lawyers acquire through it. Chapter 5 articulates how these four moral fields inform lawyers in law practice, just as their antitheses carelessness, waste, sloth, and greed would inhibit law practice.

Thus, this guide takes the reader from the study of law through law knowledge and skills, and lawyer identity, to law practice, articulating the moral basis for each in faith. If you remain willing to entertain the thought of a moral, faith-based law practice, then you have achieved faith's first accomplishment, which is to keep an open mind to faith in a setting that some insist quite wrongly is foreign to it. What lawyers do in their law practice matters to their faith. You cannot separate your work

---

[41] 2 CORINTHIANS 9:13 ("the service by which you have proved yourselves").

[42] LUKE 19:13 (" 'Put this money to work... .' ").

[43] HEBREWS 6:11 ("show this same diligence to the very end").

from your faith commitments.[44] Whether or not you appreciate it, your faith dictates your actions.[45] Because it does, it should be worth your while to give your faith direct attention in the professional context in which you study and work.

Faith

There could hardly have been a more revealing moment. The new lawyer had just graduated from law school, just walked across the graduation stage. A family member had later that day given the new lawyer a leather-bound life planner as a graduation gift. Late that same evening, still feeling flush with accomplishment, the new lawyer sat alone to look through and maybe work a little with the shiny new planner. Financial goals, career goals, family goals, recreation—the new lawyer had ready answers to record on each page. Yet then there was this odd page about faith goals. The thought dumbfounded the new lawyer. What did that mean? The new lawyer was completely unprepared to guess at what to put on the page. He just sat there, suddenly feeling a whole lot less accomplished even though his graduation was less than eight hours old. He actually thought about tearing the faith-goals page out of its little leather planner. That would take care of it, wouldn't it?

Instead, the new lawyer knew immediately that it was an important question. He was under no delusion about the power of a law career to challenge and distort a person. The new lawyer had clerked for a small firm pretty much throughout law school. He had seen there how intense practice could be, how consuming and alluring. Although the new lawyer had found reliable mentors, the new lawyer had also not seen too many of them and instead developed an uneasy sense that he had better be sure to choose his models and habits carefully. He had even seen law studies (no less law practice) distort a few of his classmates, ending in divorce, depression, disillusionment, substance abuse, and like challenges.

It took the new lawyer a few months, stretching into a couple of years, to gain a vague sense of how he might answer the planner's faith challenge. First, the new lawyer realized that some of the lawyer's classmates would have known how to fill in the planner's faith page. They had faith understanding. He met some of

---

[44] JEREMIAH 25:6 (" '[D]o not provoke me with what your hands have made. Then I will not harm you.' ").

[45] DEUTERONOMY 11:18 ("Fix these words of mine in your hearts and minds; tie them as symbols on your hands and bind them on your foreheads.").

them again here and there after law school. One of them had spent a year overseas right after law school doing some extraordinary charitable work and had come back to practice law as a first associate to a masterful solo practitioner. Chatting with his old law school classmate, the new lawyer discovered how intentional one could be about opportunities and choices when one had a distinct set of informing criteria. By contrast to his charitable friend, the new lawyer had taken what had seemed at the time as the only available route into his associate's job based on some pretty mundane criteria. He was fine with how it had turned out, but it had been providential, not planned. Apparently, there were other routes and perhaps even other destinations. Even though it was still blank, the new lawyer began to feel glad that he had not removed the faith page from his planner.

About the same time, the new lawyer joined a community of faith through which he could make fresh observations of faith outside of his profession. Because there were only a few lawyers among the community's members, it was easier for the lawyer to see how faith informed the lives, relationships, and vocations of the community's non-lawyers. On the other hand, it seemed harder for the new lawyer to find faith models within the legal profession. Either that or he had not yet learned to fully recognize faith within the profession that he was still learning. Here, in his faith community, the new lawyer had a new laboratory in which to both observe faith and to begin to adopt faith as his identity, without having to overcome the strong norms of his legal profession. The new lawyer need not yet wrestle with the professional norms he was still learning, to try to incorporate faith into skills and art in which he was in no sense a master.

The new lawyer also began to meet a wider spectrum of lawyers than that to which law school and his law clerk position in the firm had exposed him. Among those professionals, the new lawyer inevitably met lawyers who held different and in many cases larger perspectives on their roles as professionals. Those lawyers were evaluating their professional roles outside of the profession's norms against different and, it was obvious in some cases, much higher standards than those with which the new lawyer was so far familiar. These models may have been available in law school, but if so, then the new lawyer had with law school's other challenges entirely missed them. The new lawyer saw new opportunities for personal and professional growth that he had not previously imagined. Two years into a career, it becomes harder to overlook one's goals or, really, the absence of them. The new lawyer decided that it was time to fill in the last and most important page of the planner.

You have just seen in the previous section the guide's organization around moral fields in a lawyer's development from law studies to law practice. Now, consider this introduction to the subject of faith. A guide to law studies and law practice should help you anticipate and prepare for what you will encounter, so that you can make the best of it. The purpose of this guide, as it would be any guide's purpose, is to make better your experience of law studies and practice than your experience would be without it. Indeed, the first purpose of any guide is to ensure your survival during the experience.[46] Fortunately, law studies and law practice present few if any direct survival hazards. Indirect survival hazards do exist. The student's near suicide in the law school film *The Paper Chase* was only cinematic, as were the demise of so many lawyers depicted in other films and novels, John Grisham-depictions included. Yet law studies and law practice can present sufficiently serious challenges as to implicate destructive behaviors, as literature, film, infamous examples, and empirical study reflect. A guide to law studies and law practice should help you avoid, navigate, and survive those hazards by showing you an indestructible life.[47]

A second purpose of a guide is that you complete the experience rather than quitting it for lack of counsel.[48] Here, there are clearer hazards as to both law studies and law practice. Some law students drop out of law school or eschew law practice, just as some lawyers drop out of law practice. Presumably, some of those law students might have completed their legal education and begun law practice if they had the benefit of appropriate counsel, just as some of those lawyers might have continued in law practice if they had the benefit of constructive guidance. At least, many law students who do graduate are so kind as to send notes

---

[46] NEHEMIAH 9:19 ("Because of your great compassion you did not abandon them in the desert.").

[47] HEBREWS 7:16 ("the power of an indestructible life").

[48] EXODUS 13:21 ("By day the Lord went ahead of them in a pillar of cloud to guide them on their way and by night in a pillar of fire to give them light so that they could travel by day or night.").

to their advisors that they could not have done it without them. Those in legal and professional education see frequent need of encouragement and guidance about both law studies and law practice.[49] Lawyers should share that encouragement with one another, hoping that in the process law remains a worthwhile profession.

A third purpose of a guide is that you appreciate more fully the experience that the guide addresses.[50] Law school is harder for some students than it need have been, even if they ultimately graduate to enjoy its benefit.[51] Law practice is less enjoyable for some lawyers than it could be.[52] Guidance can help both law studies and law practice become and remain more enjoyable.[53] There are special things about law studies and practice, although sometimes it takes a guide to discover them or a reminder to rediscover them. Finally, a guide's last purpose is to ensure that you draw the most benefit from the experience, perhaps meaning that you end up where you should.[54] A guide can help you use your legal education to its greatest long-term effect to find and remain in the law practice that you should, with the greatest meaning and satisfaction.[55] Ultimately, a guide should lead you to your preferred destination, which we will find resides in the deepest reaches of faith.[56]

On the surface, the challenges that law studies and law practice present are intellectual. Law is deep, broad, and complex. Its practice requires applying complex concepts across the full breadth of human circumstance, meaning that those who study and practice law must appreciate the full spectrum of human

---

[49] 1 THESSALONIANS 5:11 ("Therefore encourage one another and build each other up, just as in fact you are doing.").

[50] JOHN 14:26 ("the Counselor ... will teach you all things").

[51] PSALM 33:17 ("A horse is a vain hope for deliverance... .").

[52] PSALM 39:6 ("[h]e bustles about, but only in vain"); PSALM 127:2 ("In vain you rise early and stay up late... .").

[53] ISAIAH 9:6 ("he will be called Wonderful Counselor").

[54] EXODUS 15:13 ("In your strength you will guide them to your holy dwelling."); PSALM 48:14 ("For this God is our God for ever and ever; he will be our guide even to the end").

[55] PSALM 73:24 ("You guide me with your counsel, and afterward you will take me into glory.").

[56] HEBREWS 11:6 ("without faith it is impossible to please God").

endeavor.[57] On the surface, the challenge of law studies is also psychological, testing the soundness of the mind,[58] whether our minds can withstand exponential growth, just as the challenge of law practice is psychological, whether we can help clients address the panoply of human experience. The surface challenges are also emotional, whether we can find equilibrium in the highs and lows that inevitably come with attempting to incorporate immense new knowledge and master ethereal skills within a new professional identity. The surface challenges are also relational. They include not only how we care for family and whether we can find support from and provide support to our peers but also how we relate to truth and authority. The surface challenges to law studies and law practice can be physical, whether we can read, write, counsel, advocate, and concentrate for 8, 10, or 12 hours daily. The surface challenges to law studies can also be economic, meaning the cost of a legal education while forgoing other earnings, and technological, meaning the ability to adapt to electronic tools.

Ultimately, though, the challenges of law studies and law practice are tests of faith.[59] Law students and lawyers find evidence of those faith tests in doubt, fear, anxiety, mistrust, depression, substance abuse, dropout, and divorce rates. The surface challenges translate into something deeper, testing the meaning of the pursuit.[60] Law studies and law practice are so comprehensive, detailed, social, personal, political, and analytical, that they demand an overarching rationale. They challenge all students and lawyers, both those who have not articulated faith understandings and commitments, and those who have. For law students and lawyers who have not articulated that rationale, law studies and law practice require its construction.[61] For law

---

[57] EZRA 7:10 ("For Ezra had devoted himself to the study and observance of the Law of the Lord... .").

[58] LAMENTATIONS 3:40 ("Let us examine our ways and test them... .").

[59] 2 CORINTHIANS 13:5 ("Examine yourselves to see whether you are in the faith; test yourselves.").

[60] DEUTERONOMY 13:3 ("the Lord your God is testing you"); PROVERBS 18:1 ("An unfriendly man pursues selfish ends.. .").

[61] EPHESIANS 4:14 ("Then we will no longer be infants, tossed back and forth by the waves, and blown here and there by every wind of teaching and by the cunning and craftiness of men in their deceitful scheming.").

students and lawyers who do not have a sound construction, law studies and law practice require reconstruction. Everything is a test, for which, by the way, we should not be pained but be glad.[62] These tests of faith do us great good, exactly what we need to become who we should be with everything that we should have.[63]

Because the challenges that any law student and lawyer encounter are fundamentally faith challenges, law studies and practice require acceptance, construction, and knowledge of faith. They are challenges the answers to which lawyers draw from faith, whether articulated or inarticulate. Lawyers who are able to articulate faith are more able to meet those challenges of law studies and practice. Faith is the product of hearing and accepting the constructs of faith.[64] Faith is something that a law student and lawyer can and should seek, acquire, and strengthen in the manner that they seek, acquire, and strengthen their law skills and knowledge. The symptoms of the challenges of law studies and practice may be confusion, indecision, frustration, fatigue, doubt, despair, depression, and rebellion. Yet these conditions are only symptoms of the loss of one's faith and degradation of one's faith condition,[65] that is, the inability or unwillingness to recognize the faith that defeats these challenges.[66]

Faith matters in law studies and law practice in many respects. Faith shields us against the challenges that produce these degradations.[67] Faith matters to both survival and success in law studies and law practice. Faith addresses and satisfies the

---

[62] JAMES 1:2-3 ("Consider it pure joy, my brothers, whenever you face trials of many kinds, because you know that the testing of your faith develops perseverance.").

[63] JAMES 1:4 ("Perseverance must finish its work so that you may be mature and complete, not lacking anything.").

[64] ROMANS 10:17 ("faith comes from hearing the message").

[65] PHILIPPIANS 3:8 ("I consider everything a loss compared to the surpassing greatness of knowing Christ Jesus").

[66] JOHN 5:24 (" 'I tell you the truth, whoever hears my word and believes him who sent me has eternal life and will not be condemned; he has crossed over from death to life.'").

[67] EPHESIANS 6:16 ("In addition to all this, take up the shield of faith, with which you can extinguish all the flaming arrows of the evil one.").

root of their needs.[68] It does so by giving order and meaning to study and work, making them both effective, and equipping the law student and lawyer to overcome each challenge. The constructs of faith make law studies and law practice sensible, reducing their dissonance and complexity. Faith constructs make studies and practice intelligible and meaningful. Faith supports the perseverance and trust that law studies and law practice require, trust that their disciplines will result in the acquisition and fruitful exercise of valuable knowledge and skills in an effective professional personality. Faith is reliable in part because it is so transportable. There is nothing that faith fails to touch, nothing that it fails to address, and nothing that it fails to inform.[69] Faith is also reliable because it takes so little faith to make a big difference in a law practice and career. When you consider the whole length of a lawyer's career and how just a little faith can make for big changes over the course of that career, there is a great difference between having no faith and having a little faith.[70]

Faith is also the product of the challenges of law studies and law practice.[71] Faith removes the burden from study and practice that they must be productive in themselves. Gainful pursuits of all types have as their byproduct, or perhaps as their central product, the proof of faith.[72] It is not solely that law studies and practice make a lawyer. It is more so that overcoming through faith the challenge of law studies and practice proves the value of faith to the lawyer. We labor in our law studies and law practice not

---

[68] ISAIAH 58:11 ("The Lord will guide you always; he will satisfy your needs in a sun-scorched land and will strengthen your frame.").

[69] PSALM 139:7-10 ("Where can I go from your Spirit? Where can I flee from your presence? If I go up to the heavens, you are there; if I make my bed in the depths, you are there. If I rise on the wings of the dawn, if I settle on the far side of the sea, even there your hand will guide me, your right hand will hold me fast.").

[70] MATTHEW 17:20 (" 'I tell you the truth, if you have faith as small as a mustard seed, you can say to this mountain, "Move from here to there" and it will move. Nothing will be impossible for you.' ").

[71] HEBREW 11:1 ("Now faith is being sure of what we hope for and certain of what we do not see.").

[72] 1 CORINTHIANS 4:2 ("those who have been given a trust must prove faithful").

solely for the personal or professional results of those labors, which are not always immediately evident.[73] Instead, we also labor for the proof to others and ourselves that faithful labor has its rewards in the proof of faith and the exercise of greater authority through faith.[74] The more faithfully we labor, the greater is our influence and happiness.[75] The test of faith, rule of faith, and reward of faith are what we seek.[76] Law studies and law practice are more than suitable mediums for that journey, providing many opportunities for faith's promised reward.[77] Placing law studies and law practice in that subordinate and conduit relationship to faith is our second accomplishment after having entertained the possibility of a moral vocation. Faith involves relationship.[78] We begin anew with a great advantage when we know the right relationship of law studies and law practice to faith, which is to give faith its due primacy.

Redemption

Within a couple of years of graduating from law school, the new lawyer had seen the perspective and possibilities that faith created. There were things that the new lawyer would never get to do or to be unless the lawyer had faith. Opportunity, though, is seldom enough to kindle faith. The next big step came after the new lawyer grew increasingly disappointed and then eventually disgusted not with the missteps of other lawyers or with missed opportunities but with his own moral condition. It was not that the new lawyer went out and shot someone. He did not embezzle

---

[73] ISAIAH 49:4 ("But I said, 'I have labored to no purpose; I have spent my strength in vain and for nothing.' ").

[74] ISAIAH 49:4 ("Yet what is due me is in the Lord's hand, and my reward is with my God."); 2 CORINTHIANS 9:13 ("the service by which you have proved yourselves").

[75] MATTHEW 25:21 (" 'Well done, good and faithful servant! You have been faithful with a few things; I will put you in charge of many things. Come and share your master's happiness.' ").

[76] MATTHEW 7:7 (" 'Ask and it will be given you; seek and you will find; knock and the door will be opened to you.' ").

[77] JEREMIAH 17:10 ("I the Lord search the heart and examine the mind, to reward a man according to his conduct, according to what his deeds deserve.").

[78] DEUTERONOMY 6:5 ("Love the Lord your God with all your heart and with all your soul and with all your strength.").

client funds or start chasing after secretaries. Other lawyers probably generally regarded the new lawyer as pretty much like other lawyers. Instead, as the new lawyer investigated the resources and discovered the standards of faith, he began holding himself to those standards and, in doing so, finding himself utterly wanting. Indeed, the lawyer discovered that he was so completely beyond repair that there was no use tinkering. All his life the lawyer had tried to do the right thing without faith, and here he was, finding his condition hopeless.

It was an extraordinary discovery for the new lawyer. Even well before the new lawyer had started law school, he had a sense that he was a pretty decent person, having avoided most of the more embarrassing things into which youth often fall. Law school added to that sense, especially when he found some academic success there to distinguish him in a competitive environment. You graduate in the top five percent of a top-five law school, and you must be something special, right? The new lawyer was completely unprepared to discover through faith that his behavior and condition was certainly nothing special, indeed obviously far less so than most of the modest non-lawyer members of his new faith community, who on their own did not claim to be anything special.

It would make a better story if there were a single event that triggered the lawyer's realization. There was not. There were instead a thousand cuts and nicks that so bled the lawyer's confidence in his character that he knew it was beyond recovery. The lawyer recognized for the first time that heroes do not die in a blaze of glory. They slowly sink and drown from the many small chinks in their armor. Some lawyers discover their need for redemption by falling lower than they ever imagined was possible, say, by waking up drunken one weekday morning on the office sofa. Others discover their need for redemption by seeing just how high faith sets the standard. The two discoveries may seem different, but they are really the same. Corruption is relative only when one measures corruption too narrowly. The lawyer realized that when he set the bar as high as high as faith sets it, all corruption looks pretty much the same, whether it is due to sins of omission, commission, or carelessness.

The lawyer's increasing attention to the subject of faith and how it might influence the life, health, and career of a lawyer had shown the lawyer just how preposterously inadequate he was when measured against faith's revealing standard. He knew that his moral condition on faith's absolute scale was completely beyond repair. The lawyer came to realize that despite his intentions otherwise, he still somehow managed to ruin every day and relationship with acts and attitudes that the genuine circumstances simply did not warrant. Some of those acts and attitudes looked like plain ordinariness but many looked much worse like carelessness, hardheartedness, and selfishness. The lawyer had long known faith's warning about corrupt human nature, but the lawyer had never expected to truly discover it in his own nature. "Who does?" the lawyer thought.

The lawyer felt utterly meritless, and he knew that the feeling was accurate. He had tried relying on ethics, philosophy, science, and just general good nature. The lawyer was an avid reader especially of secular self-help books. If there was any chance at helping one's self to wholeness, then the lawyer was sure that he would have accomplished it. Yet the lawyer found all of his efforts at self-improvement desperately wanting, leaving him no hope of overcoming his broken nature. Worse, he was tiring of the effort. "What's next?" the lawyer thought with more than a little worry.

The lawyer knew by then that faith had led him to his problem. The next question was whether faith would lead him to the solution. The lawyer decided to start over. After all, starting over was the only solution that the lawyer could see and, at the same time, the only solution that faith offered. The lawyer considered carefully faith's ability to satisfy the terms until the evidence convinced the lawyer that faith could do so. The lawyer accepted faith's terms. They were actually quite generous. The lawyer only wondered what changes he might perceive in his law practice. Faith seemed to demand no such changes now. The lawyer felt at ease with faith's terms and so continued with his law practice, watching for what would happen.

Strangely enough, the lawyer's discovery of his need to start completely over actually made the lawyer feel affinity for just about everyone. The lawyer certainly no longer felt that he was any better than the clients he was representing and no better than opposing counsel. The lawyer understood how his clients had gotten themselves into their problems because he had seen the root and extent of his own problem. The lawyer also saw opposing counsel in a more brotherly and sisterly light, that there was a greater sense that they were all in it, meaning law practice, together. The lawyer was also discovering some new solutions—faith solutions—to old problems, both his own problems and his clients' problems. That last discovery was what most intrigued the lawyer. The solutions came from a new perspective that faith offered, that the lawyer had not expected. The lawyer knew that he was now on a proverbial journey, and he welcomed it, already having a sense of its promised ending.

Faith remains a broad subject with many meanings and interpretations. I write this text from a Judeo-Christian perspective because Christianity is the faith that I hold. In so saying, I am not making judgments about or against other faiths. Probably, one should not judge faith from anything other than the standpoint of professing belief in that faith.[79] Whatever you believe, examine and test it to ensure that it accords with all that you learn, observe, and receive. If it does so accord, then believe it with all your heart, mind, soul, and strength. Faith by definition is something not provable.[80] Once proven, it becomes a matter of proof, not a matter of faith. Faith instead involves a confidence in things for which there is only hope and perhaps some evidence, but not something established as seen.[81] If you are an atheist or agnostic, then continue to pursue belief, for you do believe, even if you do not know what you believe.[82] Transcendent meanings are available to and employed continuously by all of us. Judge your belief by its power, authority, fitness, coherence, and consistency as you see it affect your actions.[83] I encourage you to consider the Christian truths on which this guide draws in whatever framework you most productively receive them.

For those who are not familiar with the Christian faith, it rests on a historical account of the incarnate God dying as an act of redemption.[84] God took human image[85] to announce that he

---

[79] ROMANS 14:4 ("To his own master he stands or falls."); REVELATION 4:15 (" 'I know your deeds, that you are neither cold nor hot. I wish you were either one or the other.'").

[80] 2 CORINTHIANS 5:7 ("We live by faith, not by sight.").

[81] HEBREWS 11:1 ("Now faith is being sure of what we hope for and certain of what we do not see.").

[82] ACTS 17:22-23 (" 'I see that in every way you are very religious. For as I walked around and looked carefully at your objects of worship I even found an altar with this inscription: TO AN UNKNOWN GOD. Now what you worship as something unknown I am going to proclaim to you.' ").

[83] PSALM 14:1 ("The fool says in his heart, 'There is no God.' They are corrupt, their deeds are vile; there is no one who does good.").

[84] JOHN 3:16 ("For God so loved the world that he gave his one and only Son, that whoever believes in him shall not perish but have eternal life.").

[85] JOHN 1:14 ("The Word became flesh and made his dwelling among us.").

would take responsibility for human wrong[86] by accepting in our stead the only complete punishment,[87] so long as we would accept it.[88] Christianity would make sense simply as a set of transcendent meanings, that is, as a myth rather than what it is, a historical account rooted in Judaism and spanning a couple of millennia. Authority certainly exists within the universe, whether it involves the physical laws of the universe or cause and effect in social relations. There is no getting around gravity and not much getting around elemental human things like love and hate, either. Things have properties that do not just up and change. Offend your mother-in-law, and consequences will follow. Even social events and relationships follow general rules and produce general patterns, with exceptions that merely prove the subtlety and power of the rule.

Overall, the authority must be hugely benign to have created the magnificent universe in which we live while placing us in a peculiar position and condition to observe that universe.[89] Authority is also quite visible, so that lawyers have no excuse in ignoring it.[90] For that authority to be truly benign, though, and not a distant trifler, the authority would have had to enter the authority's own creation. Redemption requires equivalent exchange. If faith would in some way have to suffer my penalty in order to redeem my wrong, then faith would have to participate in my humanity.[91] Only by doing so could faith fully suffer penalty's pain and fully redeem the wrong. Christianity says that faith did participate,[92] with the specific purpose to make existence more than merely entertaining, intelligible, or sufferable, but to redeem

---

[86] HEBREWS 1:3 ("The Son is the radiance of God's glory and the exact representation of his being, sustaining all things by his powerful word.").

[87] ISAIAH 53:5 ("by his wounds we are healed").

[88] MATTHEW 9:22 ("he said, 'your faith has healed you.' ").

[89] ECCLESIASTES 3:11 ("He has made everything beautiful in its time."); ROMANS 1:20 ("For since the creation of the world God's invisible qualities—his eternal power and divine nature—have been clearly seen, being understood from what has been made, so that men are without excuse.").

[90] ROMANS 1:19 ("what may be known about God is plain").

[91] HEBREWS 2:14 ("he too shared in their humanity so that by his death he might destroy him who holds the power of death").

[92] COLOSSIANS 1:15 ("He is the image of the invisible God, the firstborn over all creation.").

us also from its transient aspects,[93] even from our own most serious wrongs.[94]

I recognize that the concept of redemption may present a problem for some law students and lawyers, even though redemption is very much a legal concept. The concept of redemption should not present such a problem for law students and lawyers who, after all, know more than anyone the universal need for it.[95] Law books on crime brim with the consequences of sin. Horrors fill the pages of your torts casebook. The abuse and neglect that are subjects of courses on children and the law are hard examples, but we also witness human corruption and degradation in environmental law,[96] immigration law, and a hundred other law courses.[97] Every law subject involves at least to some degree our effort to constrain wrongs against one another. Most dispiriting is family law, where even the well meaning require law's intervention. Law students and lawyers know much about redemption from the depravity that they daily see the law encounter.[98]

Lawyers also learn from law more and more about their own wrongs, which is the first important step toward seeing the need for redemption.[99] Law students often enter law school thinking that they have no particular need for law but see it as a means for pursuing justice for others. They think that the course in professional responsibility is a waste of their time because they are already ethical. Yet then they see in that course and throughout the curriculum that they really had an undeveloped conscience. They had no sense of conflicts of interest, for instance, or of fiduciary duties, or of the duty of confidentiality, and on and on. The law school curriculum refines a law student's conscience, training

---

[93] 1 CORINTHIANS 15:54 (" 'Death has been swallowed up in victory.' ").

[94] ISAIAH 53:11-12 ("[B]y his knowledge my righteous servant will justify many, and he will bear their iniquities. ... For he bore the sin of many, and made intercession for the transgressors.").

[95] JOHN 3:19 ("but men loved darkness instead of light").

[96] NUMBERS 35:33 ("Do not pollute the land where you are."); ISAIAH 24:5 ("The earth is defiled by its people... .").

[97] 2 THESSALONIANS 2:3 ("the man of lawlessness is revealed").

[98] ROMANS 1:29 ("They have become filled with every kind of wickedness, evil, greed and depravity.").

[99] PSALM 51:3 ("For I know my transgressions, and my sin is always before me.").

the law student and lawyer to see and address wrong, first in themselves and then in others.[100] The faithful lawyer knows that the lawyer needs the rules of professional conduct and principles of professionalism as much as any other lawyer. There are no exceptions to the need for redemption, which is the first and greatest need.[101] Law is an incredibly special aspect of faith for revealing the constant vagaries of human selfishness and subjectivity.[102]

Yet law alone does not redeem in the full sense given that term's faith meaning.[103] Given their training in law and commitment to it, law students and lawyers should appreciate law's place in the larger scheme of things, including law's limitation. Law does not satisfy the full obligation created by its violation.[104] Law does not substitute something of equal or greater value for the obligation that arises when we injure or corrupt one another. Law does not make whole our wrongs. It does not even keep us from violating it.[105] It does not reunite us with that which we lose as we go about casting away life in wrongs or, nearly as bad, frittering away each day in petty anxieties, when we have so few days.[106] Law can only condemn.[107] Law can only tell us where we

---

[100] MATTHEW 7:5 (" 'You hypocrite, first take the plan out of your own eye, and then you will see clearly to remove the speck from your brother's eye.' ").

[101] 1 CORINTHIANS 15:3 ("For what I received I passed on to you as of first importance: that Christ died for our sins according to the Scriptures, that he was buried, that he was raised on the third day according to the Scriptures... .").

[102] ISAIAH 42:21 ("It pleased the Lord for the sake of his righteousness to make his law great and glorious.").

[103] GALATIANS 2:16 ("by observing the law no one will be justified").

[104] GALATIANS 3:10 ("All who rely on observing the law are under a curse... ."); GALATIANS 3:11 ("Clearly no one is justified before God by the law... .").

[105] ROMANS 7:16 ("And if I do what I do not want to do, I agree that the law is good.").

[106] PSALM 103:15 ("As for man, his days are like grass...; the wind blows over it and it is gone... .").

[107] ROMANS 7:7 ("Indeed I would not have known what sin was except through the law. For I would not have known what coveting really was if the law had not said, 'Do not covet.' ").

have gone wrong,[108] when we all go wrong nearly all of the time, in larger and smaller ways, despite our best intentions.[109] Law is only a signpost pointing to our need for something qualitatively different.

Faith offers that necessary solution known as redemption.[110] Faith is, in a sense, the end of law, the point at which law ceases to condemn.[111] Many people miss it, thinking that faith is all about rules and conventions that condemn you. Faith is not about rules and conventions but a complete commitment to what is right that has the effect of freeing us from rules and conventions.[112] While law condemns, faith does not condemn but redeems from condemnation.[113] Christianity's premise is that self-improvement through attention to law offers no hope of satisfactory transformation. Redemption must instead come from faith because we commit our offenses against faith.[114] Man cannot redeem. Faith, against whom we offend, must redeem.[115] Faith redeems by taking our place to suffer for the offense so that we

---

[108] GALATIANS 3:19 ("What, then, was the purpose of the law? It was added because of transgressions until the Seed to whom the promise referred had come.").

[109] ROMANS 7:15 ("I do not understand what I do. For what I want to do I do not do, but what I hate I do."); ROMANS 7:19 ("For what I do is not the good I want to do; no, the evil I do not want to do—this I keep on doing.").

[110] GALATIANS 3:24 ("So the law was put in charge to lead us to Christ that we might be justified by faith.").

[111] ROMANS 10:4 ("Christ is the end of the law so that there may be righteousness for everyone who believes.").

[112] ROMANS 2:14-15 ("they are a law for themselves, even though they do not have the law, since they show that the requirements of the law are written on their hearts, their consciences also bearing witness, and their thoughts now accusing, now even defending them").

[113] JOHN 8:11 (" 'Well, then,' Jesus said, 'I do not condemn you either. Go, but do not sin again.' ").

[114] LUKE 23:34 ("Father, forgive them, for they do not know what they are doing.").

[115] LUKE 5:12-13 ("When he saw Jesus, he threw himself down and begged him, 'Sir, if you want to, you can make me clean!' Jesus reached out and touched him. 'I do want to,' he answered. 'Be clean!' At once the disease left the man.").

might then live again in faith.[116] Faith's redemption relieves us from the prescriptive and ultimately condemning burden of rule and law.[117]

I recognize how strange it sounds in a professional setting that redemption comes through faith in the sacrificial death of an incarnate God.[118] The myth of the dying God is an ancient story, repeated in many forms in many cultures. The record of those cultures suggests that the myth was reality only once, prepared and anticipated by a millennia-long march through history of a chosen people.[119] For the faith-literate reader, I need not provide details of that history here. We will never distribute so widely any other text as the six billion copies of the sacred writings that record that history. It should suffice here to say that the same God who died first drew out a distinct people whose role it became to anticipate and herald his act of redemption.[120] God died and redeemed within the history of a people whom he created for conveying the death's message.[121] The incarnate God would die observed, on a stage that would project the death across eons in a manner that would make its meaning unmistakable to anyone who cared to watch and listen. Christianity is fundamentally historical.[122] Faith in the Christian tradition is real, not imagined.

---

[116] 2 CORINTHIANS 5:15 ("And he died for all, that those who live should no longer live for themselves but for him who died for them and was raised again.").

[117] GALATIANS 3:25 ("Now that faith has come, we are no longer under the supervision of the law.").

[118] GALATIANS 3:13 ("Christ redeemed us from the curse of the law by becoming a curse for us . . . .").

[119] COLOSSIANS 2:17 ("these are a shadow of the things that were to come; the reality, however, is found in Christ.").

[120] ISAIAH 41:8-9 ("But you, O Israel, my servant, Jacob, whom I have chosen, you descendants of Abraham my friend, I took you from the ends of the earth, from its farthest corners I called you.").

[121] ISAIAH 9:6-7 ("For to us a child is born, to us a son is given, and the government will be on his shoulders. And he will be called Wonderful Counselor, Mighty God, Everlasting Father, Prince of Peace. Of the increase of his government and peace there will be no end. He will reign on David's throne and over his kingdom, establishing it and upholding it with justice and righteousness from that time on and forever.").

[122] LUKE 1:4 ("Therefore, since I myself have carefully investigated everything from the beginning, it seemed good to me to write an orderly

Just as American lawyers can look to the Founders and Francis Lieber for their full experience of law under revolution, so lawyers of faith can look to Christianity for their full experience of faith under revolution, faith holding all things together.[123]

Above members of any other profession, law students and lawyers should recognize the dying God's unmistakable purpose to bring us newly meaningful life.[124] Day after day, we study and practice law, seeing its necessity everywhere but equally seeing how it does little more than ensnare.[125] Law is so pure.[126] We witness its perfection in reasonable care, due diligence, fiduciary duty, offer and acceptance, probable cause, duty of loyalty, character and fitness, duty of competence and diligence, and a hundred other legal concepts. Yet every one of those legal concepts does little more than afford our clients and us the opportunity to violate them.[127] The law that is to bring us order instead defines our disorder.[128] The disorder extends beyond our clients. Lawyers are not immune. We want to do well for ourselves and others but often do not do so.[129] We respect law but find ourselves challenged to satisfy it.[130] On an absolute scale—and the perfection of law demands that we consider the absolute—you can look at the

---

account for you ... so that you may know the certainty of the things you have been taught.").

[123] COLOSSIANS 1:17 ("He is before all things, and in him all things hold together.").

[124] 1 PETER 1:18 ("you were redeemed from the empty way of life handed down to you from your forefathers").

[125] ISAIAH 28:10 ("For it is: 'Do and do, do and do, rule on rule, rule on rule; a little here, a little there—so that they will go and fall backward, be injured and snared and captured.' ").

[126] ROMANS 7:12 ("So then, the law is holy, and the commandment is holy, righteous and good.").

[127] ROMANS 7:11 ("For sin, seizing the opportunity afforded by the commandment, deceived me, and through the commandment put me to death.").

[128] ROMANS 7:10 ("I found that the very commandment that was intended to bring life actually brought death.").

[129] ROMANS 7:21 ("So I find this law at work: When I want to do good, evil is right there with me.").

[130] ROMANS 7:22 ("... I delight in God's law; but I see another law at work in the members of my body, waging war against the law of my mind and making me a prisoner of the law of sin at work within my members.").

lengthy criminal history of the worst of your clients and see your-self there.[131] The violations may be different, but it is only a mat-ter of detection and degree. So far as the perfect law is concerned, we all break the rules, and to break one rule is to break them all.[132] Additionally, there is no hope of escaping detection.[133] Ev-erything is on an open record, whether or not it seems like it.[134]

The challenge for the law student and lawyer is to place in its faith context the inevitable and complete power of law to condemn. What do we make of law's awful power to identify our many transgressions? Is the law bad?[135] The dominant secular (non-religious) view is that law's purpose is instrumental, to shape behavior. In that view, law is only a guide, constraining our behavior and then providing various punishments, remedies, and adjustments of rights when our behavior transgresses. The sociological and psychological view of law is that we carry its commands in mind, for instance not to murder, not to steal, and not to exceed the speed limit. We do some of those things often (exceed the speed limit, for instance), but law serves its function by discouraging the frequent or at least the open and egregious violations. Law does not save or transform the human condition. Law merely restricts and contains the harm from the basest human instincts. The sociological view of law is a bit like the doctor treating the terminal-cancer patient. Cure is not an option. Control, and only for a time, is the goal. Anything more would require creating a new person.[136]

Faith takes a different approach, holding that law's purpose is first to make us conscious of the need for redemption through faith,[137] and that faith can then save and transform our condi-

---

[131] REVELATION 4:17 (" 'You say, "I am rich; I have acquired wealth and do not need a thing." But you do not realize that you are wretched, pitiful, poor, blind and naked.' ").

[132] JAMES 2:10 ("For whoever keeps the whole law and yet stumbles at just one point is guilty of breaking all of it.").

[133] ECCLESIASTES 12:14 ("For God will bring every deed into judgment, including every hidden thing, whether it is good or evil.").

[134] LUKE 8:17 ("For there is nothing hidden that will not be disclosed, and nothing concealed that will not be known or brought out into the open.").

[135] ROMANS 7:13 ("Did that which is good, then, become death to me?").

[136] 2 CORINTHIANS 5:17 ("he is a new creation; the old has gone").

[137] ROMANS 3:20 ("through the law we become conscious of sin").

tion.[138] Faith holds that redemption creates an opportunity for a new person no longer condemned by law.[139] Without redemption, lawyers are unable to satisfy the law and unable to help their clients do so. Faithful lawyers know it. Steeped in law, they have the constant sense of violating law and the concomitant sense of law's condemnation, both their own and their clients.[140] In law practice, faithful lawyers are keenly aware of the guilty mind, of the presence and reality of the temptation to violate law, rules, and regulation, which is actually a temptation common to all of us.[141] Lawyers know more than most that the ability to resist law breaking is beyond many of us most of the time and beyond all of us some of the time, that we lack the ability to resist temptation's constant pressure.[142] Lawyers are also constantly aware of law violations. Faithful lawyers know their need and the need of their clients for redemption through faith, without which there is no hope of anything but condemnation by a guilty conscience.[143] Redemption reconciles the faithful lawyer and willing client to the full demands of law.[144]

To satisfy the demands of law, that is, for redemption from its violation, lawyer and client need only continue in that faith.[145] Faith not only relieves lawyer and client from the burden of having violated law.[146] Faith also gives lawyer and client the willingness to submit to the authority of law, which is itself a

---

[138] DANIEL 3:17 ("the God we serve is able to save us").

[139] ROMANS 6:14 ("you are not under law, but under grace").

[140] COLOSSIANS 1:20 ("Once you were alienated from God and were enemies in your minds because of your evil behavior.").

[141] 1 CORINTHIANS 10:13 ("No temptation has seized you except what is common to man.").

[142] 2 CORINTHIANS 1:8 ("We were under great pressure, far beyond our ability to endure, so that we despaired even of life. ... But this happened that we might not rely on ourselves but on God, who raises the dead.").

[143] HEBREWS 10:22 ("having our hearts sprinkled to cleanse us from a guilty conscience").

[144] COLOSSIANS 1:22 ("But now he has reconciled you by Christ's physical body through death to present you holy in his sight, without blemish and free from accusation—...").

[145] COLOSSIANS 1:23 ("...if you continue in your faith, established and firm, not moved from the hope held out in the gospel.").

[146] GALATIANS 3:25 ("Now that faith has come, we are no longer under the supervision of the law.").

condition of redemption. There is no redemption if one continues to do that which created the need for redemption. It would be only a temporary reprieve if one were quickly to return to the same law violation that created the original need for redemption. Faith creates and reinforces within lawyer and client a consciousness of the authority of law, knowledge of the need to respect that authority, and the desire to do so.[147] The faithful lawyer develops a conscience that guides the lawyer away from law breaking and toward respect for the law. The faithful lawyer develops a keen sense of when the lawyer is complying with law and when lawyer or client may be approaching its violation. Conscience is a work of redemption.[148] Faith gives the lawyer a conscience for law.

Transformation

The lawyer smiled warmly at his friend's humor and ease. His friend always made him feel as if everything would be all right even when much seemed to be all wrong with the cases that they evaluated and shared as co-counsel. This time, the lawyer had referred a client to his friend who specialized in the field in which the client needed legal service. The two had been discussing the client's case, evaluating strategy. Their talk turned from the case to the client, who had struggled so severely that the friend had recommended to the client to a psychologist for evaluation and treatment. Then the friend said something that surprised the lawyer. "I'm surprised that she hasn't relied more on her faith," the friend told the lawyer, not critically or in condescension but as an observation.

Those words stuck with the lawyer long after he and his friend parted that day. The lawyer understood exactly what the friend meant. The client was outwardly a vocal advocate for faith in all things. Yet during the challenge of the events that led to the need for legal service, and during the course of the legal case itself, the client had shown little of that faith, not in words, emotions, or actions. The faith that the client ordinarily exuded had evaporated under these challenges. During the course of the legal case, the

---

[147] PSALM 103:5 ("who satisfies your desires with good things").

[148] ROMANS 2:15 ("they show that the requirements of the law are written on their hearts, their consciences also bearing witness, and their thoughts now accusing, now even defending them").

client had come to rely heavily on the friend's faith rather than her own, even though the friend was not at all vocal about faith. The client had strived mightily out of her own strength but in a manner that led, almost paradoxically, to her utter failure. The legal case might turn the tide of the client's failure, but only (it seemed to the lawyer) through his friend's faith, not any overwhelming merit in the client's case.

Yet the tide did turn in the case and for the client. The lawyer's friend did his usual diligent, sensible, thorough, but somehow unassuming work with the client's case. That work was, as usual, extremely effective. The client made a legal, financial, and emotional recovery, nearly becoming her old self in faith and other things. The success once again caused the lawyer to speculate on what made his friend so effective in both legal work and interpersonal relations. His friend seemed to reside in the legal work more so than to do it. His friend never seemed to strive at the work, certainly not to struggle with it, fight it, or rush it. Faith seemed to have slowed down the friend's work to its intrinsic pace, allowing him to give the work its full attention. There were many things that his friend did not understand, did not know, and could not predict. Still, his friend trusted, seeming to be rooted in something other than his own effort or competence.

Indeed, that was exactly it, the lawyer decided, after identifying a similar presence in several other highly successful lawyers. Each lawyer was different. It was not a matter of personality or style. It was not even a matter of expertise. It was truly more a matter of presence, although not each lawyer's own presence, not at all a charismatic or arrogant presence. These lawyers were the opposite of arrogant. They were instead each remarkably humble, knowing full well that they had no peculiar talent. They instead seemed to have a simple faith, not even in the judicial system but a faith in, well, faith. They just had a way of being steadfast, somehow unshakable and not in argumentation or position—they were instead often willing to concede points—but unshakable in person. They provided a foundation on which clients, judges, jurors, and others could lean, often heavily.

The lawyer had an odd advantage in observing masterful professionals. Well before law school, the lawyer had apprenticed to a master horse trainer, of all things. The lawyer had seen other apprentices take on the accent, clothing, and walk of the master trainer, so ready were they to imitate their own way to the master's success. The apprentices had indeed found some success, though never the master's success. The lawyer had learned then that imitation would only take one so far. Transformation does not occur by imitation because it is always incomplete. Imitation is not really a transformation at all but something more like a theft or charade. The lawyer had no illusion of wanting to imitate his friend or any other lawyer.

What the lawyer could do, he decided, was to take the full measure of faith. It was time to stop striving at law practice, always trying to succeed by doing more or attempting to be more, and instead to practice with more faith. Doing more never really seemed to work, indeed often seemed counterproductive. Efficiency, preparation, and competence were important. So were skill and insight. Yet work piled upon work seemed to serve no one, only to wear out the lawyer, when the professionals in whom the lawyer saw faith never seemed exhausted. Indeed, they seemed to share the energy of faith. Their faith was a source for themselves and others. That vitality was the main reason that the lawyer liked to work with his friend.

For the first time, the lawyer had a clear sense of transformation, that it depends not on effort but on reliance, and reliance not on one's self but on faith, steadfast, unmoving, and courageous, and because so, also victorious. The lawyer finally understood a little of what faith meant in that to seek one's life is to lose it and to lose one's life to find it. The lawyer was finding new life on faith's terms, which the lawyer now fully realized were the best terms for professional success. In the ensuing years, the lawyer continued to refer clients to his friend and to meet with those clients and his friend. Now, though, when the lawyer did, the lawyer had a strong sense of having joined his friend in a very special, even if unspoken, professional community. Being a lawyer within that community was a good thing, personally and professionally.

The faith view of law's role is fundamentally different from other dominant views of law like sociological and psychological views. The sociological view of law conceives of law as a social institution developed over time and set within its peculiar place and culture. Law is one institution in society among several, the aims of which the institution draws from those individuals and social groups who most influence the institution's practices. Law practice involves a competition among society's members and groups to shape and influence the institution for its individual, group, or social advantages. The psychological view of law considers how norms embodied in law's rules and practices influence human cognition and behavior. Law places an occasionally necessary constraint on individuals in order to keep one from interfering with another's life or liberty. Neither view is particularly concerned with the individual's condition. Both views are more concerned with social interactions and behaviors.

Faith has a different premise for law. Faith's premise is that law's purpose is to identify for us our need to transform rather than constrain or improve our condition.[149] Faith seeks a cure of, not an improvement in, a person's condition. Faith seeks to create the conditions for a person to form such new thoughts that it is like the person is a new person with a new mind controlling the person's life and actions for the better.[150] Like redemption, law students and lawyers may find difficult the concept of transformation, although they should not. Law knows that you cannot improve any defect sufficiently to satisfy a perfect standard.[151] You must instead begin anew with a person who no longer has the defect,[152] indeed, whose defect is so far gone and forgotten that the person has not stain or memory of it.[153] The hope is not simply to restrain the law violator—the substance-abusing drunk driver, the child-molesting felon, and the highway speeder, not to mention the board trustee who fails in breach of duties of care to read the charitable organization's monthly financial statements. The hope is instead to reform the violator, to substitute a new person who has no debt or defect, in place of the old violator.[154]

---

[149] ROMANS 7:13 ("[Law] produced death in me through what was good, so that through the commandment sin might become utterly sinful. We know that the law is spiritual; but I am unspiritual, sold as a slave to sin.").

[150] EPHESIANS 4:22-23 ("You were taught, with regard to your former way of life, to put off your old self, which is being corrupted by its deceitful desires; to be made new in the attitude of your minds; and to put on the new self, created to be like God in true righteousness and holiness.").

[151] PROVERBS 30:5 ("Every word of God is flawless... .").

[152] LUKE 17:33 ("Whoever tries to keep his life will lose it, and whoever loses his life will preserve it.").

[153] PSALM 103:12 ("as far as the east is from the west, so far has he removed our transgressions from us").

[154] ROMANS 8:3 ("For what the law was powerless to do in that it was weakened by the sinful nature, God did by sending his own Son in the likeness of sinful man to be a sin offering.").

Think for a moment of how often law attempts to transform and revivify wrongdoers, rather than improve them. The corporation emerging from bankruptcy, the convict emerging from prison, the homeowner redeeming the foreclosed residence, and the tortfeasor's insurer satisfying the tort judgment are each an example. In each case, the law accepts the futility of the legal person digging out of the figurative hole into which the person has fallen and instead allows the person to begin anew. In the law's view, a new person emerges without the old defects and the old person's attendant obligations, free of literal and figurative debt. These legal events, so familiar to law students and lawyers, are not improvement plans. They are instead transformative, substituting one legal person for another. One cannot try the convicted criminal a second time for the same crime. The Constitution prohibits doing so as double jeopardy. A creditor cannot pursue a debtor whom bankruptcy has discharged. Federal law prohibits doing so. In each case, transformation occurs when the old person takes on a new person that the law has offered as a redemptive remedy.[155]

These legal events have their faith equivalents. The faithful lawyer does not try to improve on the lawyer's thinking by the usual concentrated striving.[156] Instead, the faithful lawyer takes on a new mind in transformative event.[157] Faith includes more than hope of future transformation. It includes the means for present transformation. If a new person must substitute for the old violator, then the new person must be without the old violator's defects. Faith provides that substitutionary remedy,[158] so like the legal remedies. The old violator's acceptance of faith is the means of redemption, in much the same manner that the law

---

[155] ROMANS 8:1 ("Therefore, there is now no condemnation for those who are in Christ Jesus, because through Christ Jesus the law of the Spirit of life set me free from the law of sin and death.").

[156] GALATIANS 3:3 ("Are you so foolish? After beginning with the Spirit, are you now trying to attain your goal by human effort?").

[157] ROMANS 12:2 ("Do not conform any longer to the patterns of this world, but be transformed by the renewing of your mind.").

[158] 2 CORINTHIANS 5:21 ("God made him who had no sin to be sin for us, so that in him we might become the righteousness of God.").

provides its legal substitutionary remedies.[159] Faith takes the place of the old violator, whose new person lives on looking more and more like faith's image.[160] Each little success encourages the new person to continue in a relaxed and confident faith without that defeating sense of fruitless striving.[161] Faith's unique image for each of us is far better than the image we would make for ourselves.[162] For the lawyer, faith, like the concept of law remedies, is redemptive.

Law provides specific procedures and means for its redemptive remedies. So, too, does faith. There must be a means by which faith substitutes for the old lawyer. Law's redemptive remedy is on law's terms, not on the violator's terms. So, too, are the terms for faith's redemptive remedy on faith's terms rather than the violator's terms.[163] Faith sets the terms but makes those terms within the reach of the old violator. The old violator's recognition of faith's redemptive remedy is that means.[164] Faith presents a clear transformative formula, not a self-improvement plan but a substitute for all such plans.[165] Self-improvement plans are simply inadequate for the scope of the task of reforming the old violator.[166] The idea is no longer simply to reduce violations. It is to extinguish them, replacing them with a person incapable of violation. Faith encompasses and smothers the wrong, leaving

---

[159] ROMANS 8:6 ("The mind of sinful man is death, but the mind controlled by the Spirit is life and peace.").

[160] 2 CORINTHIANS 3:18 ("we ... are being transformed into his likeness with ever-increasing glory"); ROMANS 8:29 ("For those God foreknew he also predestined to be conformed to the likeness of his Son... .").

[161] ROMANS 9:30 ("[T]he Gentiles, who did not pursue righteousness, have obtained it, a righteousness that is by faith; but Israel, who pursued a law of righteousness, has not attained it. Why not? Because they pursued it not by faith but as if it were by works.").

[162] PSALM 139:14 ("I am fearfully and wonderfully made... ."); EPHESIANS 3:20 ("Now to him who is able to do immeasurably more than all we ask or imagine, according to his power that is at work within us...").

[163] ROMANS 8:33 ("It is God who justifies.").

[164] GALATIANS 3:24 ("So the law was put in charge to lead us to Christ that we might be justified by faith.").

[165] PROVERBS 19:21 ("Many are the plans in a man's heart, but is the Lord's purpose that prevails.").

[166] PROVERBS 20:24 ("A man's steps are directed by the Lord. How then can anyone understand his own way?").

a perfect new person. Faith provides the transformative power, not the old person, whose violations prove the old person's ineffectiveness at reformation.

The interesting thing about faith is the power of its personal formula. How effective the transformation is depends not on faith because faith has already proven perfect. The transformation's effectiveness instead depends on the simple quality of the new person's commitment.[167] Faith made the complete redemptive sacrifice on an extant and unchangeable record. Millions of transformed lives, not to mention the end of slavery and the institutional miracles of orphanages, hospitals, hospices, and thousands of others charitable organizations, prove faith's power.[168] These and other great deeds prove faith's power of individual transformation.[169] Faith's record is there for everyone to read, accept, and receive the promised blessings from it.[170] Law should be a heroic profession, not merely a serving and healing profession. Faith makes it so by the remarkable power of transformation.

What remains in question is whether the old violator accepts it. In that sense, faith presents not a formula but a relationship.[171] If you accept the faith relationship as powerful and genuine, then you receive its benefits. If you reject the relationship, then you reject its benefits and leave yourself to your own devices. The important corollary already suggested is that faith's power does not depend not on the extent of our effort.[172] Personal pursuits are unavailing. They are probably what got us into trouble and made us violators in the first place. Do substance abusers, child molesters, highway speeders, incompetents, and the slothful really have the means of changing those conditions by

---

[167] 1 KINGS 18:21 ("How long will you waver between two opinions?").

[168] JOHN 14:11 ("believe on the evidence of the miracles themselves").

[169] ACTS 26:20 ("prove their repentance by their deeds").

[170] REVELATION 1:3 ("Blessed is the one who reads the words of this prophecy, and blessed are those who hear it and take to hear what is written in it. . . .").

[171] ROMANS 8:38 ("For I am convinced that neither death nor life, . . . nor anything else in creation, will be able to separate us from the love of God that is in Christ Jesus our Lord.").

[172] GALATIANS 3:3 ("Are you now so foolish? After beginning with the Spirit, are you now trying to attain your goal by human effort?").

personal effort? Faith's commitment formula, which is really much more like a relationship, substitutes for personal effort, given that personal effort is so often unavailing.

Yet the faith premise includes more than a hope of and means for transformation. It also includes a promise of reward along with the transformation.[173] Why pursue transformation unless we know of something that we will miss without it? No life here is perfect—not even close, right?[174] Each of us suffers,[175] and yet we seem to suffer for purposes, expecting a proper end of suffering, as if we should not suffer.[176] We wake each day with a more or less eager expectation that suffering will abate,[177] even when we have little evidence of it.[178] It is that expectation that keeps us moving forward each day,[179] keeping us patient and persevering even in our worst times.[180] We anticipate a condition without suffering. We sense the possibility of an endless intimate relationship with no-suffering perfection.[181] Each of us can at least imagine not suffering, and most of us have a strong sense of something approaching an entitlement not to suffer. That sense is an indication of faith alive within us, meaning the hope of a perfection we know from experience that we will never attain on

---

[173] ROMANS 8:17 ("Now if we are children, then we are heirs—heirs of God and co-heirs with Christ, if indeed we share in his sufferings in order that we may also share in his glory.").

[174] ROMANS 8:22 ("We know that the whole creation has been groaning as in the pains of childbirth right up to the present time.").

[175] ROMANS 8:23 ("Not only so, but we ourselves, who have the first fruits of the Spirit, groan inwardly as we wait eagerly for our adoption as sons, the redemption of our bodies.").

[176] ROMANS 8:20 ("For the creation was subjected to frustration, ... in hope that the creation itself will be liberated from its bondage to decay and brought into the glorious freedom of the children of God.").

[177] ROMANS 8:18 ("I consider that our present sufferings are not worth comparing with the glory that will be revealed in us. The creation waits in eager expectation for the sons of God to be revealed.").

[178] ROMANS 8:24 ("But hope that is seen is no hope at all. Who hopes for what he already has?").

[179] ROMANS 8:24 ("For in this hope we were saved.").

[180] ROMANS 8:25 ("But if we hope for what we do not yet have, we wait for it patiently.").

[181] ECCLESIASTES 3:11 ("He has also set eternity in the hearts of men.....").

our own.[182] Faith promises us that perfection in reward for our commitment.[183]

There is another special aspect of faith's reward for transformation. When considering the length and challenges of a law career, it is good to know that faith's reward accumulates to a point that it far more than the challenges the faithful lawyer meets.[184] The more we pursue faith, the greater the reward of our future perfection.[185] We should give attention from the start to how we conceive of and conduct law practice.[186] When we build law practice on its right foundation in faith,[187] the reward is commensurately larger. There are definitely different skills with which to build.[188] I am not saying that we are in any sense all the same. Yet even though each of us labors differently, in different legal fields with different roles and gifts, faith rewards each of us according to our faithful labor.[189] Faith's demand is simply that we use the talents given us.[190] Lawyers have unusual intelligence, industry, discipline, and access to authority. Faith requires that lawyers draw appropriately on those resources. When a lawyer does so, faith rewards the lawyer.

It is also true that faith's power brings the quality of a lawyer's work to light, so that any transformation is more than show but is instead genuine.[191] The power and purity of faith have

---

[182] GALATIANS 2:20 ("It is no longer I who live but Christ who lives in me. And the life I now live in the flesh I live by faith in the Son of God, who loved me and gave himself for me.").

[183] MATTHEW 5:12 ("Rejoice and be glad, because great is your reward in heaven.... ").

[184] 2 CORINTHIANS 4:17 ("For our light and momentary troubles are achieving for us an eternal glory that far outweighs them all.").

[185] MATTHEW 5:12 (" 'be glad, because great is your reward in heaven' ").

[186] 1 CORINTHIANS 3:10 ("But each one should be careful how he builds.").

[187] 1 CORINTHIANS 3:11 ("For no one can lay any foundation other than the one already laid, which is Jesus Christ.").

[188] 1 CORINTHIANS 7:7 ("each man has his own gift from God").

[189] 1 CORINTHIANS 3:8 ("The man who plants and the man who waters have one purpose, and each will be rewarded according to his own labor.").

[190] LUKE 12:48 ("From everyone who has been given much, much will be demanded; and from the one who has been entrusted with much, much more will be asked.").

[191] 1 CORINTHIANS 3:13 ("[H]is work will be shown for what it is, because the Day will bring it to light.").

a way of testing the value of a lawyer's law practice so that the lawyer can see the lawyer's own progress or lack of progress in transformation.[192] The lawyer of faith has great insight.[193] Faith concepts have a way of breaking apart arguments, revealing just how sound or unsound the person is who makes them.[194] What survives that test is only the work built on the foundation of faith,[195] for which the lawyer earns a due reward.[196] Faith reveals to the lawyer whether the lawyer is truly meeting moral standards in the way that earns the lawyer faith's reward. Faith's reward is a specific kind of reward, proportionate not to our merit, of which we have none, but to the activity of our commitment.[197] The quality of our commitment qualifies us for reward, but the reward itself we earn by the activity of our commitment.[198] Thus, law practiced by faith has its redemptive and transformative nature, resulting in a reward worthy of the work faith produces.

The next question is whether faith's redemptive and transformative nature makes a difference in law studies and practice. Why care about these things, when one might instead live for now without them, even if mundanely? Faith's premise is that you must care, or your professional and personal life will show it.[199] Professional practice and the personal life that makes it possible have ways of revealing one's self. We get what we wish, whether in the end we find that we really wanted it.[200] We must therefore

---

[192] 1 CORINTHIANS 3:13 ("It will be revealed with fire, and the fire will test the quality of each man's work.").

[193] 2 CORINTHIANS 5:7 ("We live by faith, not by sight.").

[194] JEREMIAH 23:29 (" 'Is not my word like fire,' declares the Lord, 'and like a hammer that breaks a rock in pieces?' ").

[195] 1 CORINTHIANS 3:11 ("For no one can lay any other foundation other than the one already laid, which is Jesus Christ.").

[196] 1 CORINTHIANS 3:14 ("If what he has built survives, he will receive his reward.").

[197] MATTHEW 16:27 ("For the Son of Man is going to come in his Father's glory with his angels, and then he will reward each person according to what he has done.").

[198] 1 CORINTHIANS 3:15 ("If it is burned up, he will suffer loss; he himself will be saved, but only as one escaping through the flames.").

[199] ECCLESIASTES 12:14 ("For God will bring every deed into judgment, including every hidden thing, whether it is good or evil.").

[200] PROVERBS 20:5 ("The purposes of a man's heart are deep waters, but a man of understanding draws them out.").

examine our ways, if we desire to end up where we most want.[201] Inescapably teleological beings, we purpose,[202] and our capability of purposing forces us to choose purposes, whether we wish to or not. We should choose consistent with those purposes that will prevail for others and us in the end.[203] See in the following chapters what you think of how these truths connect with law studies, law practice, and law itself.

---

[201] LAMENTATIONS 3:40 ("Let us examine our ways and test them, and let us return to the Lord."); II CORINTHIANS 13:5 ("Examine yourselves to see whether you are in the faith; test yourselves.").

[202] PROVERBS 19:21 ("Many are the plans in a man's heart... .").

[203] PROVERBS 19:21 ("... but it is the Lord's purpose that prevails").

Chapter 1

Law Studies

CHALLENGES STRENGTHENING FAITH

Law studies precede and permeate law practice. Law students must learn vast quantities of law to pass the bar and become effective lawyers, while lawyers must continue to learn law to remain competent and effective. Do not underestimate the challenge. There is so much law in any one subject that its professors devote their careers to it and still find portions of it beyond their experience. The challenge to students who are, after all, often completely unfamiliar with those subjects, is of course far greater. The quantity of law is so vast, its complexity is so startling, and the energy, discipline, and commitment that acquiring it takes is so formidable, that law students and lawyers inevitably face challenges of faith. The challenge of law studies changes in the second year toward acquiring surprisingly subtle skills and in the third year toward integrating knowledge and skills into a professional identity, before the challenge of doctrinal studies returns, multiplied in its comprehensiveness, for the bar exam.

Lawyers then go on learning intensely for the first part of their careers,[1] where despite their studies, nearly everything seems new and unfamiliar. It can take months in law practice to gain a sense of routine and years in practice to gain a sense of mastery, meaning that learning continues to be critical to professional development and success. Throughout one's law career, the law itself changes, as do the legal challenges that our client's face, meaning that we must continually learn new law and

---

[1] PSALM 1:2 ("on his law he meditates day and night").

new forms and subjects of legal service.[2] Then, many lawyers in mid career or late career develop new practice areas or even change law careers, meaning that there are new law studies to master. Law studies do not really end at any point. As long as a lawyer continues to practice, the lawyer remains responsible to help others learn the law.[3]

It would be wrong to see law studies as a burden.[4] For the law student and lawyer, law studies become a way of living by learning. Law studies have much to recommend them as a way of life. Many feel that to live is to learn and to learn to live. Flourishing has a lot to do with gaining new knowledge and mastery. To make it so, though, it is critical to approach law studies with faith. In the challenge of law studies, faith in all its tenets matters. The tenets of faith that matter much to law studies include belief, obedience, honesty, and trust. Belief, meaning the willingness to hold propositions after testing them, fuels learning. Obedience, meaning the willingness to submit to legal authority, supports learning. Honesty, meaning the willingness to see and embrace truth, perfects learning. Trust, meaning the commitment to proceed when doubting the efficacy of doing so, rewards with learning. Read this chapter to see if you agree that faith affects how we learn, how much we learn, and what we learn, and that law studies require faith.

Belief

The lawyer sat outside in his car, waiting for his wife to finish chatting with friends and join him for the ride home. The lawyer reflected on the morning's message they had just heard that the word of faith is like a seed that, planted in the right soil, grows into a great sheltering tree. The lawyer found these rich allegories to be powerful antidotes to the overly analytical legal mind that law school had developed in him. Lawyers depend on analysis, but they also depend on communication. Stories and images inform in

---

[2] PSALM 119:78 ("I will meditate on your precepts").

[3] NEHEMIAH 8:8 ("They read from the Book of the Law of God, making it clear and giving the meaning so that the people could understand what was being read.").

[4] 1 CORINTHIANS 6:12 ("I will not be mastered by anything").

ways that analysis cannot. The lawyer had no illusion that he had any oratorical gift. He most surely did not. Yet he knew that great trial lawyers draw on images and themes, and from the morning's message, he could once again see why. In any case, the lawyer could increasingly see that the seed of faith need only take root in a lawyer's soul for the lawyer's faith and practice to become a sheltering tree to clients and others. The allegory was possible in practice. The lawyer had seen it among some of the masterful professionals with whom he had professional contact.

As the lawyer waited for his wife, who was still on the other side of the parking lot hugging friends in the chill fall air, the lawyer opened the book of faith in his lap and turned to its first page. Some years earlier, it had gradually dawned on the lawyer that as voracious a reader as the lawyer had been all of his life that the lawyer really knew no book. He had read many but had known none. Yet the lawyer had come to know illiterate men in his faith community who, despite reading so poorly that they needed help with each sentence and difficult word, could quote from memory dozens of verses from the book of faith. The realization both shamed and inspired the lawyer who, having read hundreds of books with his lawyer's gift for reading, had no book of any kind in particular to which he turned or from which he drew.

So, the lawyer had taken to reading the book of faith over and over, cover to cover. Sometimes he had read it over the course of a year. Sometimes he had read it over the course of a month, two months, three months, or six months. Repeatedly he had read its thousand-plus pages, letting its stories and words of faith sink in. He had even read it once or twice cover to cover while on his knees, not knowing particularly why but thinking that it might somehow be appropriate. Oddly, the cumulative and focused efforts of reading this one single book 18 or 20 times had still not brought him to the level of mastery of his illiterate friends. The lawyer knew why. Unlike his illiterate friends, the lawyer lived and worked within communities that did not in any direct respect share the book of faith. By contrast, the illiterate men lived and worked within a faith community that constantly celebrated and shared the book. We are whose company we keep.

Yet if the lawyer's reading effort was not much availing in producing any specific mastery of the words of faith, his effort had at least given the lawyer some ability to recognize how bound his professional community was by its non-faith culture. Reading the book of faith consistently had given the lawyer a distinct perspective on his professional community. That perspective had proven very useful. The lawyer could see more clearly how other lawyers thought and how their thinking influenced their counsel. The lawyer became gradually more able to modify some of the professional culture to serve clients who were, after all, no part of that culture. The lawyer began to be better able to switch from lawyer thinking to faith thinking to client thinking, moving from culture to culture with a new meta-cognitive skill. The lawyer determined to continue reading the book of faith in order to maintain that faith perspective, which he had found useful as a lawyer.

With the late-fall sun shining, the car grew warm inside as the lawyer waited for his wife, so he flipped the key to turn on the car's power to lower the windows just an inch before returning to reading. The lawyer's eyes traced the lines down to the middle of the book's first page to the story of faith's forming the first plants and trees bearing seed. The lawyer lifted his eyes from the page to let his mind drift back to the message that he had just heard about the seed growing into the tree of faith. The lawyer looked out across the bright parking lot warming the chill in the late-fall sun, as his mind turned over and over the message of the seed.

Just then, the lawyer saw a breeze stir some dust into a tiny swirl on the other side of the parking lot. The swirl carried a small gust of bright little maple seeds, whirly birds, across the sunny parking lot to the lawyer's waiting car, as if a person made of wind and seeds had strolled across the parking lot. It was perfectly still inside the warm car with the windows cracked just an inch. When the small whirling cloud of seeds reached the lawyer's car, one seed somehow slipped through the passenger-side window, crossed the passenger compartment to the lawyer sitting in the driver's seat, and lodged itself under the lawyer's thumb holding the middle of the book of faith right at the story of the first seed. The lawyer looked down at the book of faith with the literal seed tucked under his thumb on the words of seeds, thinking of the extraordinary providence of what had just happened.

Some persons go a lifetime without a miracle and still believe. Others receive many miracles and never believe. At that moment, the lawyer decided that although he needed no miracles in order to believe, he was so very, very glad to have just received so diaphanous, gentle, touching, and telling of a one. The lawyer then let a gentle tear fall on the tiny seed stuck under his thumb on the page as his body shook in private celebration. Anyone who feels that celebration just once understands what grandly vital life is truly possible.

It is easy to miss the significance of belief. The modern mind has a bias against belief. We think that we are enlightened, meaning that we are trusting only in those things for which there is substantial evidence, things proven to us. Instead, belief permeates our thinking, and not on subjects of faith, but on all subjects. We believe things that were never true and never in any sense proven to us but simply passed along to us.[5] We accept what others tell us, often including those whom we do not have any reason to trust. We accept assertions without rationale or justification, often simply because it fits with what we want to think of the world, our situation in it, or others.[6] Because we think that we have accepted only things proven, believing ourselves fully enlightened, we miss the large extent of our assumptions and belief. We miss that we are like sponges, soaking up belief according to whatever it is that we have last heard or read to be true. We believe ourselves enlightened from belief, when belief is instead our constant companion.

Our odd bias against the notion of belief works against faith and against us. We think that the religious are the only ones who believe without basis, when to the contrary we all believe multitudes of things without rationale or thought, simply because someone asserted them and they fit with common views of things. In our bias against belief and especially against organized belief like religion, we then make faith the one subject on which we consistently doubt, when doubt is the antithesis of faith in the law.[7] Belief is fundamental to our well-being generally and as lawyers specifically, whether it is organized and accepted religious belief or simply belief of things that do in fact serve us. We could not do without belief. Doubt would freeze us if we required proof of even a fraction of everything that we quickly accept and come to believe, and on which we then reasonably rely. Our bias against belief, when we depend fully on it, is particularly troubling when it works against our believing things compelled by faith. It is not only that it leads to a kind of condescending religious bigotry. It is also that we reject that which best serves

---

[5] 1 PETER 1:18 ("the empty way of life handed down to you from your forefathers").

[6] COLOSSIANS 2:8 ("See to it that no one takes you captive through hollow and deceptive philosophy, which depends on human tradition and the basic principles of this world rather than on Christ.").

[7] PSALM 119:113 ("I hate double-minded men, but I love your law.").

us. Belief consistent with things of faith promotes a kind of well-being that does not just improve our condition but transforms it.[8]

The same is true for law studies, that belief is critical to law student and lawyer success in learning law. We would be unable to study without belief. Belief enables us to understand law studies.[9] One can hardly think without believing. Belief is the way through which we construct our thoughts about law and on which we ultimately base our actions. One must at least hold a premise for examination in order to learn anything. We learn by accepting premise after premise, connecting one to another into a coherent and consistent whole, recognizing truth by its consistency.[10] Certainly, inquiry plays a role. Lawyers do not believe everything that they hear or read. Testing and organizing premises is an important part of learning and practicing law. Yet lawyers must accept many premises, even ones that they acknowledge may later prove wrong, like the innocence of a client. Lawyers must listen to and accept matters of faith in order to recognize, learn, recall, and employ the most sensitive and valuable of premises.[11]

Lawyers must also commit with passion to those beliefs, especially the central beliefs on which one best builds a law practice.[12] Probably, if there were anything that a lawyer might wish at the beginning of a career, it would be that the lawyer develop and maintain a passion for the practice of law. There are few things more satisfying than to work at something about which you care deeply. There are few things less satisfying than to work at something about which you do not care. Belief plays an integral role in the satisfaction of one's career. You can choose whether to have or not to have passion.[13] You can find ways through faith to engage your work with your every effort.[14] Faith

---

[8] JOHN 1:12 ("Yet to all who received him, to those who believed in his name, he gave the right to become children of God.").

[9] JOHN 12:46 ("I have come into the world as a light, so that no one who believes in me should stay in darkness.").

[10] PSALM 18:30 ("the word of the Lord is flawless").

[11] JOHN 8:47 (" 'The reason you do not hear is that you do not belong to God.' ").

[12] ROMANS 12:11 ("keep your spiritual fervor").

[13] 1 THESSALONIANS 5:19 ("Do not put out the Spirit's fire... .").

[14] 2 TIMOTHY 1:6 ("fan into flame the gift of God, which is in you").

can kindle passion for the work of a law career. If one wants to look for something that helps make one passionate about what one does, then look for faith, and the belief that faith engenders.[15] Then you will find passion for your law career.

The question is not whether to believe but what to believe.[16] If you choose the right belief, then you can build a law career that will satisfy you, impress your family and friends, and keep you from the embarrassment and shame of failure as a professional.[17] That statement includes an important point, that your belief benefits not just you but your family and friends.[18] The key is to choose the right belief, that which is most consistent with the way that the things that are subject to belief operate.[19] The challenge is to believe those truths that give us the greatest meaning in law practice and life.[20] We must avoid falling for the myths that others propagate against the truths that works so well in law practice.[21] The principal myth that we must reject is the one that says that we properly reject all belief, when in fact, we rely so constantly and appropriately on belief, and it is only a matter of recognizing consistently the right belief.[22] Overcome the myths that only the foolhardy believe, and you will find yourself and your law career open to new possibilities.

Recognize that belief is powerful, as powerful for law students and lawyers as for others. It has a powerful effect on one's

---

[15] MATTHEW 3:11 ("He will baptize you with the Holy Spirit and with fire").

[16] 1 JOHN 4:1 ("Dear friends, do not believe every spirit, but test the spirits to see whether they are from God, because many false prophets have gone out into the world.").

[17] 1 PETER 2:6 ("For in Scripture it says, 'See, I lay a stone in Zion, a chosen and precious cornerstone, and the one who trusts in him will never be put to shame.' ").

[18] ACTS 16:31 ("They replied, 'Believe in the Lord Jesus, and you will be saved—you and your household.' ").

[19] COLOSSIANS 1:17 ("in him all things hold together").

[20] JOHN 3:16 ("For God so loved the world that he gave his one and only Son, that whoever believes in him shall not perish but have eternal life.").

[21] TITUS 1:14 ("Therefore, rebuke them sharply, so that they will be sound in the faith and will pay no attention to … myths or the commands of those who reject the truth.").

[22] TITUS 1:15 ("To the pure, all things are pure, but to those who are corrupted and do not believe, nothing is pure.").

confidence and personality, not to mention one's commitment and actions. It is especially important that our actions be true because clients and others know us by our actions.[23] Belief is also really the only thing that satisfies intellectual hunger. Our thoughts constantly chase belief. To deny ourselves belief is to deny something essential to human thought, emotion, action, and character. The right kind of belief satisfies that incessant intellectual hunger that drives and in some cases haunts us, helping us to counsel right action for others while taking right actions for ourselves.[24] Satisfying that hunger with the right kind of belief, that is, with the true things of faith, makes us want to come back for more of that belief that satisfies.[25] Belief gives a lawyer and law career life, and not just any life but the best kind of life.[26]

For example, law studies and practice constantly challenge lawyers in their relationships. Law is not naturally relational. Law has the power, often exercised by lawyers, to judge, criticize, and divide. One of the greatest powers of belief is the power to fix the things that we have done poorly, incompletely, and wrong in the past. Belief helps repair professional relationships, to make up to others what we owe them but have not provided.[27] There are things that lawyers can believe that will help us overcome and make right those wrongs, so that we do not live with a sense of being a critic and judge, and with it, inadequate, a thief, and cheater. With belief, we can instead live with a sense of being special, useful, and complete, even as we study and practice law, doing things that might otherwise challenge and isolate us.[28]

Professionals need that sense of completeness and effectiveness to be a success. Belief gives us that sense of mastery that all

---

[23] PROVERBS 20:11 ("Even a child is known by his actions.... .").

[24] PROVERBS 14:15 ("The simple man believes anything, but a prudent man gives thought to his steps.").

[25] JOHN 6:35 ("Then Jesus declared, 'I am the bread of life. He who comes to me will never go hungry, and he who believes in me will never be thirsty.' ").

[26] JOHN 6:47 (" 'I tell you the truth, he who believes has everlasting life.' ").

[27] ROMANS 13:7 ("Give everyone what you owe him.... .").

[28] ACTS 10:43 ("All the prophets testify about him that everyone who believes in him receives forgiveness of sins through his name.").

professionals need.[29] Clients rely on lawyers to have the confidence and judgment to help them in their matters. The first quality that a lawyer must have is the ability to convey that confidence. It can be hard to draw confidence from law studies, but belief is an antidote to the fear that destroys confidence.[30] Belief makes all things seem possible and, by doing so, makes more things possible than we imagined.[31] Belief overcomes our doubt that we can learn, recall, and use the sheer quantity of law that a legal education and law practice require. Belief gives us the intrinsic motivation that is superior for law studies and practice over extrinsic motivations like doubt and fear. When we are confident, we attempt more, and when we attempt more, we do more, and we do it better.

Belief also helps us comply with law. It is especially important for law students and lawyers that there are things that we can believe that keep us from law's condemnation. We are law students and lawyers whom law ought not to condemn. Who wants a law-breaking lawyer, one who cannot comply with the profession's rules of conduct? Belief helps us comply with the professional rules, norms, and practices that make for sound law practice. Belief gives us that authentically innocent standing before the law that clients require.[32] Faith plays an integral role in law studies by guiding us to a proper understanding of the critical role of belief and helping us identify the right things in which to believe. All lawyers believe something. Recognize the power of belief. The lawyers who choose the right belief at the right moment when there is still little evidence for it are often those who most prosper.[33]

A faithful lawyer also avoids doubt on the fundamental things of faith. Doubt is the antithesis of belief. A lawyer who

---

[29] JOHN 3:36 ("Whoever believes in the Son has eternal life, but whoever rejects the Son will not see life, for God's wrath remains on him.").

[30] MARK 5:36 (" 'Don't be afraid; just believe.' ").

[31] MARK 9:23 (" ' "If you can"?' said Jesus. 'Everything is possible for him who believes.' ").

[32] JOHN 3:18 ("Yet to all who received him, to those who believed in his name, he gave the right to become children of God.").

[33] JOHN 20:29 ("Then Jesus told him, 'Because you have seen me, you have believed; blessed are those who have not seen and yet have believed.' ").

doubts is one who has no clear mind or has conflicting opinions about central commitments. Lawyers should instead know, believe, and hold fast to central commitments. They also should be able at any time to define those commitments firmly and clearly. Law students and lawyers should seek in law studies that kind of firm and clear belief. The goal is not to amass a huge quantity of disconnected rules. It is to connect rules to central understandings and commitments. The goal is to organize learning into a synthetic whole out of which a lawyer can make sense and share that sense with others. Clients need more than just the rule. They need a sense of how the rule connects to the whole, why there is the rule, and why the client should value the rule like the lawyer. These practices require belief.

When a lawyer doubts, the lawyer loses the foundation for everything else that the lawyer says and does.[34] Doubt has a way of first undermining the work and counsel of a lawyer, and then eventually undermining the lawyer.[35] Lawyers who doubt find little success in anything that they do. Lawyers who doubt too often on fundamental things and at critical times are hardly fit to be lawyers.[36] Belief and faith connect. Faith is the antidote to destructive doubt.[37] Faith overcomes doubt, making possible surprising things that once looked impossible,[38] particularly those things that are the greatest obstacle to us and to our clients.[39] The faithful lawyer does not doubt on central commitments.

The faithful lawyer also treats kindly clients and others who doubt, in order that those others may begin to have the faith of

---

[34] 1 CORINTHIANS 3:11 ("For no one can lay any foundation other than the one already laid, which is Jesus Christ.").

[35] JAMES 1:6 ("[H]e who doubts is like a wave of the sea, blown and tossed by the wind. That man should not think he will receive anything from the Lord; he is a double-minded man, unstable in all he does.").

[36] PSALM 119-113 ("I hate double-minded men, but I love your law.").

[37] MATTHEW 14:31 ("Immediately Jesus reached out his hand and caught him. 'You of little faith,' he said, 'why did you doubt?' ").

[38] JOHN 15:5 ("apart from me you can do nothing").

[39] MATTHEW 21:21 ("Jesus replied, 'I tell you the truth, if you have faith and do not doubt, not only can you do what was done to the fig tree, but also you can say to this mountain, "Go, throw yourself into the sea," and it will be done.' ").

the lawyer, but the lawyer does not doubt.[40] The lawyer's role is to convey belief through faith and convey it in a convincing manner that satisfies and removes the doubt of others. Law students and lawyers should recognize just how important a role belief plays in the study of law and then the practice of law. Clients hunger and pay for belief. Judges want to see it. Juries demand it. Opponents fear it. Law studies help a law student and lawyer find the right belief, the kind that is common, authentic, meaningful, and trustworthy. Belief is the goal of law studies. Belief is the product of faith.[41]

Obedience

The lawyer could not believe it. The police cruiser had turned its flashing lights on for the lawyer to pull over. The lawyer shook his head, found a parking lot, pulled his car in, and waited patiently in the darkness while the officer took his license, insurance, and registration back to the police cruiser. Time ticked by in the very early morning darkness.

The lawyer had left his home at the usual 4:30 a.m. for the long drive across the state to be at work there by 7:30 a.m. Leave any later and traffic would hopelessly mire the lawyer on the other side of the state later that morning. The lawyer had long ago grown accustomed to the once-a-week commutes between law offices. The lawyer appreciated doing the work of the law firm's main office this way each week as he developed his own clientele out of the new office. He hoped that the long drives would not last too much longer, but then, the lawyer was not going to complain about them. His law partners had been generous and under-standing in letting him try opening a new office in his wife's home town where they would raise their child. The lawyer was more than willing to make the weekly drives in exchange to make the most of their gracious accommodation.

The lawyer routinely shortened the long drives in the way that most other drivers did, by setting the car's cruise control a few miles per hour over the speed limit. Everyone knew that you could

---

[40] JUDE 22 ("Be merciful to those who doubt; snatch others from the fire and save them... .").

[41] MARK 9:24 (" 'If you can?' said Jesus. 'Everything is possible for him who believes.' Immediately the boy's father exclaimed, 'I do believe; help me overcome my unbelief!' ").

get away with five over the limit. The lawyer kept it to three or four over just to be safe. The lawyer also kept a sharp lookout for police vehicles, especially where the lawyer knew they usually waited. The lawyer knew all of the favorite lookout spots and was good at slowing to avoid detection at each of them. Yet this morning, the lawyer had been briefly inattentive at the very start of his trip, not yet even thinking that there might be a waiting officer. The officer finally came back to the car window with a ticket for going five miles per hour over the speed limit. The lawyer bit his tongue not to ask whether five over at 4:30 a.m. when there was not another car or person in sight was really an offense worth citing.

The lawyer spent the next three hours on the road mulling the answer to that question. Of course, it was an offense. A speed limit is a speed limit. It may have been a minor offense with no real victim under the circumstances. There was no one out at 4:30 a.m. other than the offending lawyer and apprehending officer. Yet as the lawyer turned the question repeatedly in his mind, he realized that there was a greater offense involved in his actions. The lawyer had been deliberately violating the law by driving three to four miles per hour over the speed limit—five over early this morning. The lawyer had been doing so day after day, pretty much wherever and whenever he was driving, as a constant habit.

The lawyer continued to reflect while the sun gradually lightened the dark early-morning sky. The lawyer realized that to accommodate the fact that he was consistently breaking the law, the lawyer had also adopted what he now recognized to be an anti-detection ethic. The lawyer had been thinking that he would have been an offender only if someone had detected his wrong. The truth was that he was a constant offender, guilty whether or not apprehended. The law is the law, and a violation is a violation, whether or not someone catches the violator. The lawyer realized how completely wrong his attitude toward the law had been and how deeply his wrong had affected his driving behavior. The lawyer also realized that his offense had a victim, and he was that victim.

On the long drive home that evening, the lawyer adjusted his speed to the limit, not three, four, or five over the limit. At first, it seemed frustrating to let all those other cars go rushing by. He would also be 10 to 15 minutes later than usual arriving home that evening. Yet as the miles ticked slowly by, the lawyer realized that he was no longer anxiously squinting ahead to see if there was a police vehicle hidden behind a guardrail or overpass. He was also no longer tucking in behind other vehicles as they passed the slower cars, using the speeding offense of others to hide his own offenses. The lawyer had no need for a guilty mind. He was no longer an offender. The lawyer smiled at the realization that he could drive without worry wherever he wanted so long as he stayed within the speed limit. The lawyer saw that in law there is not constraint but is instead liberty. The constraints are in law's violation.

The lawyer's relief and the other insights he drew from the ticketing that morning helped him to see the event through a different perspective. The grumbling that he wanted to do that morning dissipated, replaced with an odd appreciation for the officer's action. It had been, after all, an inexpensive lesson, one that the lawyer should appreciate for correcting his outlook. He knew that others that day would not have had that correction, indeed that everyone seemed to be able to get away with driving five over. Why not the lawyer? Yet the lawyer was strangely glad that he was now not able to drive five over, that the perspective of faith had held him to its higher and true standard. The lawyer's realization led the lawyer to wonder in what other areas of his daily life he was living by that same desultory anti-detection ethic. If he discovered any, then he was now committed to eradicating it.

Not that the lawyer was now perfect. Over the next few weeks, the lawyer realized how powerful the tendency to justify one's violations is. He continued to want to speed. He never really lost the temptation. The temptation to speed was so strong that the lawyer one day realized that he had developed a sophisticated but reliable method to combat it: take his foot off the accelerator whenever his speed exceeded the limit. He chuckled deeply at his sophisticated method, realizing just how hard the mind works to justify misconduct and how easy it really is to stop it. What the lawyer did was to lose the ability to justify, as he realized that each justification relied on a corrupt ethic. He continued for a long time to enjoy the humor behind his sophisticated lift-the-foot-from-the-pedal method.

The lawyer also appreciated that staying within a posted speed limit is only formal compliance. Obedience of the faith kind goes beyond formal compliance to genuine respect for authority. In addition, it mattered just as much where the lawyer drove as it did how fast or slow he got there. Obedience to authority has both substantive and procedural dimensions. The lawyer began filling the long drives back and forth to the main office with thoughts of those substantive ends of obedience including the professional relationships the travel represented, the welfare of the clients the lawyer served, and the objectives of their claims and defenses. The lawyer now appreciated that whatever he thought of his obedience to the right ends was, in the right way of thinking about it, perfectly transparent. The omniscience of faith had replaced the ethic of anti-detection, and the lawyer felt much, much better for it.

Faith during law studies helps law students and lawyers recognize and respect the role of authority and our relationship to it. It should be obvious that authority and a lawyer's obedience to it play central roles in law studies and practice. Law is authoritative.[42] Law's authority is the central point of law studies and practice. Because authority and obedience to it are so central to law studies and practice, law students and lawyers must develop and maintain the right attitudes about authority and obedience.[43] The question is how we do so. If law studies do not teach a law student about authority and obedience, then law practice will surely teach the lawyer obedience. Yet it is a hard way to learn obedience on the wrong end of a trial judge's contempt sanction, witness's grievance, or client's malpractice suit. Law studies should teach law students and lawyers to respect and obey authority.[44] Faith is the source for understanding authority's nature and for understanding what it means to obey authority.

What is it that faith teaches lawyers about authority? Authority is a universal attribute, meaning that it lies inherent in every environment in which lawyers and others work.[45] Faith, not every lawyer appreciates, is authoritative.[46] More obviously, to the lawyer, law as a manifestation of faith is also authoritative.[47] History and current events certainly teach us that man should live under law rather than under man, that law constrains power in a way necessary to fair governance. Of necessity, we live under the rule of law, which means that we each owe the duty to submit to

---

[42] PSALM 119:120 ("My flesh trembles in fear of you; I stand in awe of your laws.").

[43] ECCLESIASTES 12:13 ("Fear God and keep his commandments, for this is the whole duty of man.").

[44] ISAIAH 1:17 ("Stop doing wrong, learn to do right!").

[45] ROMANS 13:1 ("[T]here is no authority except that which God has established."); MATTHEW 28:20 (" 'All authority in heaven and on earth has been given to me.' ").

[46] ISAIAH 48:11 ("I will not yield my glory to another").

[47] ROMANS 7:1 ("[T]he law has authority over a man only as long as he lives.").

governance under law.[48] You cannot have the rule of law without obedience to law, in which lawyers obviously play a principal role.

Law is not self-administering. Law establishes governing authorities. Some of those authorities are judges and lawyers. Citizens owe obedience to judges and occasionally also to lawyers as representatives of the law.[49] It is natural and necessary, then, that as law students and lawyers, we commit ourselves and urge others to obey the law and those appointed to administer it.[50] As lawyers, we are careful about the law, trying to make sure that both others and we comply with it.[51] Lawyers have little hope of succeeding in law practice without obeying the law and encouraging others to do so. Yet by obeying, lawyers find that it goes well for them in law practice.[52] Obedience to governing authorities is critical to law studies and practice.[53] To reject governance is to reject the rule of law.[54] To reject governance is also to reject and dishonor those who govern.[55] Lawyers should support the work of those who govern.[56] The personal consequence of rejecting governance is to bring judgment against and condemnation to one's self.[57] Rejecting governance also brings

---

[48] ROMANS 7:1 ("Everyone must submit himself to the governing authorities....").

[49] ROMANS 7:1 ("The authorities that exist have been established by God.").

[50] TITUS 3:1 ("Remind the people to be subject to rulers and authorities, to be obedient, to be ready to do whatever is good, to slander no one, to be peaceable and considerate, and to show true humility toward all men.").

[51] JOSHUA 1:7 ("being careful to act in accordance with all the law").

[52] DEUTERONOMY 6:3 ("be careful to obey so that it may go well with you").

[53] JOSHUA 1:7 ("do not turn from it to the right hand or to the left, so that you may be successful wherever you go").

[54] ROMANS 7:2 ("Consequently, he who rebels against the authority is rebelling against what God has instituted....").

[55] HEBREWS 13:17 ("Obey your leaders and submit to their authority. They keep watch over you as men who must give an account.").

[56] HEBREWS 13:17 ("Obey them so that their work will be a joy, not a burden, for that would be of no advantage to you.").

[57] ROMANS 7:2 ("and those who do so will bring judgment on themselves").

fear of governing authorities, violation of the law, and attendant punishment.[58]

We generally see authority as oppressive to our activities and nature, and think of obedience as a limitation. Yet faith teaches us that the view of authority as constraining is a false view. Conversely, obeying authority brings liberty.[59] Authority and obedience to it liberate us particularly when we follow the dictates of faith on authority.[60] That is, when we accept authority and obedience as articles of faith and act on them by choice, we lose the sense of authority and obedience as oppressive. We recognize that we cannot disobey authority and choose our own way without being inconsistent with the requirements of faith. That recognition makes us a partner with authority rather than a subject of it, which is the exact stance that lawyers must take. We then follow the course that is best for those whom we serve and for us.

To the faithful lawyer, faith is authoritative, the sole source of both law and judgment.[61] The faithful lawyer follows it as a matter of obedience, knowing that it will be best for the lawyer and others.[62] The faithful lawyer does not make extensive, circuitous, and risky plans to avoid authority. The faithful lawyer knows that complex plans to side-step authority can be worse than useless in that they can lead the lawyer and clients away from sound decisions and actions.[63] Better than complex plans is

---

[58] ROMANS 7:4 ("But if you do wrong, be afraid, for he does not bear the sword for nothing. He is God's servant, an agent of wrath to bring punishment on the wrongdoer.").

[59] ROMANS 7:3 ("For rulers hold no terror for those who do right, but for those who do wrong.").

[60] JAMES 1:25 ("the man who looks intently into the perfect law that gives freedom").

[61] ISAIAH 45:23 ("Before me every knee will bow... ."); JAMES 4:12 ("There is only one Lawgiver and Judge... .").

[62] PROVERBS 16:9 ("In his heart a man plans his course, but the Lord determines his steps.").

[63] JAMES 4:13–14 ("Now listen, you who say, 'Today or tomorrow we will go to this or that city, spend a year there, carry on business and make money.' Why, you do not even know what will happen tomorrow. What is your life? You are a mist that appears for a little while and then vanishes.").

obedience to law and faith.[64] Those of us, particularly law students and lawyers, who develop and maintain a consciousness of law and then follow that conscience, avoid condemnation and its punishments.[65] We live free of anxiety and help our clients also do so.[66] Faith helps us obey, especially as we accept that faith is authoritative.[67] Lawyers who have faith are more willing to accept what they hear from authoritative sources rather than disagreeing with and rejecting authority.[68]

Faith also aids law studies by teaching us the distinction between authority and the authoritarian. As every law student and lawyer learns, there are rulers whose false authority we are not to follow.[69] Faith helps us distinguish true authority from false authority, meaning the authoritarian.[70] Faith helps lawyers distinguish the arbitrary rule of man, in the nature of the authoritarian, from the sound rule of law, in the nature of authority. As lawyers, we devote ourselves to the support of authorities so that peace and order may prevail.[71] Yet as law students and lawyers, we also stand firm and with courage against authoritarian rulers who exercise power without law's authority.[72] Faith helps lawyers see that properly constituted law is the basis for

---

[64] JAMES 4:15 ("Instead, you ought to say, 'If it is the Lord's will, we will live and do this or that.' ").

[65] ROMANS 7:5 ("Therefore, it is necessary to submit to the authorities, not only because of possible punishment but also because of conscience.").

[66] ROMANS 7:3 ("Do you want to be free from fear of the one in authority? Then do what is right and he will commend you.").

[67] EZEKIEL 36:27 (" 'And I will put my Spirit in you and move you to follow my decrees and be careful to keep my laws.' ").

[68] PROVERBS 10:8 ("The wise in heart accept commands.....").

[69] EPHESIANS 6:12 ("For our struggle is not against flesh and blood, but against the rulers, against the authorities, against the powers of this dark world and against the spiritual forces of evil in the heavenly realms.").

[70] MARK 13:22 ("false prophets will appear and perform signs and miracles to deceive").

[71] 1 TIMOTHY 2:2 ("I urge, then, first of all, that requests, prayers, intercession, and thanksgiving be made for everyone—for kings and all those in authority, that we may live peaceful and quiet lives in all godliness and holiness.").

[72] EPHESIANS 6:13 ("Therefore put on the full armor of God, so that when the day of evil comes, you may be able to stand your ground, and after you have done everything, to stand.").

governing authority. Faithful lawyers respect and obey judges and governing authorities while confirming that their authority emanates from law. Lawyers also stand firm on the side of law against the authoritarian.[73]

Faith's article that authority is in law and faith, not in the whims of those who exercise authority, helps lawyers constitute authority properly. Wherever there is authority, there is right and wrong. You cannot find authority without standards of right and wrong action that authority establishes.[74] When appealing to and invoking authority, lawyers stand for truth and against falsehood.[75] Lawyers invoke authority for doing the right things over the wrong things.[76] Faithful lawyers are able to discern how and when to invoke authority because faith informs and prepares those lawyers.[77] Faithful lawyers distinguish properly established authority from the authoritarian by relying on the instruction of faith like that illustrated in this guide.[78] Faithful lawyers discern false authoritarianism because they understand the principles, nature, and goals of faith.[79]

Faithful lawyers also know that legitimate authorities can sometimes exceed their authority, leading into authoritarianism. Faith shows lawyers how to approach authorities to distinguish legitimate authority from false authoritarianism. The obedience and discernment that come from faith help lawyers avoid transgressing legitimate authority even as they test, resist, and correct the authoritarian.[80] The kind of diplomatic, respectful, and sensitive action that faith supports in a lawyer gives the faithful lawyer

---

[73] 2 THESSALONIANS ("stand firm and hold to the teachings we passed on to you").

[74] GENESIS 1:4 ("he separated the light from the darkness").

[75] EPHESIANS 6:14 ("Stand firm then, with the belt of truth buckled around your waist....").

[76] EPHESIANS 6:14 ("with the breastplate of righteousness in place").

[77] EPHESIANS 6:14 ("and with your feet fitted with the readiness that comes from the gospel of peace").

[78] EPHESIANS 6:17 ("Take the helmet of salvation and the sword of the Spirit, which is the word of God.").

[79] DANIEL 1:8 ("But Daniel resolved not to defile himself with the royal food and wine...").

[80] DANIEL 1:8 ("... and he asked the chief official for permission not to defile himself this way.").

favor even with those senior to the lawyer and even with the authoritarian.[81] A lawyer of faith may avoid the wrath of the authoritarian when resisting the authoritarian's false authority. Even the authoritarian will often see the wisdom within faithful action and will submit to it.[82] In that way, faithful lawyers inform, guide, and correct governing authorities by relying faithfully on authority.

In distinguishing between the authoritative and the authoritarian, law students and lawyers recognize how the belief system of our professional peers, clients, and others affects what we do as lawyers. As lawyers of faith, we develop and exercise the capacity to modify our counsel to counteract the false belief systems and counsel of others that would lead a client to the wrong decision for the wrong reasons.[83] The faithful lawyer does not give up the lawyer's own faith when counseling others. Rather, the faithful lawyer recognizes what others believe. The faithful lawyer sees how others will understand and interpret the lawyer's counsel. Lawyers of faith shape their counsel and actions accordingly, so that their counsel does not miss its mark. In other words, faith is wise about false beliefs and wise about how to counteract them. The faithful lawyer knows that others will recommend many possible courses only a small number of which are right. The faithful lawyer discerns the authoritative route and counsels clients to follow it.[84]

Another way to understand and respect authority is for a lawyer to recognize that obedience is an aspect of every relation-

---

[81] 1 PETER 3:15 ("Always be prepared to give an answer to everyone who asks you to give the reason for the hope that you have. But do this with gentleness and respect, keeping a clear conscience, so that those who speak maliciously against your good behavior in Christ may be ashamed of their slander.").

[82] DANIEL 1:9 ("Now God had caused the official to show favor and sympathy to Daniel... .").

[83] MATTHEW 15:14 (" 'If a blind man leads a blind man, both will fall into a pit.' ").

[84] MATTHEW 7:13 (" 'Enter through the narrow gate. For wide is the gate and broad is the road that leads to destruction, and many enter through it. But small is the gate and narrow the road that leads to life, and only a few find it.' ").

ship. Faith certainly involves right relationship to others,[85] not solely right relationship to faith's author.[86] Right relationship often means acknowledging the role, expertise, standing, or rights of others and treating them as authoritative. It also often means recognizing where others do not have authority and thus where their demands are only authoritarian, for the lawyer to challenge or ignore. In the end, and often after some struggle and challenge, faith proves effective in constraining and embarrassing the authoritarian.[87] Faith teaches law students and lawyers to relate to authority with respect, obedience, and submission but also to distinguish and overcome the authoritarian.[88] Faith does so by reserving the lawyer's devotion for things of faith, while having the lawyer obey temporal authority.

Law students and lawyers encounter authority constantly in law studies. Law students encounter forms of authority in the law school and its policies and administrators. Law schools develop and maintain policies having to do with character, fitness, timely submission of academic work, and attendance specifically to qualify law students for licensure and prepare law students for law practice. The authority found within the policies and administrators of a law school is prelude to the authority of the rules of professional conduct, grievance officials, and judges that lawyers encounter. For instance, law graduates must convince bar authorities that they have the character and fitness to join the bar, just as law students must convince law school admissions officials that they have the character to matriculate. Law students also encounter a form of authority in law professors, clinic directors, and extern field supervisors.[89]

---

[85] JOHN 13:34 (" 'A new command I give you: Love one another. As I have loved you, so you must love one another.' ").

[86] HEBREWS 12:2 ("Let us fix our eyes on Jesus, the author and perfecter of our faith.").

[87] COLOSSIANS 2:15 ("And having disarmed powers and authorities, he made a public spectacle of them, triumphing over them by the cross.").

[88] MARK 12:17 (" 'Give to Caesar what is Caesar's and to God what is God's.' ").

[89] MATTHEW 7:29 ("[H]e taught as one who had authority, and not as their teachers of the law."); TITUS 2:15 ("These, then, are the things you should teach. Encourage and rebuke with all authority.").

Yet most of all, law students and lawyers encounter authority in the common law and its cases, constitutions and treaties, codes and statutes, rules and regulations, and other authorities that comprise the law. Lawyers are relatively seldom in front of judges, spending much of their time in offices, yet lawyers are constantly aware in their office practices of the presence and authority of the law. Faith teaches law students and lawyers the nature of authority, that it is constantly present, not simply present when embodied in a judge or other official. Authority permeates the law school curriculum in every subject and legal fields in every activity, so much that law students and lawyers hardly notice its omnipresence. We are like fish swimming in a sea of authority, not recognizing authority because we live and breathe it.

Disobedience to authority is a challenge that both law students and lawyers face and must learn to identify, overcome, and manage. A lawyer's biggest challenge is often the lawyer's own self to overcome.[90] We all have at least a little bit of a rebellious nature, and many of us encourage that rebellious nature in others.[91] Popular culture tends to encourage that rebellious nature in each of us, or at least it does not always value obedience. Words like obedience and submission even have an odd ring to the ear, meaning that the concept of obedience in submission to authority is that unfamiliar to us. Yet authority implies obedience.[92] Because the law is authoritative, you cannot be a lawyer without recognizing and obeying authority, and maintaining the right relationship to it. There is little doubt that disobedience to authority destroys the reputations and careers of lawyers.[93] Some lawyers still pursue that destructive course,[94] mostly in ways that

---

[90] LUKE 9:23 ("he must deny himself and take up his cross").

[91] PROVERBS 24:21 ("do not join with the rebellious").

[92] JOHN 14:15 ("If you love me, you will obey what I command.").

[93] PROVERBS 13:13 ("He who scorns instruction will pay for it, but he who respects a command is rewarded.").

[94] MATTHEW 7:13 ("[W]ide is the gate and broad is the road that leads to destruction, and many enter through it.").

they attempt to hide behind a show of compliance.[95] Others hide their disobedience behind arrogance.[96]

It may be the case that relatively few lawyers are truly and thoroughly obedient to authority inside and out. Most of us, perhaps all of us, nurture at least some small disobedience.[97] Those faithful lawyers who are obedient to authority fully as they should be tend to find respect and honor.[98] You seldom see bar leaders honored without at the same time seeing how respectful they are toward authority[99] to the point of humility.[100] The success and honor given faithful lawyers prove that your attitude toward authority is important. The choices that you make in how you regard authority and whether you accept, respect, and obey it matter to your professional career and reputation.[101] Law students and lawyers who obey authority find confidence and security.[102] They also serve their clients better.[103] The faithful lawyer is obedient in just the way that properly constituted authority requires of it. Disobedience is a sure way to spoil a law career and lawyer.

Honesty

"Sure, yes, thank you," the lawyer was telling his legal assistant as he lifted the telephone to his ear to take the insurance claim representative's call. That was fast, the lawyer simultaneously thought, having just the other day sent the insurance company the introductory retention letter. A new client had come into the office a few days earlier complaining of an injury for which the insurance

---

[95] 1 SAMUEL 15:22-23 ("To obey is better than sacrifice, and to heed is better than the fat of rams. For rebellion is like the sin of divination... .").

[96] 1 SAMUEL 15:23 ("and arrogance like the evil of idolatry").

[97] ROMANS 7:18 ("I know that nothing good lives in me... .").

[98] MATTHEW 7:14 ("[S]mall is the gate and narrow the road that leads to life, and only a few find it.").

[99] PSALM 84:11 ("the Lord bestows favor and honor").

[100] PROVERBS 15:33 ("humility comes before honor").

[101] 1 TIMOTHY 3:13 ("Those who have served well gain an excellent standing... .").

[102] LUKE 11:28 ("Blessed are those who hear the word of God and obey it.").

[103] 1 JOHN 5:3 ("This is love for God: to obey his commands."); 2 JOHN 6 ("This is love: that we walk in obedience to his commands.").

company's insured likely had liability. The new client had shown the lawyer an off-work slip signed by the client's physician, indicating that the client was to be off work for three months because of his injuries. The lawyer believed from that record alone that the new client's claim had sufficient value to investigate further. The new client had signed the lawyer's contingency-fee agreement and given the lawyer the name of the insurance claim representative with whom the client had already had some preliminary dealings. The lawyer had promptly sent the insurer the retention letter indicating that complete medical records and other documentation of the claim would follow. Maybe the claim representative was already calling with an offer, thought the lawyer, smiling to himself that law practice is not always as challenging as made out to be.

"Just thought I'd give you a call before you get fully into this one, Counselor," the claim representative told the lawyer. The lawyer immediately detected something different from the usual bravado in the claim representative's voice. The claim representative then explained quickly. Before contacting the lawyer, the client had given the claim representative the same three-months-off-work slip that the client had later given to the lawyer. The client had also given the claim representative an authorization to get complete medical records from the physician, with which the claim representative had done so. In doing so, the claim representative had discovered that the client had altered the off-work slip. The physician had written that the client was to be off work for three days, not three months. "Just thought I'd let you know, Counselor," the claim representative concluded, offering to fax the lawyer the unaltered work slip.

As shocked and disappointed as he was, never having anything like it happen, the lawyer had no doubt of what he was going to do. He calmly asked the claim representative to do nothing regarding his retention letter until the lawyer had reviewed the original record at the physician's office and met again with the client. The lawyer also took care to thank the claim representative for bringing the matter to the lawyer's attention so quickly. Immediately after the call ended, the lawyer headed for the physician's office, where he presented the client's signed authorization for release of medical records. The office manager showed the lawyer the original off-work slip indicating three days, not three months, off work. The manager and the lawyer looked at the copy that the client had given the lawyer and examined the medical file, confirming that there was no such three-months-off record. With the original and the copy side by side, the lawyer could even now see evidence of the record's alteration. The lawyer flipped through the medical file, confirming with the manager that there was no indication of a more serious injury. Indeed, the client had not even been back to the physician's office.

At the lawyer's request, the lawyer's legal assistant had the new client back in the lawyer's office later that same day. The lawyer had the legal assistant sit in on the consultation. The lawyer watched the client's face closely for reaction as the lawyer calmly explained the circumstances of the altered record. The client showed no resistance. At most, the client may have shown a little disappointment and resignation, but the client said nothing. The lawyer explained the potential civil liability and criminal convictions that could result from presenting false evidence for insurance settlements and asked if the client wanted to explain anything about the altered record. The client shook his head back and forth once but still said nothing. "Is there anything that I have said that you do not understand?" the lawyer ended as he slid across his desk the letter indicating that the lawyer had terminated the client relationship. The client shook his head once back and forth, rose, and left quickly and quietly. The lawyer then faxed the claim representative a letter confirming that the lawyer had terminated the representation.

Later that month, the lawyer hired a new legal assistant. On the new legal assistant's first day of work, the lawyer overheard her say to a caller that the lawyer was "in court" when in fact the lawyer was in an office conference with a client. The lawyer immediately apologized to the client, stepped out to the new legal assistant's desk, and patiently explained to the legal assistant that everything that they said and did in the office, including responding to callers' queries about the lawyer's availability, must be truthful. Although in some firms an innocuous misrepresentation that a lawyer was "in court" when the lawyer was instead in the office might be acceptable, this firm would not accept it. The lawyer and legal assistant agreed that the legal assistant would say that the lawyer was or was not available now and take any emergency messages straight to the lawyer. The firm had clients who called more often than they needed and whose calls could be distracting. Yet there was no justification for even the smallest dishonesty.

Faith during law studies also helps law students and lawyers recognize the role of truth in the practice of law and a lawyer's relationship to it. Truth and its corollary attribute honesty are critical components of law studies and practice. The idea of truth is that there are things that a lawyer can know definitively. Not everything is a matter of opinion or viewpoint. While there are certainly different perspectives and viewpoints, there are also truths and, with them, falsehoods.[104] Everyone listens to viewpoints. Everyone has an opinion. Law studies, though, must lead law students and lawyers to seek, recognize, accept, and communicate truth, while recognizing and rejecting falsehoods. Truth implicates both a lawyer's willingness to be truthful, that is, to be honest, and to communicate truth, that is, to speak honestly in representation of faith.[105] Lawyers must become honest counselors to their clients and advocates on behalf of their clients in what should amount to figurative battles for truth and against falsehoods.[106]

Make no mistake. Lawyers are to contend for truth.[107] There is a battle aspect to counsel, in which the lawyer must advocate with passion for right action. When lawyers fight for truth, faith ensures that truth wins even when the odds seem very much against it.[108] When lawyers counsel in faith, faith carries the fight, then, for the faithful lawyer. When faith carries the fight, faith also determines the outcome in the faithful lawyer's favor. The faithful lawyer need only stand firmly and confidently on behalf of truth in those instances, watching faith carry the battle.[109] Honest counsel has that kind of power. The faithful lawyer does not overlook it but continues the firm fight for truth until the matter is finished.[110] Faith determines truth, not in a rigid or doctrinaire

---

[104] 1 JOHN 4:5 ("They are from the world and therefore speak from the viewpoint of the world, and the world listens to them. We are from God, and whoever knows God listens to us; but whoever is not from God does not listen to us. This is how we recognize the Spirit of Truth and the spirit of falsehood.").

[105] NUMBERS 22:38 (" 'I must speak only what God puts in my mouth.' ").

[106] EPHESIANS 6:14 ("with the belt of truth buckled around your waist").

[107] JUDE 3 ("I felt I had to write and urge you to contend for the faith....").

[108] 2 CHRONICLES 20:15 ("Do not be afraid or discouraged because of this vast army. For the battle is not yours, but God's.").

[109] EXODUS 14:14 ("The Lord will fight for you; you need only to be still.").

[110] 2 TIMOTHY 4:7 ("I have fought the good fight, I have finished the race, I have kept the faith.").

manner but like an extremely sensitive and subtle guide on which a lawyer can fully rely.[111]

Faith teaches lawyers that truth has an active ingredient. Law students and lawyers learn that truth is not simply a set of words standing for propositions.[112] Lawyers must speak truth, and speak it at the right time and place for the right reasons. Truth has a time, place, and purpose. Truth in one setting may not be truth in another, at least in the sense that context inevitably changes meaning. Truth itself does not change, but the time, place, and manner of its expression must change to fit the circumstances for truth to remain truth having its true meaning. Truth involves actions fitting to the full circumstances requiring those actions.[113] In that sense, the faithful lawyer does not flail about in advocacy but speaks truth in a targeted manner, meaning concisely and effectively.[114]

Truth is in that sense personal, not impersonal, and practical, not abstract.[115] Truth requires of a lawyer faith in action. Truth resides in faith.[116] Law students and lawyers find truth in faith. The faithful lawyer listens carefully to and follows the words of faith in order that the truth that derives from faith would give them and their clients the greatest meaning and liberty.[117] Truth informs and guides lawyer and client by connecting lawyer and client with essential and trustworthy meanings. Law students and lawyers who follow the truth have nothing to hide because there is no falsehood or artifice in them.[118] Lawyers commit themselves

---

[111] JOHN 16:13 ("But when he, the Spirit of truth, comes, he will guide you into all truth.").

[112] 1 JOHN 3:18-19 ("[L]et us not love with words or tongue... .").

[113] 1 JOHN 3:18-19 ("[L]et us ... love ... with actions and in truth.").

[114] 1 CORINTHIANS 9:26 ("Therefore I do not run like a man running aimlessly; I do not fight like a man beating the air.").

[115] JOHN 14:6 (" 'I am the way and the truth and the life.' ").

[116] JOHN 18:37 (" 'In fact, for this reason I was born, and for this I came into the world, to testify to the truth.'").

[117] JOHN 8:31-32 (" 'If you hold to my teaching, you are really my disciples. Then you will know the truth, and the truth will set you free.' ").

[118] JOHN 3:21 (" '[W]hoever lives by the truth comes into the light, so that it may be seen plainly that what he has done has been done through God.' ").

to pursuing truth as their professional calling.[119] The faithful lawyer finds professional solace in truth, meaning a resting place free from challenge and worry.[120] Truth becomes the lawyer's shelter and safe harbor in every challenge. Lawyers rely on truth for its protection and safety, like a mountain climber relying on a rope or a firefighter on a ladder.

The faithful lawyer makes truth a solid foundation for law practice.[121] There is nothing more reliable in law practice than truth. Build a law practice on truth, and it will stand against many challenges that would topple a law practice built on marketing, personality, timing, or momentum. For a lawyer to pursue truth in law practice takes a working attitude toward the language that lawyers use. Language has such a surprising capacity to mislead. The faithful lawyer ensures that the lawyer's communications do not distort truth but instead respect and convey it.[122] The faithful lawyer examines each communication, ensuring that it represents itself, the lawyer, and truth squarely and fairly, knowing that it is better that the lawyer judge the lawyer's own self than others judge the lawyer.[123] Lawyers make every communication, not just court papers, stand the test of truth, including every email and correspondence they write, and every document and memorandum.

Lawyers go to great lengths to find and hold onto truth and the wisdom that comes from it.[124] Faithful lawyers pursue truth because it is of great value, greater than other things on which other lawyers mistakenly rely, like cleverness, friendship, or loquaciousness. Some lawyers try novelty or originality, to be

---

[119] 1 JOHN 3:19 ("This then is how we know that we belong to the truth, and how we set our hearts at rest in his presence whenever our hearts condemn us.").

[120] 1 JOHN 3:19 ("[W]e set our hearts at rest in his presence whenever our hearts condemn us.").

[121] MATTHEW 7:24 (" 'Therefore everyone who hears these words of mine and puts them into practice is like a wise man who built his house on the rock.' ").

[122] 2 TIMOTHY 2:15 ("Do your best to present yourself to God as one approved, a workman who does not need to be ashamed and who correctly handles the word of truth.").

[123] 1 CORINTHIANS 11:31 ("But if we judged ourselves, we would not come under judgment.").

[124] PROVERBS 23:23 ("Buy the truth and do not sell it; get wisdom, discipline and understanding.").

convincing. Others try to rely on networks of friendships. Others try to speak around issues, to overwhelm clear thought with verbiage. The faithful lawyer sticks to the truth, relying on faith to ensure that the lawyer speaks truth on all occasions. Faith has a way of judging truth, making the true seem truer and falsehoods seem more false. The faithful lawyer knows that pursuing faith helps the lawyer discern truth and, with it, to practice with wisdom.[125] Lawyers see truth through faith, and when they put that truth into practice in their counsel and action, truth becomes wisdom.

Law students learn and lawyers know that truth divides. We know that truth requires one to take sides for or against it.[126] There is a delicate aspect to taking sides for truth. Lawyers of faith are constantly discovering and confronting their own dishonesty, just as they see dishonesty's prevalence among those around them.[127] Some think mistakenly that they are never or rarely dishonest, and only then with good cause. Yet dishonesty is a challenge that all law students and lawyers face, especially when one accepts that truth includes consistency between what is inside and what is outside. Faith wants us to be truthful inside and out, not just outwardly.[128]

Being truthful inwardly can mean to recognize one's own faults.[129] We all have them, assuming that we are willing to look,[130] and assuming that we are willing to apply the high standards of faith rather than our own low standards.[131] Our faults are especially apparent when we listen to our own corrupt thoughts

---

[125] 2 TIMOTHY 3:15 ("the holy Scriptures ... are able to make you wise for salvation through faith").

[126] JOHN 18:37 (" 'Everyone on the side of truth listens to me.' ").

[127] ISAIAH 6:5 ("Woe is me! I am lost, for I am a man of unclean lips, and I live among a people of unclean lips.").

[128] PSALM 51:6 ("You desire truth in the inward being; therefore teach me wisdom in my secret heart.").

[129] 1 JOHN 1:9 ("If we confess our sins, he is faithful and just and will forgive us our sins and purify us from all unrighteousness.").

[130] PSALM 51:3 ("For I know my transgressions; and my sin is ever before me.").

[131] PSALM 51:4 ("Against you, you only, have I sinned and done what is evil in your sight, so that you may be justified in your words and blameless in your judgment.").

that no one else can hear but that, if we truly listen, we know readily condemn us.[132] Imagine a transcript of your own thoughts, and you will get the picture. When we deny our own faults, we are being untruthful with ourselves in the worst of ways.[133] We are actually then quite dishonest, turning truth into falsehood and falsehood into truth, and placing ourselves beyond the reach and help of faith.[134] That kind of self-deception, to mislead us about our own condition, is most harmful. We should avoid it at all costs.

Dishonesty also challenges non-lawyers,[135] yet dishonesty does more damage to lawyers than it does to others. Dishonesty destroys the careers and reputations of law students and lawyers because lawyers are trained, licensed, and expected to speak and write truth. Truth is the lawyer's stock in trade, as is transparency. Lawyers must be genuine in law practice, taking stances that attract constituencies to them. Dishonesty makes a lawyer hide the lawyer's true thoughts and actions, when lawyers are supposed to be reasoning and transparent.[136] Dishonesty destroys the kind of authenticity, respect, and standing lawyers must have to be successful in law practice. Even with little things, the lawyer must be honest. If you cannot trust a lawyer to be honest with the little things, then you will not be able to trust the lawyer to be honest with the big things, either.[137] The faithful lawyer tells the truth all of the time, not just when the truth seems to be important.

---

[132] PSALM 51:6 ("you delight in truth in the inward being, and you teach me wisdom in the secret heart").

[133] 1 JOHN 1:8 ("If we claim to be without sin, we deceive ourselves and the truth is not in us.").

[134] 1 JOHN 1:10 ("If we claim we have not sinned, we make him out to be a liar and his word has no place in our lives.").

[135] 1 JOHN 1:6 ("If we claim to have fellowship with him yet walk in the darkness, we lie and do not live by the truth.").

[136] JOHN 3:20 (" 'Everyone who does evil hates the light, and will not come into the light for fear that his deeds will be exposed.' ").

[137] LUKE 16:10 ("Whoever can be trusted with little can also be trusted with much, and whoever is dishonest with very little will also be dishonest with much.").

It is also a waste of time for a lawyer to try to conceal the lawyer's dishonesty.[138] It is a funny thing, but against truth, there is really no hiding. The faithful lawyer knows that the truth will always come out one way or another, that in a sense, judgment is omniscient.[139] Lawyers do not operate on a conceal-if-you-can ethic. The faithful lawyer especially discloses the lawyer's own wrongs, knowing that doing so is the best way to avoid its worst consequences.[140] The faithful lawyer does everything assuming that it will stand up to examination later, even those things that the lawyer may for the time being keep confidential. Although we should always avoid dishonesty, we should take special care to avoid dishonesty when speaking to frequent acquaintances and avoid telling lies against those whom we know. Doing so destroys the sense of community we should share with one another.[141] It also condemns us within that community, when we should instead evoke its respect and delight.[142] Indeed, building a practice of truth can take community. The faithful lawyer avoids keeping the company of those who are constantly curious but unwilling consistently to speak and acknowledge truth, remaining fundamentally dishonest.[143] Truth makes a lawyer, as if it were a part of the lawyer's character.

Just as truth is in some respects incarnate, filling and vitalizing the lawyer who speaks it, so is dishonesty, destroying the lawyer who speaks lies.[144] Lies destroy.[145] Some simply will not

---

[138] MATTHEW 10:26 (" 'There is nothing concealed that will not be disclosed, or hidden that will not be made known.' ").

[139] PSALM 139:1-3 ("O Lord, you have searched me and you know me. You know when I sit and when I rise; you perceive my thoughts from afar. You discern my going out and my lying down; you are familiar with all my ways.").

[140] PROVERBS 28:13 ("He who conceals his sins does not prosper.... .").

[141] EXODUS 20:16 ("You shall not give false testimony against your neighbor."); EPHESIANS 4:25 ("Each of you must put off falsehood and speak truthfully to his neighbor, for we are all members of one body.").

[142] PROVERBS 12:22 ("The Lord detests lying lips, but he delights in men who are truthful.").

[143] 2 TIMOTHY 3:5, 7 ("Have nothing to do with [those who are] ... always learning but never able to acknowledge the truth.").

[144] JOHN 8:44 ("There is no truth in [the devil]. When he lies, he speaks his native language, for he is a liar and the father of lies.").

acknowledge truth—indeed will not even acknowledge that there is such a thing as truth.[146] They instead seek out those who say what they want to hear, in a way that keeps them from having to confront their own dishonesty.[147] Those persons turn instead to things that make no sense and have nothing to do with the truth, even though some of those things have can have the vague sound of truth or another kind of false allure.[148] They talk about things without the need to talk, and in so doing move farther from the truth and closer to dishonesty.[149] They do so because they are self-seeking, the result of which is to bring trouble to them.[150] Those who are self-seeking tend, when challenged by law studies, toward brooding and self pity.[151] Instead, law students and lawyers maintain the pursuit of truth.

Trust

"Are you sure that we shouldn't be urging him to settle?" the new lawyer kept asking the highly experienced law partner. The new lawyer knew that the partner was a risk taker who was used to winning and losing big cases. The new lawyer was not a risk taker, especially when it came to risks of this size. The firm had put hundreds of hours of attorney time and probably a hundred thousand dollars in expenses into a contingency-fee case that was going to trial tomorrow. The trial court had dismissed one defendant, and two others had settled for a pittance because of the weakness of the plaintiff's case against them. It looked like the

[145] PROVERBS 19:9 ("A false witness will not go unpunished, and he who pours out lies will perish.").

[146] JOHN 18:38 (" 'What is truth?' Pilate asked.").

[147] 2 TIMOTHY 4:3 ("For the time will come when men will not put up with sound doctrine. Instead, to suit their own desires, they will gather around them a great number of teachers to say what their itching ears want to hear.").

[148] 2 TIMOTHY 4:4 ("They will turn their ears away from the truth and turn aside to myths.").

[149] 2 TIMOTHY 2:16 ("Avoid godless chatter, because those who indulge in it will become more and more ungodly.").

[150] ROMANS 2:8 ("But for those who are self-seeking and who reject the truth and follow evil, there will be wrath and anger.").

[151] JONAH 4:3-4 (" 'Now, O Lord, take away my life, for it is better for me to die than to live.' But the Lord replied, 'Have you any right to be angry?' ").

lone remaining defendant was willing to offer just enough money to reimburse the firm's expenses, put a little money in the seriously injured plaintiff's pocket, and earn the firm a contingency fee that, if calculated on an hourly basis, would amount to little more than minimum wage. Yet the new lawyer would have taken it. The partner gave a quick little shake of his head back and forth, like he was shaking off a fly or mosquito, not even saying anything or looking at the new lawyer. The two lawyers returned to preparing for trial.

As it turned out, the partner was right—this time. The jury seemed like a good draw for both sides, fair and balanced. The partner made a good opening statement for the plaintiff, as did counsel for the defendant. The plaintiff's proofs went in easily over the course of a week, ending on the perfect high note. The turning point probably came early the next week on the new lawyer's cross-examination of the defense expert, in which the expert admitted the plaintiff's liability theory in surprisingly dramatic fashion. The partner made a good closing argument. Defense counsel, who in 19 tries had never lost one of these cases, seemed on closing to be trying too hard to make up for his expert's damning admission. The new lawyer gave the plaintiff's rebuttal closing argument to what seemed like reasonably good effect. There was reason for the plaintiff to be optimistic, even more so when deliberations stretched into the evening. The jury returned a seven-figure verdict. The plaintiff and partner celebrated, while the new lawyer breathed a huge sigh of relief.

The new lawyer had always had a hard time trusting. Yet the new lawyer was beginning to see substantial evidence of the need for it. In this case, the partner and plaintiff client had been trusting. In another case, the new lawyer watched as his experienced co-counsel calmly reassured their plaintiff client that the decision whether to settle was the client's decision and that the lawyers would give their best to back up the client's decision. The client in that case had settled, but co-counsel's trust and confidence had made a deep impression on the new lawyer. Then in the courthouse hallway one day, the new lawyer had seen another well known but not-much-respected plaintiff's lawyer loudly chastising his cowed client and threatening to withdraw if the client did not settle. The ugly scene embarrassed the new lawyer, who finally put it together. Trust was a critical component to law practice.

The new lawyer learned that technical competence, though a good thing, was not enough. Neither were good judgment, strong oratorical skills, great preparation, and ample resources. The new lawyer saw repeatedly, in his own cases, those of his law partners, and the actions of other lawyers, that a masterful lawyer also had to be trusting. The new lawyer saw excellent trial lawyers walk away from severe losses not with a tirade but with a shrug, still trusting. The new lawyer gradually learned to do likewise. Sure, there was pain in every loss. Yet every loss taught the new lawyer more than any of the victories taught the lawyer. Some of the losses actually also turned around and became victories on appeal or in post-trial settlements. The new lawyer's enthusiasm for preparation, insight, discretion, and wise counsel in no sense abated. The new lawyer was not going to play the fool in any situation. Yet still, the new lawyer had learned that the critical response to every situation was trust, not borne of foolishness but of faith. Trusting then, and still trusting.

Faith during law studies also helps law students and lawyers develop and demonstrate trust. The truth-seeking faith that law students and lawyers must exercise in law studies and practice involves more than belief leading to commitment. It also involves trusting in and coming to rely on that commitment and all that it entails.[152] Faith, belief, and obedience imply more than lip service or a one-time thing. Law students and lawyers must trust in the truths that they learn and practice, knowing that doing so will honor faith while also working well for them.[153] They must rely on those truths, not leaning too heavily on their own impressions of how to construct a career but instead seeing the value of relying on faith's constructions.[154] Sometimes, we sell faith short, believing that there are certain things that we must do or take for ourselves, even though it may not be the right time for them. The faithful lawyer learns that nothing takes too long or is too hard for faith to accomplish in the way of career and professional development, even though it may seem to us that we should take shortcuts.[155]

---

[152] NAHUM 1:7 ("He cares for those who trust in him... .").

[153] ROMANS 8:28 ("in all things God works for the good of those who love him, who have been called according to his purpose").

[154] PROVERB 3:5 ("Trust in the Lord with all your heart, and lean not on your own understanding... .").

[155] JEREMIAH 32:17 ("Ah, Sovereign Lord, you have made the heavens and the earth by your great power and outstretched arm. Nothing is too hard for you.").

A lawyer's knowledge and skill tend to make the lawyer self-reliant, as if the lawyer can think and do for the lawyer's own self. Yet often, do-it-yourself action leads to the most trouble and longest detours from professional success. What is hard for a lawyer is to rely on faith rather than on the lawyer's own knowledge and skill, when the power of faith is so much greater.[156] What we would create for ourselves is puny compared to what pursuing faith offers for us. Faith's challenge is that faith requires a trusting belief, even when the evidence for that trust is not yet apparent. That is the nature of faith, to require trust in the right things before the basis for that trust is evident. Trust would not be trust without the commitment to it before it appears fully warranted. Trust implies a willingness to rely before reliance appears fully justified. When faith guides us, we receive what we need in order to trust.[157] Those things we receive from faith that help to build trust include confidence, peace, and rest, without which we would be less trusting.[158]

When we rely on ourselves too much in our law studies, turning our attention to our own progress and condition, we begin to lose faith because our progress is often not so evident. The professional development of a lawyer is a subtle thing, not always apparent especially to the law student or lawyer who is undergoing that development. When we lose faith, we begin to lose trust, and once we lose trust, we stop progressing in professional development. It is at that point that the law student or lawyer once again needs the rescue of faith.[159] If we turn to our own strength and to other artificial things, relying too much on formulas and methods, then we face even more challenges than before.[160] Our strength is never as great as faith's strength, that

---

[156] 1 CHRONICLES 29:12 ("In your hands are strength and power to exalt and give strength to all.").

[157] PSALM 23:1 ("The Lord is my shepherd, I shall not be in want.").

[158] PSALM 91:1 ("He who dwells in the shelter of the Most High will rest in the shadow of the Almighty.").

[159] MATTHEW 14:31 ("Immediately Jesus reached out his hand and caught him. 'You of little faith,' he said, 'why did you doubt?' ").

[160] ISAIAH 31:1 ("Woe to those who go down to Egypt for help, who rely on horses, who trust in the multitude of their chariots and in the great strength

is, in trusting in the eventual productivity of faithful right action.[161]

Trust is a critical aspect of faith. Trust has a way of vitalizing us.[162] Trust implies accepting that faith is always conscious of and interested in our progress,[163] always giving us opportunity and the strength to pursue it.[164] The more we trust, the more we see that faith has an unfathomably high, wide, and deep quality in particular where it comes to the study of law and pursuit of justice.[165] There is something utterly distinct and remarkable about faith's justice that attracts lawyers.[166] Trust, though, also implies that we will not know everything about the good that faith does for us. If every power of faith were immediately evident to us, then our relying on faith would not be trust but would instead be simply reason. Trust means something more in the nature of not knowing but still being willing to rely. Faith must in part remain a mystery. The faithful lawyer accepts that faith has unimaginably extensive powers that the lawyer will never know directly.[167]

When we trust in complete faith while studying law, that trust makes our studies more productive. Trust changes our performance, and not just our performance. Trust also changes

---

of their horsemen, but do not look to the Holy One of Israel, or seek help from the Lord.").

[161] 1 JOHN 4:16 ("God is love, and those who abide in love abide in God, and God abides in them.").

[162] LAMENTATIONS 3:22 ("Because of the Lord's great love we are not consumed, for his compassions never fail."); ISAIAH 40:28-30 ("The Lord … will not grow tired or weary… .").

[163] PSALM 73:23-24 ("I am always with you; you hold me by my right hand. You guide me with your counsel, and afterward you will take me into glory.").

[164] ISAIAH 40:31 ("He gives strength to the weary and increases the power of the weak.").

[165] PSALM 36:5 ("Your love, O Lord, reaches to the heavens, your faithfulness to the skies. Your righteousness is like the mighty mountains, your justice like the great deep.").

[166] PSALM 84:10 ("Better is one day in your courts than a thousand elsewhere… .").

[167] PSALM 145:3 ("his greatness no one can fathom").

us.[168] The more that we trust, the more apparent our faith is to others, and the more that others trust in us. Then, the more that others trust in us, the more encouragement we receive to persevere. Faith promises that persevering will produce its own reward, especially when the trials that a lawyer faces are severe.[169] Trusting in faith gets to be like an upward spiral, reversing the downward spiral of doubt and distrust.

By trusting in faith during law studies and practice, we also reduce and eliminate fear and anxiety.[170] The faithful lawyer knows that worry does no good.[171] Worry is distracting and draining. Law studies and practice are hard enough without worrying. Add worry to the challenge of law studies and practice, and you have an unsavory challenge. Anxiety is simply too heavy a burden for the law student and lawyer.[172] The exercise of faith and the good practices that follow it are ways to remove the anxiety that comes when we do not trust during law studies and practice.[173] Faith begins to lessen worry and anxiety, creating more reliance on faith.

Fear and anxiety interfere with law studies and practice. Anxiety is like a weight on us when studying law,[174] crushing our sense of possibility and accomplishment.[175] Trust is the antidote to anxiety and fear.[176] When others see us trusting and persevering, they help us. We receive strength from trusting alone

[168] PSALM 37:5-6 ("Commit your way to the Lord; trust in him and he will do this: He will make your righteousness shine like the dawn.").

[169] JAMES 1:12 ("Blessed is the man who perseveres under trial, because when he has stood the test, he will receive the crown of life that God has promised to those who love him.").

[170] ROMANS 8:15 ("For you did not receive a spirit that makes you a slave again to fear, but you received the Spirit of sonship.").

[171] LUKE 12:25 ("Who of you by worrying can add a single hour to his life?").

[172] PROVERBS 12:25 ("An anxious heart weighs a man down... .").

[173] PSALM 42:5 ("Why are you downcast, O my soul? Why so disturbed within me? Put your hope in God, for I will yet praise him, my Savior and my God.").

[174] PROVERBS 12:25 ("An anxious heart weighs a man down, but a kind word cheers him up.").

[175] PROVERBS 17:22 ("A cheerful heart is good medicine, but a crushed spirit dries up the bones.").

[176] ISAIAH 41:10 ("Do not fear, for I am with you; do not be dismayed, for I am your God.").

and then help when we gain strength through trust as we study.[177] We call and draw on faith in those times when we are most anxious and fearful in our law studies. The result is a confidence that has the effect of giving credence once again to our faith.[178] We tend to believe that fear and anxieties are unavoidable products when to the contrary they can be manageable when we exercise control over them.[179] Faith demands that we take courage, rejecting the sense that anxiety, fear, and discouragement are conditions beyond our control.[180] Faith influences our emotions and state of mind, helping us take hold of and control those emotions and states of mind that seem so elusive when we try to control them directly.[181] Faith makes a lawyer bold in the manner that lawyer should be bold and when a lawyer should be bold.[182] We should know that even in law studies, peace and security are the products of a steadfast trust borne of faith.[183] Let faith help you trust and, by trusting, eliminate fear and anxiety.

In these ways, through belief, obedience, honesty, and trust, faith informs and supports law studies. Next, consider how faith connects with law knowledge.

---

[177] ISAIAH 41:10 ("I will strengthen you and help you; I will uphold you with my righteous right hand.").

[178] PSALM 50:15 ("Call upon me in the day of trouble; I will deliver you, and you will honor me.").

[179] PROVERBS 29:11 ("a wise man keeps himself under control"); ROMANS 8:6 ("the mind controlled by the Spirit is life").

[180] JOSHUA 1:9 ("Have I not commanded you? Be strong and courageous. Do not be terrified; do not be discouraged, for the Lord your God will be with you wherever you go.").

[181] 2 TIMOTHY 4:5 ("But you, keep your head in all situations.").

[182] PROVERBS 28:1 ("the righteous are as bold as a lion").

[183] ISAIAH 26:3-4 ("You will keep in perfect peace him whose mind is steadfast, because he trusts in you. Trust in the Lord forever, for the Lord, the Lord, is the Rock eternal.").

Chapter 2

Law Knowledge

FAITH AT LAW'S FOUNDATIONS

Just as faith informs law studies by developing obedience, honesty, and trust, faith also helps law students and lawyers develop, organize, and recall broad, deep, and coherent law knowledge.[1] Law doctrine finds its foundation in faith.[2] To be effective, lawyers must know much law. They have to develop, maintain, and continually update an active knowledge base.[3] Lawyers must also connect that knowledge base to meanings that their clients understand and respect. Law is not solely or even primarily a technical knowledge. A lawyer's working knowledge matters to clients, not a lawyer's static knowledge. Clients must be able to understand and use a lawyer's counsel. A lawyer's mastery lies in the depth and breadth of the lawyer's knowledge base, but it is faith that makes that knowledge base actionable and profound.[4] Indeed, knowledge alone tends to make a law student or lawyer unduly proud, as if there were something valuable simply in knowing.[5] The real value is in being able to use knowledge in service of another.[6] The faithful lawyer is cautious about knowledge because the moment that we think we know

---

[1] DANIEL 1:17 ("To these four young men God gave knowledge and understanding of all kinds of literature and learning.").

[2] PROVERBS 1:7 ("The fear of the Lord is the beginning of knowledge.... .").

[3] PROVERBS 12:1 ("Whoever loves discipline loves knowledge.... .").

[4] DANIEL 1:17 ("And Daniel could understand visions and dreams of all kinds.").

[5] 1 CORINTHIANS 8:1 ("Knowledge puffs up ...").

[6] 1 CORINTHIANS 8:1 ("... but love builds up.").

something is probably the moment that we do not.[7] We should instead treat knowledge as a pursuit of faith, that faith would know us rather than we would know much.[8]

The need of lawyers to know much law in a way that lawyers can use it is why law schools devote the substantial portion of the curriculum to doctrinal courses. This chapter shows how the doctrinal courses and concepts of the law school curriculum find their foundation in faith. The connection should not be surprising. Law and theology have always had a close connection. Even a child recognizes that law, rule, and regulation are fundamentally moral. Law is natural. Law students and lawyers benefit by knowing that it is so and keeping it so. It makes law easier to learn, recall, and use, if one connects its fields, concepts, and rules to one's faith. It also makes law practice more meaningful when one connects the law with which lawyers constantly work to articles of faith. It takes faith to approach the deep truths of law and the deep meanings of legal fields and concepts, even while law students and lawyers of faith know that as hard as we study, there will always be more great truths to discover.[9]

While this guide is about a law student's and lawyer's faith, it is also about learning. Lawyers are lifelong learners. They have to be (or get to be, to take a more accurate view of learning) learners, as law and law practice change. From a pedagogical standpoint, the first thing that a program of instruction should do is to connect your new learning with something you already know. Educators call that process *anchoring*. In cognitive theory, you have established conceptual structures from your prior education and life experience. You already know something. You learn new matters best when you can connect those new matters to your prior learning. You might connect your law studies and practice to anything you already know. Law students and lawyers draw on many different personal experiences and interests to which to connect their new law learning. Yet what better

---

[7] 1 CORINTHIANS 8:2 ("The man who thinks he knows something does not yet know as he ought to know.").

[8] 1 CORINTHIANS 8:3 ("But the man who loves God is known by God.").

[9] ROMANS 11:33 ("Oh, the depth of the riches of the wisdom and knowledge of God! How unsearchable his judgments, and his paths beyond tracing out!"); EPHESIANS 3:7 ("the unsearchable riches of Christ").

structure is there to which to connect your law studies and practice than your existing faith? As you learn how law and its practice connect with and draw on your faith, you learn law subjects more quickly, confidently, deeply, and effectively. Reading this chapter of the guide on law knowledge could make you a better learner and therefore a better law student and lawyer.

Love

Acting as a case evaluator all day on panels of three evaluators were the days that always convinced the lawyer that he loved tort practice. The lawyer was on panels in three counties, so his turn came up regularly, every couple of months it seemed. The lawyer's civil-litigation practice involved personal-injury, wrongful-death, business, and civil- and employment-rights cases, all of which involved to tort claims. Most of the cases that the panels evaluated were torts cases. The lawyer was in his practice element. He knew many of the lawyers, judges, insurers, treating and examining physicians, and expert witnesses, and even some of the corporate defendants. The law was thoroughly familiar. Yet each case still seemed unique. Sometimes it was the liability theory that was different. Sometimes the way in which the injury came about (causation) was unusual. Often, the plaintiffs' circumstances were unique. There was just so much variety in human activity and circumstance. Just when you thought you had seen it all, you saw something new in the way that people injured one another.

Most interesting to the lawyer was how the people involved in the cases regarded the parties' various tort-law duties. A tort claim revealed the character of the plaintiff, individual defendant or corporate employees, lay and expert witnesses, claim representatives, and even the lawyers. Some plaintiffs and their lawyers balanced to near perfection the rightful sense of injury, need, and justice with countervailing mercy, reasonableness, and forgiveness. Others came across as whiny, malingering, exaggerating, demanding, vengeful, and unforgiving. Some defendants and their lawyers came across as responsibly remorseful, others as callous. Some witnesses seemed uninterested, others over-involved. Some experts appeared independent and virtuous, others biased. On and on it went, the tort claims litmus to each participant's character.

The lawyer had seen the same spectrum of attitudes in his own tort practice. It was just that when the lawyer was evaluating cases for others, the lawyer could look at the people involved as an observer would look at them rather than as a participant. The lawyer remembered in two of his own cases deposing two very different women in two different jails. Prosecutors had convicted each of the women for the drunk driving that had injured the lawyer's clients. The lawyer had deposed each woman in ensuing civil suits both to confirm their individual liability but also to discover claims against the bars where they had been drinking. One of the women was so thoroughly contrite about the serious injuries that she had caused that the lawyer felt bad for her as a guard led her back to her jail cell after the deposition. The other woman was so thoroughly disdainful of those whom she had nearly killed that the lawyer hoped that she spent long enough in jail to come to a different attitude. Tort law revealed the character of each woman like a genetic profile.

The lawyer had also seen tort law change individuals. The lawyer had seen angry victims turn into the forgiving healed. Sometimes it just took time and evidence. The lawyer had seen callous perpetrators turn into concerned apologetics. Sometimes it just took a gentle but searching cross-examination on deposition. Other times it took years of intense litigation. The outcomes were often just as surprising. The lawyer had seen over-reaching claimants burned with no-cause verdicts, under sung lawyers turned into heroes, and stingy defendants and insurers forced to generosity. The lawyer's own attitude toward tort law had changed over the years. He once saw it as something artificial and created, a contrivance overlaid across society for the benefit of victims and lawyers. After seeing tort law operate on the character of the participants in these cases, the lawyer saw the care that enlivened tort law as something more fundamental than even the humanity of the system's participants. Love has such power to reveal, the lawyer decided, in his paean to tort law.

Faith places love at the core of social relationship, as its prime tenet, while also connecting love to law doctrine.[10] Love is the heart and foundation of law.[11] It is the application of law,

---

[10] GALATIANS 5:14 ("The entire law is summed up in a single command: 'Love your neighbor as yourself.'").

[11] ROMANS 13:10 ("Love does no harm to its neighbor. Therefore love is the fulfillment of the law.").

making law active beyond its mere knowledge.[12] The kind of love about which faith instructs is not the kind of love that some readers would think. There should be more words for love because love has more meanings than one word implies. To mistake one kind of love for another in this or any other context can be unfortunate. We have one kind of love for a spouse with whom we are intimate, hold another kind of love for a brother or sister, and have yet another kind of love for food or art or other things of general stimulation and pleasure. There is also the kind of awe-stricken love that we reserve for the person whom or thing that we give ourselves over to such a degree as to call it something like worship or adoration. None of these forms of love represents the law of love. They are each important and each inform us to some degree, but they do not provide the basis for social relationship in the way that another form of love does.

The form of love informing law has to do with regarding others as we regard ourselves.[13] Tort law is the clearest example, although it is only one of many examples where the law requires us to consider others. Any time that we act creating risks to others, we must consider their interests including their safety and the security of their property, as we would consider ourselves and our own property. The other-regarding form of love suffuses law in our every action and relationship. The faith form of love requires us to limit our self-seeking just at those points where it would interfere with the welfare of others.[14] The faith form of love is actually not that constraining because self-seeking does not bring us the self-fulfillment for which we hope. Oddly, we tend to gain that elusive self-fulfillment by seeking the well-being and fulfillment of others.[15] As strange as it seems, in faith's form of love we rise in stature primarily by stooping to serve the needs

---

[12] EPHESIANS 3:18-19 ("to grasp how wide and long and high and deep is the lover of Christ, and to know this love that surpasses knowledge").

[13] MATTHEW 7:12 ("In everything, do to others what you would have them do to you, for this sums up the Law and the Prophets.").

[14] 1 CORINTHIANS 13:5 ("Love ... is not self-seeking.... .").

[15] MATTHEW 10:39 ("Whoever finds his life will lose it, and whoever loses his life for my sake will find it.").

of others.[16] Faith has that self-sacrificial sense, that to love is not to feel sentimental about others but to give something up of our own for others.[17]

Yet no matter how we feel about it, the faith form of love makes us consider others and do things for others in certain circumstances as if they are just as important as we are.[18] There is no going about thinking and acting as if we have rights superior to others. Indeed, love would require a lawyer to rebuke a client who does so.[19] Law requires that we care for others in certain ways and at certain times, whenever we act in ways that may injure others or damage their property, just as we care for ourselves. Tort law imposes that duty on every one of in every situation. Indeed, faith's form of love requires that we care for others even when those others seem to be working against us.[20] It really does not matter what others are doing, whether we like them or not, if we know them or not, or if they are competing against us or not. If we know or should know that our actions may harm them, then we owe them due consideration as a matter of law informed by faith.

As strange as it may seem, caring for others even when they are working against us actually makes practical sense. It overcomes their resistance and turns them toward working for us rather than against us.[21] Faith's form of love is important in society, encouraging us to choose to think of others whether or not they are thinking of us. When tort law requires that we show reasonable care for others, and permits us to expect reasonable care in return, it builds relationships even where they did not

---

[16] MATTHEW 20:26 ("Whoever wants to become great among you must be your servant, and whoever wants to be first must be your slave... .").

[17] MATTHEW 20:28 ("[T]he Son of Man did not come to be served, but to serve, and to give his life as a ransom for many.").

[18] JOHN 13:14–15 ("Now that I, your Lord and Teacher, have washed your feet, you also should wash one another's feet. I have set you an example that you should do as I have done for you.").

[19] REVELATIONS 3:19 (" 'Those whom I love I rebuke... .' ").

[20] MATTHEW 5:43 ("You have heard that it was said, 'Love your neighbor and hate your enemy.' But I tell you: Love your enemies ... that you may be sons of your Father in heaven.").

[21] ROMANS 12:21 ("Do not be overcome by evil, but overcome evil with good.").

exist. It creates a community of care even in such rough-and-tumble places as the freeway or the marketplace. Faith's form of love instills an authentic and indeed enforceable sense of civility not only between friends and acquaintances but also among strangers and opponents.[22] Faith knows that kindness toward an opponent makes it very hard for that opponent to be unkind, even while it rewards the one who is so kind.[23] It may take a small sacrifice to stay within the speed limit, for instance, but then tort law requires that we do so unless we are prepared to pay for any resulting wrong.

Do not mistake the simplicity of this do-unto-others formulation for a lack of profundity or, for that matter, take it simply as a formula. The rule of love is something more like a living thing than a rule at all. There is no end of depth and subtlety to it, and it is powerful.[24] The philosopher Immanuel Kant developed several ways to describe it but even in doing so reduced it to less than it is. To Kant, it became a categorical imperative, that anything we do we should be able to make its doing equally a rule for everyone. If we cannot, then we should not do it. Each of our actions we should be able to generalize into a rule of action for everyone, and if we cannot—if disorder would instead result—then we should abandon that action. To Kant, the rule was not to treat another as a means but instead always as an end, as having intrinsic and infinite value.

Yet these formulations are still inadequate. They do not plumb the depth or cover the breadth of other-regarding love. We would almost have to see love in full action, embodied, to appreciate it. What makes faith's other-regarding form of love special is its sacrificial aspect.[25] To love another in the sense of treating

---

[22] MATTHEW 5:44 (" 'Love your enemy, and pray for those who persecute you, that you may be sons of your Father in heaven.").

[23] PROVERBS 25:21-22 ("If your enemy is hungry, give him food to eat; if he is thirsty, give him water to drink. In doing this, you will heap burning coals on his head, and the Lord will reward you.").

[24] 2 TIMOTHY 1:7 ("For God did not give us a spirit of timidity, but a spirit of power, of love and of self-discipline.").

[25] ROMANS 12:1 ("Therefore, I urge you, brothers, in view of God's mercy, to offer your bodies as living sacrifices, holy and pleasing to God—this is your spiritual act of worship.").

them as we would treat ourselves, we must often give up something of ourselves, meaning something that if it were not for caring for the other, we would take it or do it ourselves.[26] To show reasonable care for another, we must at times put aside ourselves. In faith's terms, we must put ourselves aside at times as the only way to regard others as we would regard ourselves, as intrinsically worthy.[27] The very thought of putting one's self aside for another is so foreign that it makes faith's form of love something unique and almost incomprehensible.

There is one way to understand that unique aspect of other-regarding love as the law of love. It is not so much that we first learn to love as a matter of principle in this way. It is instead that we first see how completely love of this kind cares for us.[28] Once you see how much this kind of love cares for you, it gets easier to see how much our showing that kind of love cares for others. Knowing the depth and richness of this other-regarding kind of love, we are more readily able to commit ourselves fully to it.[29] It makes it easier to live out that kind of love, whether in law studies or practice, to know how faith's love lives for us.[30] As law students and lawyers, we can then embrace loving others.[31] When we truly know love, we find that we must love accordingly.[32]

---

[26] 1 JOHN 3:16 ("This is how we know what love is: Jesus Christ laid down his life for us. And we ought to lay down our lives for our brothers.").

[27] 1 JOHN 4:9 ("This is how God showed his love among us: He sent his one and only Son into the world that we might live through him.").

[28] 1 JOHN 4:10 ("This is love: not that we loved God, but that he loved us and sent his Son as an atoning sacrifice for our sins. Dear friends, since God so loved us, we also ought to love one another.").

[29] DEUTERONOMY 6:5 ("Love the Lord your God with all your heart and with all your soul and with all your strength.").

[30] 2 CORINTHIANS 5:14 ("Christ's love compels us, because we are convinced that one died for all, and therefore all died.. And he died for all, that those who live should no longer live for themselves but for him who died for them... .").

[31] 1 JOHN 4:11 ("Dear friends, since God so loved us, we also ought to love one another.").

[32] MATTHEW 22:37-39 ("Jesus replied: 'Love the Lord your God with all your heart and with all your soul and with all your mind.' This is the first and greatest commandment. And the second is like it: 'Love your neighbor as yourself.' "); 1 JOHN 4:21 ("Whoever loves God must also love his brother.").

Once a law student or lawyer learns the true nature of this other-regarding kind of love that the law adopts and enforces, then the law student or lawyer can love others more deeply and genuinely.[33] Other-regarding love is transparent and accountable, not something vague. It often means simply to obey the moral commands of faith.[34] Morality may require of us literally hundreds of small things, depending on the circumstances. It might be something as simple as giving our devotion to worthwhile things rather than things that harm others. It might mean not to envy or hate.[35] It might mean to provide for ourselves and then for others. Other-regarding love encourages us to learn and do those moral things. It also often means to use our words and actions to limit the worst effects of the wrongs of others.[36] Other-regarding love has the protective nature to it.

Again, we see it most in tort law, which we recognize as the law of care. In the manner that the law of care requires caring for one another as we care for ourselves, love has a fully other-regarding nature to it, as if we are not to make greater account of ourselves than of others. The greatest example of other-regarding love might be if someone actually gave up his or her life for us.[37] Self-sacrifice is an extraordinarily self-sacrificial, all-embracing kind of love of the kind one would hardly expect to see.[38] One who did so would have to be the image of other-regarding love, the greatest of possible examples.[39] If we have that kind of example, then it gets easier to understand how powerful that kind of other-regarding love really is.

---

[33] 1 PETER 1:22 ("Now that you have purified yourselves by obeying the truth so that you have sincere love for your brothers, love one another deeply, from the heart.").

[34] JOHN 14:23-24 ("Jesus replied, 'If anyone loves me, he will obey my teaching. ... He who does not love me will not obey my teaching.").

[35] PROVERBS 14:30 ("envy rots the bones").

[36] 1 PETER 4:8 ("Above all, love each other deeply, because love covers over a multitude of sins.").

[37] REVELATION 12:11 ("they did not love their lives so much as to shrink from death").

[38] JOHN 13:34 ("A new command I give you: Love one another. As I have loved you, so you must love one another.").

[39] 1 JOHN 4:16 ("God is love.").

Fortunately, we tend to have challenges that are more mundane. Our challenges and the challenges of our clients are to remain consistently within the standards of that love.[40] The law actually requires it, when you think of it. Lawyers must practice to standards of care. How do we do that? We keep our actions consistent with what is reasonable and right under each different circumstance. It takes real attention. That other-regarding love helps make the faithful lawyer consistent. To love in that way does not necessarily mean that we have to like our clients. To love is always to think of how to protect the other.[41] Love encourages lawyers to trust others when trust is what the situation needs to move matters forward.[42] Love also encourages lawyers to be optimistic about the possibilities in a situation, when optimism is what the situation requires.[43] It also urges us to move diligently forward with matters expecting their just resolution, things working out for the better.[44]

A community of lawyers, whether in a law firm or a bar, each member of which is duly caring for others, can be a special community. So can a community of non-lawyers. Reasonable care toward one another is a community asset that lawyers should promote at all times. When we all do remain loving toward one another, there is no liability to one another.[45] Our clients need not even be concerned about tort liability so long as they maintain the right attitude.[46] When you see a client worrying about liability, you know that they have probably already done something wrong in not keeping the right attitude toward others.[47] In a sense, worry over liability is another selfish concern. It disregards that one is willing to be careless toward others but concerned only

---

[40] 1 JOHN 4:8 ("Whoever does not love does not know God, because God is love.").

[41] 1 CORINTHIANS 13:7 ("It always protects ...").

[42] 1 CORINTHIANS 13:7 ("... always trusts ...").

[43] 1 CORINTHIANS 13:7 ("... always hopes ...").

[44] 1 CORINTHIANS 13:7 ("... always perseveres.").

[45] 1 JOHN 4:17 ("In this way, love is made complete among us so that we will have confidence on the day of judgment....").

[46] 1 JOHN 4:18 ("There is no fear in love. But perfect love drives out fear, because fear has to do with punishment.").

[47] 1 JOHN 4:18 ("The one who fears is not made perfect in love.").

about the law holding one to account for their harm. A client cannot truly claim to be law-abiding if the client does not care for others.[48]

Law incorporates this other-regarding sense of care into its most fundamental precepts of justice.[49] It does so from the first-year foundational courses in property, contracts, and criminal law, across such other fields as family law, business organizations, environmental law, and securities regulation, but most obviously in tort law. The basis of tort law is duty to the other. Fundamentally, tort law represents the faith conception of love as giving due regard to the other. The central concept of tort law is one of care for others, that kind of care that one would have for oneself. You should recognize faith's Golden Rule in that concept, that we ought to do unto others as we would have done unto ourselves.[50] Tort law imposes as a matter of law precisely what faith would require of us, which is due regard for the other. Tort law does so in every social interaction, whether direct or indirect, for example when providing medical care or legal services, manufacturing a product, building a home or roadway, maintaining a sidewalk, performing an appraisal, or doing any of the countless other things we do daily.

Faith also shapes tort law's remedial and redemptive nature. Tort law does not bar individual action. One can be as careless as one wish, and tort law will do nothing about it until someone suffers injury. Tort law merely requires a person to provide a fitting and complete remedy when a person intentionally injures another[51] or that person's actions are careless.[52] Informed by faith, tort law fosters the greatest liberty and responsibility, both at

---

[48] 1 JOHN 4:21 ("Whoever loves God must also love his brother.").

[49] HOSEA 10:12 ("Sow for yourselves justice, reap the fruit of steadfast love.").

[50] GALATIANS 5:14 ("The entire law is summed up in a single command: 'Love your neighbor as yourself.'").

[51] EXODUS 21:17 ("If men quarrel and one hits the other with a stone or with his fist and he does not die but is confined to be, ... he must pay the injured man for the loss of his time and see that he is completely healed.").

[52] EXODUS 21:33 ("If a man uncovers a pit or digs one and fails to cover it and an ox or a donkey falls into it, the owner of the pit must pay for the loss; he must pay its owner... .").

once. Indeed, so long as we are ordinarily careful, we have perfect liberty, although recognize that ordinary care is in an ordinary sense perfect.[53] Lawyers find tort law's generous but responsible care-or-liability principles in one form or another in nearly every other law subject, for example, in the duties of diligence in business organizations, the obligations of an executor of a will, the responsibilities of a taxpayer, and so on.

While faith supports the foundational duty of reasonable care in tort law and fashions tort law's redemptive remedy, faith also supports the myriad of subtle doctrines that accompany that foundational care duty. In comparative negligence, we see that faith demands that we care for ourselves before burdening others with care for us.[54] In objective standards of care, faith shows that one's own subjective view can be distorting even with good intentions,[55] while in subjective standards faith shows that intention remains important. In defenses of intra-family and governmental immunity, faith shows us that relationship affects duties. In defamation law, faith shows us the power of words to do good and evil. In misrepresentation claims, faith shows us the reality of fairness and honesty. In every tort claim and defense, there is the seed of faith's morality. Faith holds that we are nothing without love,[56] and so law places an obligation of love within every action and relationship. To love only oneself without loving another is to reject faith.[57] When law students and lawyers see that connection between law and faith, law draws on the strength, purpose, clarity, and meaning of faith.

---

[53] MATTHEW 5:48 (" 'Be perfect, therefore, as your heavenly Father is perfect.' ").

[54] TITUS 3:14 ("Our people must learn to devote themselves to doing what is good, in order that they may provide for daily necessities and not live unproductive lives.").

[55] 1 CHRONICLES 28:9 ("[T]he Lord searches every heart and understands every motive beind the thoughts.").

[56] 1 CORINTHIANS 13:2 ("If I . . . have not love, I am nothing.").

[57] 2 TIMOTHY 3:2 ("People will be lovers of themselves... , without self-control, ... rather than lovers of God—having a form of godliness but denying its power.").

Covenant

"What's the lesson? What's the lesson?" the lawyer remembered his Contracts professor haranguing students after discussing each case, and then answering his own question, "Don't deal with jerks!" Law practice taught the lawyer the value of the lesson. Exhibit A was a client who had sold the small business that it had taken the client a lifetime to develop, to "investors" who turned out to be a whole lot worse than common crooks. The client was selling his business because he was going blind. He could no longer manage his employees, contractors, and customers. The client planned to use the investors' small lump-sum payment for a down payment on a Florida condominium and to live off the investors' monthly $5,000 payments. The payments lasted just two months. The investors raided the business for its every asset including customer funds held in trust, leaving the blind client facing undeserved civil lawsuits and criminal investigation. The Contracts professor's lesson came back to the lawyer: "Don't deal with jerks!"

The problem, the lawyer realized, is identifying the jerks before making contracts with them. There were plenty of other examples. A single mother saves up a couple thousand dollars, giving it to a contractor running a special for new gutters on her home. The contractor absconds with the single mother's money and the deposits paid by a dozen others for the elusive special. A couple advances a builder the funds to complete their new home, but the builder uses the money on another job and then files for bankruptcy. A putative filmmaker dupes a friend interested in the arts to loan thousands for a phantom film project. A subscription service defrauds a blind elderly woman into purchasing dozens of magazines that she cannot even read, the magazines piling up in great stacks around her tiny unkempt home. The lawyer had seen case after case of people losing their hard-earned savings through contracts. "Don't deal with jerks!" the professor's lesson repeated.

Now faith was extending the Contracts professor's lesson. More and more, the lawyer realized that contracts have a community or covenantal aspect. The modern notion of arm's-length transactions between strangers evaluating the merits of deals in an invisible market seemed inadequate. Contracts are seldom that discrete, neat, and compartmentalized. Contracts are instead often heavily relational. They often include payment schedules, security interests, non-competes, confidentiality clauses, claw-back provisions, and other terms that force the parties to trust one another long after the ink is dry and the first consideration changes hands.

91

Whether they recognize and appreciate it or not, the parties to a contract are joining one another in a community of exchange, trusting that the other is a worthy partner in the covenants that formed their relationship. Contract law only enforces the covenants. It gives no guarantees that the parties will fulfill them.

The lawyer was learning that when choosing a covenant partner, one needed to consider whether the partner had a relationship with faith. In case after case, the lawyer saw that the good faith of the parties to the contract mattered as much or more than the literal terms of the contract. If the contracting party had no good faith, then there was little hope of avoiding conflict and loss through it. The first time that the contract required something that the faithless party did not want to perform, there would be a problem. The faithless party would make it the faithful party's problem. A contract is only as good as the word, meaning the character, of the parties. The word and character of a party depends on the party's relationship to faith. The party must have made a covenant with faith for the party's word and character to be reliable.

As hard as it was, the lawyer saw these lessons sink in on some of the consumer and business clients whom the lawyer represented. In a sense, these clients were often as blameworthy as their opposing party was, even when the opposing party had failed to perform the covenant. While the opposing party had failed to perform, these clients had failed to choose a covenant partner wisely. Indeed, they had often known that they were preparing to contract with an unreliable, faithless party. In entering into contracts with parties whom they knew to be untrustworthy because the terms appeared sufficiently advantageous to do so, they had set their own gain ahead of their faith covenant. They had willingly entered the charlatan's realm, deciding that the wares that they saw there were of greater value than what their faith would have provided. They had breached their own covenant with faith, one tenet of which was like the Contracts professor's adage, not to deal with jerks, or you just may become one.

While law studies begin with tort law, which faith teaches us to recognize as the law of care or love, law studies also begin with contract law, which faith teaches us to recognize as the law of promise or covenant. Promises, like care, are at the core of social relationship, meaning that they are also at the core of law. We first care for one another in at least the sense of not harming others, as we would wish that others not harm us. We then seek positive, voluntary, and mutually beneficial relationship, making and relying upon promises, the basis of contract law. The old-fashioned word for promising is to covenant. The law continues to use the old-fashioned word in phrases like a covenant not to compete. Although a law term, the word covenant also carries with it a faith connotation, indeed that faith implies a special form of covenant[58] that in a sense makes plain old promises obsolete.[59] The law of some states today even recognizes covenant marriage as a new form of marriage. Promise, so like covenant in its meaning, is also a fundamental faith concept.

Just as faith informs the basis of contract law, whether we identify contracts as based on promises or covenants, the faith concept of promise or covenant informs other aspects of law practice. The lawyer of faith recognizes four aspects of faith within the concept of promise or covenant. One faith meaning to promises, the most pedestrian but still an important form, has to do with the relationship between parties to a contract. A second faith meaning to promises has to do with the lawyer's relationship to the client, which is a special form of contract. A third faith meaning to promises has to do with the lawyer's relationship to faith itself, in the sense of the promises of faith to the individual lawyer. And a fourth faith meaning has to do with the relationship of a community or nation to faith itself, in the sense of the reciprocal commitments of the community or nation to faith and of faith to the community or nation.

The first faith concept of promise involves a relationship between parties to a contract. Faith indicates that a promise involves placing one's well-being in another's hands, taking a position of vulnerability. In faith's terms, the effect of a promise is to make promisors part of a continuous moral community of peace in which each promisor recognizes the humanity of the others and the position of trust each holds toward others.[60] We make promises to fulfill them, not break them. Although law students and lawyers study efficient breach, broken promises by nature are

---

[58] HEBREWS 12:24 ("Jesus the mediator of a new covenant").

[59] HEBREWS 8:13 ("he has made the first one obsolete").

[60] EZEKIEL 34:25 (" 'I will make a covenant of peace with them and rid the land of wild beasts so that they may live in the desert and sleep in the forests in safety.' ").

exceptions, not the rule. In a perfect world, the perfect person would fulfill all promises to create and preserve a perfectly moral community.[61] Faith helps us see the first form of promise, the bargain between two parties, as more than merely economic, even though commerce is a fundamental aspect of it. Faith helps us see bargain as involving the community that the bargain forms and in which the bargain takes place. By keeping the covenantal sense of contract law in mind, lawyers expand their understanding and deepen the authority of their counsel.

A second faith concept of promise involves the relationship between lawyer and client. Law practice itself relies on covenants between lawyer and client. When a lawyer and client agree on the lawyer's representing the client, they have a contract for legal services. The faith concept of covenant imbues that contract, like other contracts, with those greater moral meanings that make the practice of law more than a business. These faith-inspired meanings transform the nature of promises between lawyer and client. They bring lawyer and client together as part of a larger moral community in which the members are more significant than the benefits each hope to extract from the specific promises that brought them together. There is more than the possibility of entering into future promises. There is membership within the moral community of promising. Relationship within that community is continuous and enduring beyond the contract's duration. Even after the contract term ends, the lawyer owes the client duties of confidentiality and loyalty, and other duties associated with membership within the moral community.[62]

With this faith-inspired understanding of promises between lawyer and client, the lawyer of faith expects more from a client relationship than a fee in exchange for service. The lawyer of faith expects the covenant between lawyer and client to change both lawyer and client. The lawyer expects to bend the lawyer's knowledge and skill to the client's service, changing the nature of

---

[61] JOSHUA 23:14 (" 'Now I am about to go the way of all the earth. You know with all your heart and soul that not one of all the good promises the Lord your God gave you has failed. Every promise has been fulfilled; not one has failed.' ").

[62] PROVERBS 25:9 ("do not betray another man's confidence").

the knowledge and skill in so doing, and changing the quality of the lawyer and client. The lawyer hopes that the client receives more than the accomplished legal objective. The lawyer also hopes that the client gains a sense of having had the relationship affect the client in a way that makes the client stronger for the next challenge. Promises in their faith-inspired meanings transform lawyer and client into fellow sojourners within the same moral community, each having equal value, and each owing a duty to serve and benefit the other that goes beyond the face of the contract into the humanity of the other.

A third faith concept of promise involves faith's own commitment to the lawyer, and the lawyer's reciprocal commitment to faith.[63] The nature of faith's promise is important. Faith's promise is first reliable.[64] Faith does not change faith's mind about keeping faith's promise.[65] It is the most reliable of foundations, giving us security at every moment.[66] Faith's promise is also lasting.[67] It endures as long as endure. The basis for covenant is in faith because faith promises us its rewards so long as we maintain our covenant with faith. Faith does not break faith's promise.[68] Faith simply asks that we not make promises that are inconsistent with faith and that would make us members of immoral communities.[69] After all, there are moral communities that strengthen their members, and there are immoral com-

---

[63] PSALM 119:57 ("I have promised to obey your words.").

[64] JOSHUA 23:14 (" 'You know with all your heart and soul that not one of all the good promises the Lord your God gave you has failed. Every promise has been fulfilled; not one has failed.' ").

[65] PSALM 110:4 ("The Lord has sworn and will not change his mind.").

[66] HEBREWS 6:18-19 ("God did this so that, by two unchangeable things in which it is impossible for God to lie, we who have fled to take hold of the hope offered to us may be greatly encouraged. We have this hope as an anchor for the soul, firm and secure.").

[67] GENESIS 9:16 ("Whenever the rainbow appears in the clouds, I will see it and remember the everlasting covenant between God and all living creatures of every kind on the earth.").

[68] JUDGES 2:1 (" 'I will never break my covenant with you...' ").

[69] JUDGES 2:2 (" '... and you shall not make a covenant with the people of this land, but you shall break down their altars.' ").

munities whose members destroy.[70] Lawyers should be members of moral communities.

Faith's promise is also active, pressing upon and transforming the lawyer, subsuming the lawyer into a relationship with faith, just as other promises draw promisors into moral community.[71] Faith's promise gives the lawyer access to a moral community in a way that no other reform could, enabling the lawyer to participate in additional but otherwise-unavailable promises.[72] Faith's promise is in that sense redemptive, making something of us that we could not make of ourselves without faith.[73] Faith's promise to us is also historical, having its roots in recorded world events.[74] Faith's promise also requires our performance of faith's terms, like other covenants require other performances.[75] A significant challenge to our performance of our part of the faith bargain is that we must trust in faith's power to fulfill faith's promise to us, if we are to fulfill our promise to faith.[76] Like other promises, faith requires our vulnerability to and confidence in the other party.[77]

Faith's promise to the faithful lawyer is also expansive. It extends beyond the lawyer to the lawyer's children, meaning that by serving in faith the lawyer gains the benefit of faith's promise

[70] ISAIAH 10:7 ("his purpose is to destroy").

[71] JEREMIAH 31:33 (" 'This is the covenant I will make with the house of Israel after that time,' declares the Lord, 'I will put my law in their minds and write it on their hearts.'").

[72] 2 PETER 4 ("Through these he has given us his very great and precious promises, so that through them you may participate in the divine nature and escape the corruption in the world caused by evil desires.").

[73] GALATIANS 3:14 ("He redeemed us ... so that by faith we might receive the promise of the Spirit.").

[74] GALATIANS 3:14 ("He redeemed us in order that the blessing given to Abraham might come to the Gentiles through Christ Jesus... .").

[75] ACTS 2:38-39 (" 'Repent and be baptized, every one of you, in the name of Jesus Christ for the forgiveness of your sins. And you will receive the gift of the Holy Spirit. The promise is for you... .' ").

[76] ROMANS 4:21 ("Yet [Abraham] did not waver through unbelief regarding the promise of God, but was strengthened in his faith and gave glory to God, being fully persuaded that God had power to do what he had promised.").

[77] HEBREWS 10:23 ("Let us hold unswervingly to the hope we profess, for he who promised is faithful.").

as if the lawyer's children had also served in faith.[78] Faith's promise is in that sense enduring.[79] Faith may have made the promise to a parent or even earlier generation, but faith keeps the promise to the child. It is extraordinary to consider, but faith's promise extends even to strangers[80] and others whom only faith knows and intends.[81] Fortunately, faith's promise is also timely, its fulfillment coming immediately.[82] Faith's promise to the lawyer is also rich in both worldly terms[83] and faith terms.[84] Faith's promise is also entire, meaning whole and complete.[85] Faith does not offer only a little consideration or even measured consideration. Faith offers all that faith has.

A fourth faith concept of promise involves the commitment of a community or nation to faith, and faith's reciprocal commitment. Faith does not limit faith's promise to the individual. Promise or covenant also has a community-building function. Faith forms a covenant with whole communities and nations.[86] Faith's covenant with nations lasts over generations.[87] Faith's promise to communities and nations is to distinguish them from unfaithful communities and nations through an abundance of blessings,[88] to make faithful communities and nations far better

---

[78] ACTS 2:39 ("... and your children...").

[79] 1 TIMOTHY 4:8 ("For physical training is of some value, but godliness has value for all things, holding promise for both the present life and the life to come.").

[80] ACTS 2:39 ("...and for all who are far off...").

[81] ACTS 2:39 ("—for all whom the Lord our God will call.").

[82] 2 PETER 3:9 ("The Lord is not slow in keeping his promise, as some understand slowness.").

[83] 1 KINGS 8:20 ("The Lord has kept the promise he made: I have succeeded David my father and now I sit on the throne of Israel, just as the Lord promised... .").

[84] ACTS 2:38-39 (" 'Repent and be baptized, every one of you, in the name of Jesus Christ for the forgiveness of your sins. And you will receive the gift of the Holy Spirit. The promise is for you... .' ").

[85] 1 CORINTHIANS 11:25 ("This cup is the new covenant in my blood... .").

[86] EXODUS 24:7 ("Then he took the Book of the Covenant and read it to the people.").

[87] 1 KINGS 8:21 ("the covenant of the Lord that he made with our fathers when he brought them out of Egypt").

[88] EXODUS 3:17 (" 'And I have promised to bring you up out of your misery in Egypt into ... a land flowing with milk and honey.' ").

places in which to live than unfaithful places.[89] Faith makes those who hold it citizens of a higher community, committed to higher ends, held to higher standards, and rewarded accordingly.[90] Faith is earnest, even passionate, in its promise, treating a covenanting nation not off-handedly but with such devotion as to be a treasured possession.[91] Faith's promise to nations is comprehensive, replete with other advantages.[92] It is also complete. Faith keeps every aspect of every promise to faithful communities and nations.[93]

This expansive faith reading of the nature of promise reaches beyond contract law and into constitutional law. Countries found themselves on self-evident premises of faith[94] in covenant with faith, promising that they will not deny their citizens the rights and benefits of faith. Faith's form of promise or covenant is nation founding, defining a people and creating a national community out of them based on their consent under faith. Faithful lawyers especially keep their promises to faith in connection with the constitution of a community and nation.[95] In these and other ways, faith imbues the law of promise with its most significant and purposeful meanings. The faithful lawyer connects the law of promise with its faith meanings.

Provision

"Now, this turn of events is going to make for an interesting challenge," the lawyer thought to himself, about as charitably as he

---

[89] DEUTERONOMY 26:19 ("He has declared that he will set you in praise, fame and honor high above all the nations he has made and that you will be a people holy to the Lord your God, as he promised.").

[90] PHILIPPIANS 3:20 ("But our citizenship is in heaven.").

[91] DEUTERONOMY 26:18 ("[T]he lord has declared this day that you are his people, his treasured possession as he promised. . . .").

[92] ROMANS 9:4 ("Theirs is the adoption as sons; theirs the divine glory, the covenants, the receiving of the law, the temple worship and the promises.").

[93] JOSHUA 21:45 ("Not one of all the Lord's good promises to the house of Israel failed; every one was fulfilled.").

[94] GENESIS 1:27 ("So God created man in his own image, in the image of God he created him, male and female he created them.").

[95] NUMBERS 30:2 (" 'When a man takes a vow to the Lord or takes an oath to obligate himself by a pledge, he must not break his word but must do everything he said.' ").

could possibly spin it. It had been a tough year for the law practice, complicated by a tough year for family. The lawyer had pretty much maintained the same practice as always: a good mix of civil litigation, some of it hourly defense work but much of it contingency fee, with large and small cases across several fields including personal injury, civil rights, business, and even some family law. That mix had always managed to even out the cash flow suitably for the small firm in which the lawyer was a partner. In nearly a decade and a half of working for the firm, much of it as a partner, the lawyer had never missed a paycheck and seldom missed a year-end bonus. With prudent financial management and reliable earnings, the lawyer and his wife had paid off law school loans, paid off their modest home, and saved for their young daughter's college education.

The challenges had begun with the lawyer's parents who had recently lost their palatial home and filed for bankruptcy. The parents had first asked their son, the lawyer, to lend them larger sums of money than the lawyer could risk losing. He declined, painfully but wisely as it turned out, when another family member made and lost the loan without in any respect having helped the parents. The lawyer had been wiser. The parents had then struggled with other family members' help to maintain housing over the next few months. It had been a turbulent time for everyone involved with one parent angrily threatening suicide while the other parent struggled to get along with other family members—not what the lawyer had expected.

After much consideration, the lawyer and his wife had decided to buy a home for the lawyer's parents. A key part of the lawyer's decision, undoubtedly the difference, had been the moral admonition that a person of faith who fails to care for his family is worse than a person without faith who does care for his family. The lawyer and his wife bought a home for the lawyer's parents, expecting challenges but acting on principles of faith. They knew it would not be easy, either financially or in the unsteady relationship with the lawyer's parents. Yet they also felt that if they could get the parents into a stable home, owned and eventually paid for by the lawyer and his wife, then at least the parents' financial and housing issues would settle down. The lawyer and his wife could care for the lawyer's parents in their last years without worrying about housing. So they found a modest home acceptable to the lawyer's parents and then closed on the home.

That was when the fun started. The next day after the closing, the managing partner of the lawyer's small firm told the lawyer that the lawyer would not receive a paycheck for a little while because of some cash-flow issues within the firm. The news shocked the lawyer and his wife. The lawyer had never missed a paycheck until now, the day after he and his wife had made one of the biggest moral commitments and financial risks of their lives. Then, the little while stretched into a couple of months and finally a season without a paycheck, even as the lawyer continued daily to do the challenging legal work for the firm, and the lawyer and his wife continued to pay for the home now occupied, comfortably and happily, by the lawyer's parents. Imagine working without pay for several months under those conditions, and you can see how easily it could have destroyed the lawyer's marriage, law firm, and faith.

Yet it did not. Strangely, that long season of hard work without compensation became one of the most satisfying times of the lawyer's marriage and career. The lawyer and his wife knew that they were acting morally while trusting in and drawing on the rich resources of faith. They had not a single argument that whole summer about money or any other subject. They had decided to say nothing to the lawyer's parents or other family members about their unexpected financial challenge, a decision that made their commitment to one another and their faith even stronger. The lawyer appreciated deeply his wife's sacrifice for his parents, while the wife learned deeper appreciation and trust for her husband.

The lawyer also grew to appreciate his firm's commitment to its staff, no member of which ever missed a paycheck that summer. The partners ensured that they paid everyone else responsibly, even if they did not pay themselves. The lawyer also grew to respect even more his law firm's managing partner, who in return undoubtedly grew even more to respect the lawyer's commitment to the firm and managing partner. The lawyer knew that his own practice was a big part of the cash-flow issue. He had always been one of the firm's reliable workhorses on profitable cases. Yet over the past year he had worked 800 uncompensated hours on contingency fee in a civil-rights case. His firm trusted his skill and judgment, just as he trusted the skill and judgment of the managing partner on other long-pending contingency-fee matters.

Finally, at the end of a long, hot summer of working without pay, the lawyer received a paycheck. In that check was every dollar of compensation that he and his wife had missed all summer. A client for whom the firm had worked on another matter for 10 years without compensation had finally paid the firm, and the lawyer had won the civil-rights case into which he had put so many uncompensated hours, resulting in a fee award that the opposing party's insurer had finally paid. The firm paid off its line of credit and restored its financial order, just as the lawyer restored the financial order of the lawyer's household. The lawyer and his wife knew, though, that the real victory was a more subtle and important one. Their faith had grown and, with that growth, blessed themselves and their family.

The trust that the lawyer and his wife had shown, and the way in which faith had ultimately honored their trust, made them more generous and consistent in their other giving in the ensuing years. They also received more in return. They learned to give a fixed percentage of their income to their faith home. They found that they soon had enough that they were able to give cars and housing to others. Each of these actions freed them further from concerns about financial security, even as their finances also grew more secure. They had trusted in faith's provision, and faith had rewarded them not only with provision but also with confidence, blessing, and a new kind of security.

Perhaps most satisfying, though, was that their 12-year-old daughter had watched as the lawyer and his wife did the right thing for the lawyer's parents that summer. Their daughter knew (as only a child can) that the decision had come at substantial cost, that it had not been an easy decision. Yet their daughter also saw them succeed with real grace despite unexpected challenge. The faith of the lawyer and his wife deepened the faith of their daughter through the promise of faith's provision. The lawyer realized that money actually matters little when it comes to passing these blessings of faith from generation to generation. What matters more is one's attitude toward money and toward the faith that secures those blessings.

Law studies include property law among tort law and contract law as the foundations of civil society. Faith teaches that we are not only to care for others, as tort law would have us do, and benefit from covenanting with others, as contract law would support. We are also to provide for ourselves and our families as part of our individual and social responsibility.[96] In other words, we are to work so that our industry brings us what we need in the way of daily provision.[97] We are capable of working and producing, and that capability when exercised duly earns us our keep.

---

[96] 2 THESSALONIANS 3:10 (" 'If a man will not work, he shall not eat.' ").

[97] 2 THESSALONIANS 3:8 ("we worked night and day, laboring and toiling so that we would not be a burden to any of you").

To those who do not work when they could, we legitimately urge that they do so in order that they, too, adequately provide for themselves.[98] In that way, faith teaches us that property law is an important incident to both the responsibility to provide and the ability to do so. When we acquire and accumulate property through our industry, we fulfill our duty to provide for ourselves and our families.

The faithful lawyer trusts that faithful pursuit and execution of a lawyer's professional duties will result in sufficient provision for the lawyer and the lawyer's family.[99] The faithful lawyer does not worry about not having enough.[100] The faithful lawyer instead takes faith from what the lawyer sees others earning, particularly those whose work does not appear to have the same merit, that the lawyer's right work will also earn its due and even greater reward.[101] Faith's promise is that the faithful lawyer will receive sufficient provision.[102] Provision may come repeatedly to the lawyer of faith from unexpected sources.[103] Provision is not always a matter of marketing and establishing new practice areas. Lawyers often find rewarding work from sources that are naturally close to them and from long-established relationships.[104] Fundamentally, lawyers receive provision by working for the good of others, ensuring that others are prospering, with the lawyers who work faithfully for others receiving their own

---

[98] 2 THESSALONIANS 3:11-12 ("We hear that some among you are idle. They are not busy; they are busybodies. Such people we command and urge in the Lord Jesus Christ to settle down and earn the bread they eat.").

[99] PROVERBS 28:19 ("He who works his land will have abundant food. . . .").

[100] MATTHEW 6:26 (" 'Look at the birds of the air; they do not sow or reap or store away in barns, and yet your heavenly Father feeds them. Are you not much more valuable than they?' ").

[101] MATTHEW 6:30 (" 'If that is how God clothes the grass of the field, which is here today and tomorrow is thrown into the fire, will he not much more clothe you, O you of little faith?'").

[102] EZEKIEL 34:26 (" 'I will bless them and the places surrounding my hill. I will send down showers in season; there will be showers of blessing.' ").

[103] 1 KINGS 17:5 ("The ravens brought him bread and meat in the morning and bread and meat in the evening. . .").

[104] 1 KINGS 17:5 (". . . and he drank from the brook.").

provision in return.[105] Faithful labor has a way of earning its sure reward, even when and sometimes especially when odds seem stacked against the faithful lawyer.[106] The harder the challenge, the greater the reward, and the greater support that faith gives to the faithful lawyer.[107]

The faithful lawyer also knows that accumulating and protecting property can itself be an important means of continuing to produce and provide for our families and ourselves. We do not acquire property to squander it. The accumulation of wealth and its orderly transfer from generation to generation protects families against unexpected need.[108] Property can be a buffer against need. Property is also a means of producing wealth. The means of producing can require substantial capital. Lawyers, for instance, require research services, offices, and staffing in order to offer legal services. Without capital, lawyers cannot be productive, just as a lawyer's client will need capital to produce (although it is good to keep in mind that faith is capital of another kind[109]). Capital owned is better than capital borrowed, meaning credit relying on someone else's capital.[110] Owning property does more than enable us to work. It also increases our incentive to work.[111] We work best for ourselves when we own the means of

---

[105] RUTH 2:12 ("Boaz replied, '… May the Lord repay you for what you have done. May you be richly rewarded by the Lord, the God of Israel, under whose wings you have come to take refuge.' ").

[106] JUDGES 7:2 ("You have too many men for me to deliver Midian into their hands.'").

[107] DEUTERONOMY 31:8 (" 'The Lord himself goes before you and will be with you; he will never leave you nor forsake you.' ").

[108] LUKE 15:13 (" 'There was a man who had to sons. The younger one said to his father ,"Father, give me my share of the estate." So he divided his property between them. Not long after that, the younger son got together all he had, set off for a distant country and there squandered his wealth in wild living. After he had spent everything, there was a severe famine in that whole country, and he began to be in need.' ").

[109] 2 PETER 1:8 ("For if you possess these qualities in increasing measure, they will keep you from being ineffective and unproductive.… .").

[110] PROVERBS 22:7 ("the borrower is servant to the lender").

[111] ECCLESIASTES 11:1 ("Cast your bread upon the waters, for after many days you will find it again.").

our production.[112] Property law serves faith by protecting property against theft and destruction, helping persons to accumulate property, and helping persons organize around and share property.

Faith also informs lawyers in the cause for and outcome of property-law disputes. Faithful lawyers recognize and avoid greed, of which there is too much around.[113] Greed has a way of destroying a lawyer and the lawyer's family.[114] Faith cautions against placing too great an emphasis on the pursuit of money and material goods because they are not really the best part of life.[115] We are not to allow money to become our master and should caution our clients against doing so.[116] We should work diligently and creatively in order to provide for ourselves and our family.[117] Yet it is wrong to take everything possible from our work, leaving nothing for others.[118] There are times when the faithful lawyer should counsel the rich client to share wealth and, by doing so, be happier and better for it.[119] It is simply harder for those who have riches to be faithful in all respects because riches have a way of distracting one from the essentials of life.[120] The faithful lawyer knows that for a client to love money rather than the good that money might do in the right hands can bring a client plenty of trouble.[121]

---

[112] NEHEMIAH 5:5 ("we are powerless because our fields and our vineyards belong to others").

[113] LUKE 12:15 (" 'Watch out! Be on your guard against all kinds of greed....' ").

[114] PROVERBS 15:27 ("A greedy man brings trouble to his family.").

[115] LUKE 12:15 (" '...a man's life does not consist in the abundance of his possessions.'").

[116] LUKE 16:13 (" 'No servant can serve two masters. Either he will hate the one and love the other, or he will be devoted to the one and despise the other. You cannot serve both God and money.' ").

[117] 1 TIMOTHY 5:8 ("If anyone does not provide for his relatives, and especially for his immediate family, he has denied the faith and is worse than an unbeliever.").

[118] LEVITICUS 19:9 ("When you reap the harvest of your land, do not reap to the very edges of your field or gather the gleanings of your harvest.").

[119] MARK 10:21 (" 'One thing you lack,' he said. 'Go, sell everything you have and give to the poor, and you will have treasure in heaven.' ").

[120] MARK 10:23 (" 'How hard it is for the rich to enter the kingdom of God!' ").

[121] 1 TIMOTHY 6:10 ("For the love of money is a root of all kinds of evil.").

Sharing wealth rather than hoarding it can also bring security. Our clients sometimes think that money will protect them, but sometimes money wisely spent makes friends where one most needs it for that protection. There is something in faith about being a shrewd manager of resources for the longest-term ends.[122] Faith cautions against taking too much security in wealth, which is always elusive and hard to protect.[123] Lawyers counsel clients who are making substantial money and acquiring substantial property, more than they need. Wise counsel can be to be sure to accumulate the permanent things that make a difference to real life, not just property.[124] The more property we accumulate, the more property we want.[125] Once you start to desire money, you can never get enough.[126] The faithful lawyer knows that property is not what counts in the end.[127]

Faith also teaches lawyers to be patient in accumulating property and to counsel their clients to do so because our life is not really in what we manage to accumulate.[128] Our life is instead in how we use property fairly with respect to others. We must be careful and ensure that our clients are careful not to hoard property accumulated by cheating others.[129] Hoarders who have

---

[122] LUKE 16:9 ("I tell you, use worldly wealth to gain friends for yourselves, so that when it is gone, you will be welcomed into eternal dwellings.").

[123] MATTHEW 6:19 (" 'Do not store up for yourselves treasures on earth, where moth and rust destroy, and where thieves break in and steal.' ").

[124] MATTHEW 6:20 (" 'But store up for yourselves treasures in heaven, where moth and rust do not destroy, and where thieves do not break in and steal.").

[125] MATTHEW 6:21 (" 'For where your treasure is, there your heart will be also.' ").

[126] ECCLESIASTES 5:10 ("Whoever loves money never has money enough; whoever loves wealth is never satisfied with his income.").

[127] LUKE 12:15 ("a man's life does not consist in the abundance of his possessions").

[128] LUKE 12:15 ("Then he said, 'Watch out! Be on your guard against all kinds of greed; a man's life does not consist in the abundance of his possessions.").

[129] JAMES 5:1, 4 ("Now listen, you rich people, weep and wail because of the misery that is coming upon you. ... You have hoarded wealth in the last days. Look! The wages you failed to pay the workmen who mowed your fields are crying out against you.").

cheated others in order to accumulate more property than they deserve face the condemnation of law and faith.[130] We know the reason for hoarding. It has to do with our desire to live in ease, pursuing our own desires even at our own cost and the cost of innocent others whose property we have taken from others with the ease of our advantage.[131] How many times have we seen people pursuing that course because they do not maintain the right relationship to property? It does a lawyer nothing to get rich but lose character and reputation, just as it does a client nothing, even when there may be great wealth to gain. A person is worth more than riches.[132]

For that reason, we best accumulate property slowly at first in order that we learn how best to manage it. The better we are at managing it, the more property we acquire and accumulate. The lawyer who does right with a little property will receive more property of greater value to manage in the future.[133] The worse we are at managing property, the less we acquire and accumulate.[134] The lawyer who misuses a small piece of property or small amount of money belonging to a client will never get the opportunity to handle large properties and sums of money.[135] Lawyers give wise counsel when encouraging clients to be patient and trustworthy.

The best way to look at property is that it belongs to faith, not to us.[136] We hold it only briefly and should hold it in that

---

[130] JAMES 5:4 ("The cries of the harvesters have reached the ears of the Lord Almighty.").

[131] JAMES 5:5-6 ("You have lived on earth in luxury and self-indulgence. You have fattened yourselves in the day of slaughter. You have condemned and murdered innocent men, who were not opposing you.").

[132] MARK 8:36 (" 'What good is it for a man to gain the whole world, yet forfeit his soul?' ").

[133] LUKE 16:10 (" 'Whoever can be trusted with very little can also be trusted with much....' ").

[134] LUKE 16:10 (" '... and whoever is dishonest with very little will also be dishonest with much.' ").

[135] LUKE 16:11 (" 'So if you have not been trustworthy in handling worldly wealth, who will trust you with true riches?' ").

[136] PSALM 24:1 ("The earth is the Lord's and all that is in it, the world, and those who live in it.").

trust that all things belong to faith.[137] There is impermanency to ownership, that even law regards ownership as contingent on various obligations to pay taxes, not destroy or waste, and under the conventions of title.[138] To think about property in that manner can give the faithful lawyer great peace and liberty. We are, after all, here and gone rather quickly. And so, we hold property in trust in that perspective, that we have a sort of dominion over it,[139] in which it is ours[140] but to treat it as if we were stewards of it, to make the best of it while caring for it.[141] Property is not something that we grasp with any permanency but something that we know outlasts us, belonging to the faith that created it.[142] We have no claim to property beyond that faith's own claim to it.[143]

Faith abhors when we desire the property of another unjustly. That kind of longing for the property of another, especially those whose property is conveniently within our reach, is ruinous, and so faith commands that we not court that kind of desire.[144] Faith recognizes that we are acquisitive by nature, that there is little end to our unjust desires. We desire not only real and personal property but also the labor and intimacy of others, when it seems just within our reach but someone else whom we know owns it.[145] Faith further abhors when we take property without it

---

[137] GENESIS 1:1 ("In the beginning, God created the heavens and the earth.").

[138] LEVITICUS 25:23 (" 'The land must not be sold permanently, because the land is mine and you are but aliens and my tenants.' ").

[139] GENESIS 1:26 ("Then God said, 'Let us make man in our image, in our likeness, and let them rule over the fish of the sea and the birds of the air, over the livestock, over all the earth, and over all the creatures that move along the ground.' ").

[140] PSALM 115:16 ("The highest heavens belong to the Lord, but the earth he has given to man.").

[141] GENESIS 2:15 ("The Lord God took the man and put him in the Garden of Eden to work it and take care of it.").

[142] DEUTERONOMY 10:14 ("To the Lord your God belong the heavens, even the highest heavens, the earth and everything in it.").

[143] JOB 41:11 ("Who has a claim against me that I must pay? Everything under heaven belongs to me.").

[144] EXODUS 20:17 ("You shall not covet your neighbor's house.").

[145] EXODUS 20:17 ("You shall not covet your neighbor's wife, or his manservant or maidservant, his ox or donkey, or anything that belongs to your neighbor.").

belonging to us. It is one of the prime tenets of faith, as it is of property law, that we leave to others that which is theirs and not take it from them.[146] It is especially perilous to be dishonest with one's own faith when it comes to money. The consequence of distorting the truth of one's faith over greed for holding onto money is the death of one's faith.[147] We should fear being dishonest about money within our faith as much as we fear anything.

Community

    The lawyer chuckled knowingly at what were apparently exaggerations in the case-evaluation brief. The lawyer knew well the law firm from the other side of the state. The lawyer had defended a couple of cases against the firm and its lawyers when he had worked on the other side of the state nearer the firm. The firm had a statewide reputation for overly aggressive presentation and pursuit of its cases. It would be an interesting case evaluation tomorrow, the lawyer thought, seeing how the case-evaluation panel of which the lawyer was a member would treat the out-of-town lawyer who had written the over-the-top brief. Local lawyers did not treat their cases in that fashion. They associated flamboyant over-reaching with lawyers from the large metropolitan area on the other side of the state.

    Indeed, the case evaluation was highly interesting, fulfilling perfectly the lawyer's expectations. The lawyer was the neutral evaluator, so he felt that he could sit back a bit and watch it all happen. The plaintiff's lawyer from the firm on the other side of the state made his flamboyant presentation, placing a value on the case about five times what a local lawyer would have. Before he had even finished, the defense evaluator was all over him, saying how ridiculous the valuation was and arguing with the plaintiff's lawyer while the defense lawyer just grinned. The defense lawyer made a brief presentation, followed by more arguing between the defense evaluator and the plaintiff's lawyer. The lawyers on the case then stepped out of the room while the evaluators made their decision. It was actually an easy case to evaluate, with a well-

---

[146] EXODUS 20:15 ("You shall not steal.").

[147] ACTS 5:3-4 ("Then Peter said, 'Ananias, how is it that ... you have lied to the Holy Spirit and have kept for yourself some of the money you received for the land? ... What made you think of doing such a thing? You have not lied to men but to God.").

established settlement range. The neutral evaluator ensured that the panel picked a figure right in the middle of the range and then went to the door to call the lawyers on the case back into the room.

The defense evaluator, still seated behind the conference table where the lawyers had argued, shoved the case-evaluation results across the table, glaring at the plaintiff's lawyer as he approached. The plaintiff's lawyer looked down at the evaluation figure and erupted. The other lawyers had to step between the plaintiff's lawyer and the defense evaluator to cut short the loud argument. The neutral evaluator escorted the still-fuming plaintiff's lawyer from the room and returned to his seat at the conference table for the next evaluation. The defense evaluator was still red-faced, shaking his head, and muttering about those out-of-town big-shot lawyers. The neutral evaluator smiled and nodded calmly in agreement, reassuring the defense evaluator that while his assessment of the plaintiff's lawyer was dead-on, it really did not make any difference in their evaluation of the case. The defense evaluator nodded in agreement and turned to prepare for the next case.

The lawyer had first learned as every law student and new lawyer learns that lawyers are a distinct community with their own rules and norms. The lawyer had then learned from traveling the state and country that each local bar was its own professional community maintaining its own norms. When the lawyer had taken a case to file on the other side of the country, the lawyer had wisely retained local counsel and had watched and listened closely to that local counsel to adapt to local norms. The lawyer had learned that local judges and lawyers hold out-of-town lawyers accountable to local norms. Case evaluation was one way that they do so, although the lawyer was sure that they had evaluated this case at the figure they would have assigned any case, whether handled by a local or out-of-town lawyer.

The lawyer had also learned the value of a society having distinct communities, particularly communities of faith. The lawyer had also learned the value of being a member of a faith community. In joining a faith community, the lawyer saw how its members helped one another learn and hold to its truths, ones that the larger culture did not consistently recognize or honor. The lawyer saw how a faith community holds its members accountable to the community's understanding and commitments. The lawyer saw how the company one keeps influences heavily the views one accepts and behaviors and attitudes one adopts, especially toward one's own condition and conduct. The lawyer saw how a faith community could develop and maintain among its members an intense concern for the welfare of each individual member of the community and for non-members.

That concern was what the defense evaluator had shown when confronting the exaggerating out-of-town lawyer, the lawyer decided. The defense evaluator was letting the out-of-town lawyer know that the local bar valued integrity more than showmanship, that its members could trust one another to present their cases fairly, without exaggeration, and receive what was due in the way of professional consideration. The out-of-town lawyer had first tried over-the-top emotional appeals and had then tried to bully the evaluators with his eruption. The defense evaluator called him on it, hoping that by embarrassing the out-of-town lawyer that he might learn to conform his conduct to the community's norms, or if not that, then to at least preserve those norms among its members. There may be another community that required its members to exaggerate every claim or defense and to appeal to the passion and prejudices of its members, but not in this community, not before the defense evaluator. The lawyer appreciated and respected the defense evaluator, making a note to be likewise prepared to defend the professional commitments of his professional community and the faith commitments of his faith community.

Law studies include constitutional law among property law, tort law, and contract law as the foundations of civil society. Faith recognizes constitutional law as the law of community, participation, decision, and consent. A constitution forms a community, whether a nation, state, city, or other territory. It does so by calling a people to decide, announce, and commit to the terms on which they will participate in the community. A constitution determines the terms on which citizens will allow governors to decide matters that are so important to them as to define the contours of the community. Constitutional-law disputes are about who gets to decide, meaning whether the individual or the federal or state government, and if government, then which branch. Constitutional-law disputes are also about what decisions governments get to make following what processes and on what terms. Constitutions declare the commitments of a people collectively to one another.

Faith informs constitutions by defining a people's fundamental commitments.[148] Faith forces a people to distinguish itself from ordinary history and tradition.[149] Just as constitutions require clarity, faith both allows a people to choose, creating an option, and forces a people to choose, compelling corporate definition, sometimes following history and local culture, but at other times sometimes transcending it to create a new people.[150] Faith shows a people the option of writing a constitution that will bring the people out of the history, traditions, and culture that made them less than those whom they ought to have been.[151] The faithful lawyer knows that a constitution is the community's covenant out of which a people's governors will draw the community's laws,[152] with the constitution a witness to their original and fundamental commitments.[153]

Faith teaches that constitutions involve commitments, meaning decisions defining the community. People divide over many things including what it means to be a certain people. [154] Constitutions force them to decide on common things defining them as a people.[155] Constitutions usually arise when a people face self-inflicted crises so deep as to require the people to seek redefi-

---

[148] JOSHUA 24:14 ("Now, fear the Lord and serve him with all faithfulness.").

[149] JOSHUA 24:14 ("Throw away the gods your forefathers worshiped beyond the River and in Egypt, and serve the Lord.").

[150] JOSHUA 24:15 ("But if serving the Lord seems undesirable to you, then choose for yourselves this day whom you will serve, whether the gods your forefathers served beyond the River, or the gods of the Amorites, in whose land you are living.").

[151] JOSHUA 24:16-17 ("Then the people answered, 'Far be it from us to forsake the Lord to serve other gods! It was the Lord our God himself who brought us and our fathers up out of Egypt, from that land of slavery ... .' ").

[152] JOSHUA 24:25 ("On that day, Joshua made a covenant for the people, and there at Shechem he drew up for them decrees and laws.").

[153] JOSHUA 24:26 ("And Joshua recorded these things in the Book of the Law of God. Then he took a large stone and set it up there under the oak near the holy place of the Lord.").

[154] 1 KINGS 18:21 ("How long will you waver between two opinions?").

[155] 1 KINGS 18:21 ("If the Lord is God, follow him; but if Baal is God, follow him.").

nition.[156] A new constitution admits and declares that faithless old ways have failed and that the community must adopt new ways that will faithfully provide for the people.[157] Faith urges that people decide on and adopt the common things that will both unify them in their commitments and provide for them materially as a people.[158] In discerning those corporate commitments, a people will often look to individuals whose commitments have already met similar challenges. The shape of a new constitution may arise out of the experience of leaders of faith whose ways have already proven to meet the challenges of the people.[159]

Faith also informs how individuals relate to a constituted community. While constitutions require a high degree of unity among the people in order to obtain their peaceful adoption,[160] constitutions also recognize that individuals within the community must have distinct identities and functions for the community to function.[161] Constitutions provide for individual liberty for the benefit not solely of the individual but of the community. In the strongest of communities, members of the community do not use their liberty for individual gain that destroys others. They use

---

[156] HEBREWS 3:7-9 ("So, as the Holy Spirit says: 'Today, if you hear his voice, do not harden your hearts as you did in the rebellion, during the time of testing in the desert, where your fathers tested and tried me and for forty years saw what I did.").

[157] HEBREWS 3:10-11 ("That is why I was angry with that generation, and I said, 'Their hearts are always going astray, and they have not known my ways.' So I declared on oath in my anger, 'They shall never enter my rest.' ").

[158] ACTS 4:32 ("All the believers were one in heart and mind. No one claimed that any of his possessions was his own, but they shared everything they had.").

[159] HEBREWS 11:24-26 ("By faith Moses, when he had grown up, refused to be known as the son of Pharaoh's daughter. He chose to be mistreated along with the people of God rather than to enjoy the pleasures of sin for a short time.").

[160] EPHESIANS 4:3 ("Make every effort to keep the unity of the Spirit through the bond of peace.").

[161] ROMANS 12:4-5 ("Just as each of us has one body with many members, and these members do not all have the same function, so in Christ we who are many form one body, and each member belongs to all others. We have different gifts, according to the grace given to us.").

liberty to strengthen and draw together the whole community,[162] making each member of the community strong.[163] Each member of the community regards each other member with due concern, especially those members who are not already visible leaders.[164] In other words, the community reserves its greatest concern for the weakest among it.

Communities seek to ensure that each member of the community knows the constitution and can instruct others in it.[165] When a member of the community disrupts it, violating a community norm, other members of the community, particularly lawyers who know the community's norms, should instruct the member until the member reforms.[166] Those who do the instruction should ensure at the same time that they are not also violating the norm. They should not allow the violating member to convince them to ignore the constitution.[167] Communities should highly value lawyers who are effective at helping individuals and corporations reform before larger problems arise.[168] Communities should embrace members who do reform, so that they may resume being effective members of the community.[169] Yet if a member refuses to reform, then other members should

---

[162] EPHESIANS 4:11-12 ("It was he who gave some to be apostles, some to be prophets, some to be evangelists, and some to be pastors and teachers, to prepare God's people for works of service, so that the body of Christ may be built up...").

[163] EPHESIANS 4:13 ("... until we all reach unity in the faith ... and become mature, attaining to the whole measure of the fullness of Christ.").

[164] 1 CORINTHIANS 12:24-25 ("... God has combined the members of the body and has given greater honor to the parts that lacked it, so that there should be no division in the body, but that its parts should have equal concern for each other.").

[165] ROMANS 15:14 ("I myself am convinced, my brothers, that you yourselves are full of goodness, complete in knowledge and competent to instruct one another.").

[166] GALATIANS 6:1 ("Brothers, if someone is caught in a sin, you who are spiritual should restore him gently.").

[167] GALATIANS 6:1 ("But watch yourself, or you also may be tempted.").

[168] JAMES 5:20 ("Whoever turns a sinner from his way will save him from death and cover over a multitude of sins.").

[169] 2 CORINTHIANS 2:7-8 ("Now instead, you ought to forgive and comfort him, so that he will not be overwhelmed by excessive sorrow. I urge you, therefore, to reaffirm your love for him.").

avoid that member.[170] It may be that the member will gradually reform under this kind of influence.[171]

To maintain the community's constitution and law-abiding nature without unnecessary litigation, a community should generally use a progressive form of discipline with its members. In general, lawyers whom clients retain to address another's wrong should first make a confidential demand to the wrongdoer, giving the wrongdoer the opportunity to reform privately.[172] If the wrongdoer does not reform, then the lawyer should gather more evidence and present it to the wrongdoer again, involving others to show the wrongdoer that it is not just the lawyer's own view.[173] Only if the wrongdoer continues to refuse to reform should the lawyer file a lawsuit, invoking public legal procedures.[174] A lawyer should not hesitate to pursue legal proceedings against a person who or entity that will not correct misconduct that violates the community's laws.[175] Correction through instruction and then, if necessary, legal proceedings is an important aspect of preserving a flourishing community.[176] The indi-

---

[170] 1 CORINTHIANS 5:11 ("you must not associate with anyone who calls himself a brother but is sexually immoral or greedy, an idolater or a slanderer, a drunkard or a swindler").

[171] 2 THESSALONIANS 3:14 ("If anyone does not obey our instruction in this letter, take special note of him. Do not associate with him, in order that he may feel ashamed. Yet do not regard him as an enemy, but warn him as a brother.").

[172] MATTHEW 18:15 ("If your brother sins against you, go and show him his fault, just between the two of you.").

[173] MATTHEW 18:16 ("But if he will not listen, take one or two others along, so that 'every matter may be established by the testimony of two or three witnesses.' ").

[174] MATTHEW 18:17 ("If he refuses to listen tot hem, tell it to the church...").

[175] MATTHEWS 18:17 ("... and if he refuses to listen even to the church, treat him as you would a pagan or a tax collector.").

[176] REVELATION 2:2 (" 'I know your deeds, your hard work and your perseverance. I know that you cannot tolerate wicked me, that you have tested those who claim to be apostles but are not, and have found them false.' ").

vidual who rejects correction will regret it.[177] The community that fails to enforce its laws will suffer.[178]

Commitment to a unifying identity, one that leaders and visionaries have shown serves as a faithful guide, keeps the community constituted.[179] To maintain their unity and vitality, communities constituted by constitutions should publicly celebrate their unifying identity whenever the occasion arises.[180] One way in which they do so is to welcome publicly new members when those members meet the constitution's requirements.[181] Welcoming qualifying new members helps a community celebrate its constitution. Another way that communities remain unified is to choose their leaders carefully. Leaders should first of all be able to control themselves, then be willing to serve the interests of all community members, and finally be fully committed to the community's constitution, appreciating its great worth and value.[182] Leaders must not hesitate to warn the community when it strays from the commitments of its constitution and must convince its members to return to those commitments. Whenever the community suffers for ignoring its constitution, the leaders who failed to guide it will suffer with it.[183]

---

[177] PROVERBS 15:10 ("he who hates correction will die").

[178] REVELATIONS 2:14-16 (" 'I have a few things against you: You have people there who hold to the teaching of Balaam, who taught Balak to entice the Israelites to sin ... . Repent therefore! Otherwise, I will soon come to you and will fight against them with the sword of my mouth.' ").

[179] EPHESIANS 2:19-20 ("You are no longer foreigners and aliens, but fellow citizens with God's people and member's of God's household, built on the foundations of the apostles and prophets, with Christ Jesus himself as the chief cornerstone.").

[180] HEBREWS 10:25 ("Let us not give up meeting together, as some are in the habit of doing, but let us encourage one another—and all the more as you see the Day approaching.").

[181] PHILEMON 15 ("Perhaps the reason he was separated from you for a little while was that you might have him back for good—no longer as a slave, but better than a slave, as a dear brother.").

[182] ACTS 20:28 ("Keep watch over yourselves and all the flock of which the Holy Spirit has made you overseers. Be shepherds of the church of God, which he bought with his own blood.").

[183] EZEKIEL 33:7-9 ("Son of man, I have made you a watchman for the house of Israel; so hear the word I speak and give them warning from me. When I say to the wicked, 'O wicked man, you will surely die,' and you do not

speak out to dissuade him from his ways, that wicked man will die for his sin, and I will hold you accountable for his blood.' ").

Chapter 3

Law Skills

FAITH INFORMING SERVICES

If lawyers must know things consistent with the moral fields of faith, then lawyers must also do things in the same manner. Clients retain lawyers to act, not to know. A lawyer who knows law but has no skill in using it is completely ineffective. While knowledge must have its expression in action, law's skill must be faithful action, just as law's knowledge must be faithful knowledge. The moral fields of faithful action include reason, relationship, counsel, and discernment. Lawyers must act logically, clearly, and reasonably as they apply their law knowledge. A lawyer's action logic depends on the faithful form of reason. A lawyer's actions must also be in relationship, usually to a client but often to others and always to the law and legal profession. Faithful relationship is a critical aspect of the skills of a lawyer. Lawyers must be effective in giving counsel, meaning that faith must inform their counsel. Finally, lawyers must be wise and discerning in all things, meaning that faith must inform their counsel.

It takes faith to serve effectively as a lawyer, just as it takes faith to embrace the deep truths of law knowledge. Consider in detail how the moral fields of reason, relationship, counsel, and discernment inform a lawyer's skills.

Reason

The jury verdict of nearly a million dollars shocked the lawyer and his partner who had defended the case. Yet then again, it did not. The plaintiff's case had been as weak as the lawyer and his partner had expected. They had clearly won the trial. Indeed, the fact that the defendants' victory had been so obviously imminent was what caused the problem. In closing argument, the plaintiff's lawyer had made several deliberate appeals to the jury to ignore the law and facts, and to consider false, irrelevant, and prejudicial matters that were not in the trial record. Each time, the partner had objected, and the trial judge had sustained each objection. Yet plaintiff's counsel continued making objectionable arguments. With each of the last couple of objections, the trial judge had called counsel to a sidebar at the bench to warn and chastise plaintiff's counsel. When the argument was over, the trial judge excused the jury and then excoriated plaintiff's counsel, saying that he knew what plaintiff's counsel was doing, prejudicing the jury because plaintiff's counsel figured that he had already lost the case. The trial judge wasted no time in throwing out the telltale verdict and entering judgment notwithstanding the verdict.

That case was just one of many in which the lawyer saw how important the reasons were that lawyers gave for the justice that they advocated. The lawyer learned quickly that you could not make just any argument. Each argument, in whatever setting a lawyer offered it, had to be grounded. Sure, it had to have supporting law and facts. Every law student quickly learns that a frivolous argument can result in court sanctions. Yet the lawyer soon learned that each argument also had in some larger sense to make sense, to fit, to resonate. For a lawyer to really gain and hold the respect of the bench, bar, and larger community, the lawyer had to reason in a fashion in some sense representative of a more fundamental justice.

Another case provided several examples, indeed probably dozens of them given the case's wide scope and endless duration. A dispute erupted between parties who had once been close. Both the stakes and the feelings ran high in the situation. One party hired counsel who had the technical acumen to plead and argue just about anything. Therefore,, counsel did. Counsel filed several lawsuits in different courts, each pleading several theories, multiplying the claims and forums. Yet what that counsel did not seem to have was one wit of sense. Just because counsel can argue something, does not mean counsel should argue it. At first, it seemed like every claim that counsel pled might have been at least tenable. Complex civil proceedings have a way, though, of testing and proving the character of a case, party, and counsel. Before long, counsel's cases were unraveling. Unfortunately, the unraveling just gave counsel more opportunities for make-waste arguments. Motions for reconsideration, appeals, and appeals of appeals—on and on it went for a decade. One might have thought counsel was doing it for the money or to burden and aggravate the opposing party, but here it seemed to be just senseless argument.

Over the years, the lawyer realized what a refreshing contrast his law partner made to the senseless counsel. The lawyer's law partner was either not particularly adept at or interested in legal analysis, or at least did not care to show it. What the partner did do was to exercise sound reason and judgment consistently, connected somehow to a clear and constant sense of what was fair and reasonable in both argument and outcome. Repeatedly, the partner's positions proved right. It did not seem to matter who had the smarter or richer client or who had the sympathies, which of course it should not have mattered. In other cases, it did not even seem to matter who had the better law or facts. Sometimes the law alone is not quite enough, when there are countervailing equities, and sometimes there are other facts not yet seen. The partner was able to see each case's largest sense of justice. The partner exhibited no particular skill in articulating his sense of justice, not relying on oratory. The partner simply had a way of seeing and saying what mattered most to justice. The lawyer decided that his law partner was the kind of lawyer that the lawyer would most like to become, one with good sense and a willingness to rely on it.

In exercising the skills of a lawyer, a faithful lawyer does not proceed thoughtlessly.[1] The thoughts and words of a lawyer must make sense, not nonsense, if the lawyer and the lawyer's clients are to thrive.[2] Reasoning is in large part what makes the work of a lawyer, and sound reasons are what make the work of a lawyer effective.[3] The faithful lawyer always has a reason ready for proceeding with a work from which the lawyer expects a good

---

[1] LEVITICUS 5:4 ("[I]f a person thoughtlessly takes an oath to do anything, whether good or evil[,] ... he will be guilty.").
[2] PROVERBS 10:8 ("a chattering fool comes to ruin").
[3] PROVERBS 11:29 ("the fool will be servant to the wise").

result.[4] Lawyers of faith help others discern right action by exploring the right basis for action, for those lawyers have found their own right basis for law practice.[5] The faithful lawyer has a way of articulating sound reasons for sound courses of action. Faith is not blind. Faith does not authorize irrational or arbitrary courses. Faith requires a lawyer to proceed with reason. Faith is articulate, cohesive, consistent, and sound, and makes a lawyer be so. The faithful lawyer has the skill of reasoning.

The faithful lawyer, though, gives reasons not with affront or challenge but with respect.[6] The faithful lawyer does not really argue, if by argument one means trying to overcome the humanity of a person who holds a contrary view. Rather, the faithful lawyer reasons with others, accepting their humanity and independence, and letting the reasoning do its work rather than depending on advantage or coercion. In doing so, the faithful lawyer does not think that the lawyer is better than those others are.[7] Instead, the lawyer evaluates reasoning against its moral standard, compelled to do the same for the lawyer's own reasoning rather than thinking that everything the lawyer concludes is right.[8] To put it another way, lawyers separate the truth of a person's reasoning from the personality of the one who is doing the reasoning, holding each argument up to the test of moral standards, no matter who has given the reason.[9] The lawyer's reasoning skill is actually distinct from the way that most people think. Most people accept things based on who said them rather than what the person said. The lawyer considers the proposition, not the person.

---

[4] 1 PETER 3:15 ("Always be prepared to give an answer to everyone who asks you to give the reason for the hope that you have.").

[5] HEBREWS 7:16 ("one who has become a priest not on the basis of a regulation ... but on the basis of the power of an indestructible life").

[6] 1 PETER 3:15-16 ("But do this with gentleness and respect, keeping a clear conscience... .").

[7] ROMANS 12:3 ("Do not think of yourself more highly than you ought ...").

[8] ROMANS 12:3 ("... but rather think of yourself with sober judgment, in accordance with the measure of faith God has given you.").

[9] ACTS 10:34 (" 'God does not show favoritism but accepts men from every nation who fear him and do what is right' ").

To the faithful lawyer, to reason is in a sense to reach out to, consult, and invoke faith.[10] When evaluating reasoning, the faithful lawyer reflects most on those things that are true, plumbing the lawyer's reasoning against known and proven moral standards.[11] Lawyers look consistently for the noble statements that elevate an argument toward moral truths.[12] They connect their own and their clients' circumstances to those truths, particularly truths of faith.[13] They search for reasons that fit the complete circumstances and that leave the sense that they are right reasons.[14] The faithful lawyer connects reasoning to faith, letting faith do the work in due course as sound minds consider sound reasons. That kind of patient, persistent, and accountable reasoning is different from the argumentation often associated with lawyers. Some think that those who have faith are naïve, when to the contrary they are more perceptive of people and their motivations, even while they also have a way of elevating the discourse.[15]

A faithful lawyer wants the lawyer's reasoning to include nothing other than what matters, that is, to be without irrelevant and distracting matters.[16] The faithful lawyer wants others to see something proportional in their reasoning, almost as if it were aesthetically attractive.[17] Lawyers admire reasoning not for its ornamentation or flair but in the sense that others see, respect, and accept its fitness.[18] You will seldom see lawyers admiring showboating and fancy oratory.[19] Lawyers instead evaluate

---

[10] ISAIAH 1:18 (" 'Come now, let us reason together,' says the Lord.").

[11] PHILIPPIANS 4:8 ("Finally, brothers, whatever is true, ... think about such things.").

[12] PHILIPPIANS 4:8 ("... whatever is noble ..."); ISAIAH 32:8 ("the noble man makes noble plans").

[13] ROMANS 4:9-10 ("... Abraham's faith was credited to him as righteousness. Under what circumstances was it credited? ... [T]hat he had ... faith.... ").

[14] PHILIPPIANS 4:8 ("... whatever is right ...").

[15] MATTHEW 10:16 ("be as shrewd as snakes and as innocent as doves").

[16] PHILIPPIANS 4:8 ("... whatever is pure ...").

[17] PHILIPPIANS 4:8 ("... whatever is lovely ...").

[18] PHILIPPIANS 4:8 ("... whatever is admirable ...").

[19] JOB 15:3 (" 'Would he argue with useless words, with speeches that have no value?' ").

reasoning on its connection to principles, and not the desultory practices that pass for principle among unprincipled persons,[20] but on principles accountable to the constructs of faith. Lawyers respect reasoning based on faith constructs including fitness, soundness, consistency, and proportion, because that kind of reasoning is effective. Clients who accept that kind of sound reasoning based in faith tend to accomplish the good ends that lawyers desire for their clients.[21]

The faithful lawyer's commitment to reasoning on faith constructs is important because the work of a lawyer must not be merely to provide a rationale or justification for senseless wrong action. Lawyers do not rationalize and justify wrongs, as many persons do among their cohorts, leading ultimately to their own condemnation.[22] It would be one thing to reason accountably to moral standards. It is another thing to purport to give rationales for what has already been decided based on wrong reasons.[23] Faith helps lawyers reveal where others are manipulating reasoning for their own ends, to their detriment and the detriment of others.[24] Lawyers of faith reason their way toward discovering and confirming right action, separating that action from the selfish interests of the one who advocates it. In that way, the faithful lawyer gives sound counsel without needing others to counsel and correct the lawyer.[25]

---

[20] GALATIANS 4:9 ("But now that you know God—or rather are known by God—how is it that you are turning back to those weak and miserable principles? Do you wish to be enslaved by them all over again?").

[21] ISAIAH 55:11 ("[S]o is my word that goes out from my mouth: It will not return to me empty, but will accomplish what I desire and achieve the purpose for which I sent it.").

[22] LUKE 16:15 (" 'You are the ones who justify yourselves in the eyes of men, but God knows your hearts. What is highly valued among men is detestable in God's sight.' ").

[23] LUKE 10:29 ("But he wanted to justify himself, and so he asked Jesus, 'And who is my neighbor?' ").

[24] 1 CORINTHIANS 3:19 ("As it is written, 'He catches the wise in their craftiness'....").

[25] 1 CORINTHIANS 2:15 ("The spiritual man makes judgments about all things, but he himself is not subject to any man's judgment....").

Faithful lawyers are also not self-deceiving in their reasoning.[26] They do not adopt whatever happens to be the trite convention of the day and then base their counsel on it, thinking that they are doing their clients a favor.[27] Faithful lawyers see beyond the foolishness of the day and reject it.[28] They are willing instead to take a stance that may initially seem wrong because it is unfamiliar but that soon proves effective.[29] Popular thinking can be misleading. Often, the popular thought of the day is what a faithful lawyer must challenge with sound reasoning. What looks right measured by what everyone is doing can be wrong when measured against faithful reasoning, accountable to moral standards.[30] Effective lawyers recognize and reject the trite phrases or shallow thinking that others use to rationalize wrong actions.[31] They recruit others to their sound reasoning, making reason a community property centered on faith.[32]

The faithful lawyer's reasoning is also not abstract and theoretical. The reasoning of a faithful lawyer always accounts for the circumstance in which and the persons to whom it applies. That is the nature of moral standards, that they account for the circumstances and require fitting action. Lawyers reason to avoid problems for their clients and to bring clients out of problems and into better conditions. They reason to make everyone better by seeking justification in the improvement of all, from whatever is their present situation. Lawyers do not argue for argument's sake.[33] Faithful reasoning is essentially positive, normative,

---

[26] 1 CORINTHIANS 3:18 ("Do not deceive yourselves.").

[27] 2 PETER 1:16 ("We did not follow cleverly invented stories... .").

[28] ISAIAH 29:14 ("the intelligence of the intelligent will vanish"); 1 CORINTHIANS 1:19 ('the intelligence of the intelligent I will frustrate").

[29] 1 CORINTHIANS 3:18 ("If anyone thinks he is wise by the standards of this age, he should become a 'fool' so that he may become wise.").

[30] ROMANS 12:2 ("be able to test and approve what God's will is").

[31] 1 CORINTHIANS 3:19 ("For the wisdom of this world is foolishness in God's sight.").

[32] ISAIAH 1:18 (" 'Come now, let us reason together... .' ").

[33] ROMANS 5:18 ("Consequently, just as the result of one trespass was condemnation for all men, so also the result of one act of righteousness was justification that brings life for all men.").

remedial, and hopeful. Lawyers find justification in giving life, not bringing about never-ending condemnation.[34]

The faithful lawyer's reasoning is not as difficult as it may seem. First, it readily recognizes how commonly we fall into problems due to our own actions and omissions, and our own faults, until those problems discourage us.[35] Faith is familiar with the common problems that we cause ourselves, and it is effective in addressing them.[36] Faithful reasoning recognizes how readily right thinking, meaning thinking based in faith, gets us out of those problems. The faithful lawyer uses reasoning of a redemptive kind, linking reasons directly to justice rather than using reasoning to avoid or minimize justice.[37] The faithful lawyer solves problems instead of ignoring or justifying them. The faithful lawyer uses reasoning to recognize and address problems rather than to justify one's way around them.[38] The faithful lawyer leaves justification to faith, which then both justifies and rewards the lawyer.[39]

Faithful reasoning issues not from abstract principles but from the active life of faith with which faithful lawyers have direct and personal experience.[40] In some respects, reasoning takes on the nature of following one's conscience. Lawyers and their clients often tend to know what the right course is.[41] Sometimes, the greatest challenge for a client is simply in not justifying some

[34] ACTS 13:39 ("Through him everyone who believes is justified from everything you could not be justified from by the law of Moses.").

[35] PSALM 40:12 ("For troubles without number surround me; my sins have overtaken me, and I cannot see. They are more than the hairs of my head, and my heart fails within me.").

[36] PSALM 54:7 ("he has delivered me from all my troubles").

[37] ROMANS 3:24 ("[A]ll have sinned and fall short of the glory of God, and are justified freely by his grace through the redemption that came by Christ Jesus.").

[38] ROMANS 3:25-26 ("God presented him as a sacrifice of atonement, through faith in his blood. He did this to demonstrate his justice ..., so as to be just and the one who justifies those who have faith in Jesus.").

[39] ROMANS 8:30 ("those he called, he also justified; those he justified, he also glorified").

[40] EZEKIEL 37:5 ("I will make breath enter you, and you will come to life.").

[41] ISAIAH 30:21 ("Whether you turn to the right or to the left, your ears will hear a voice behind you, saying, 'This is the way; walk in it.' ").

other course when the right course is apparent. Faithful lawyers do not allow clients to use their counsel to ignore their conscience. They also do not accept that different legal fields or client circumstances warrant different moral standards. Faith does not abandon a lawyer to other standards at certain times in certain arenas. Moral standards exist at all times in all arenas.[42] Clients are always coming up with plans, some of them making no sense and actually being harmful, but the faithful lawyer will counsel which are the right plans.[43]

On the other hand, faithful reasoning is not like a cookie-cutter, the same for every person and circumstance. Effective lawyers draw on their own experience of how faithful reasoning works to justify each individual in exactly their own circumstances, based on faithful reasoning's redemptive work.[44] With the help of a faithful lawyer's counsel, clients can and do find unique paths that make great sense and lead to good results.[45] Some of those paths will indeed seem unfamiliar to the client, but the lawyer and client must learn to trust in the capability of faithful reasoning to find the right path down which a client may go without creating more problems.[46]

Faithful reasoning also often finds new ways to draw on the overlooked strengths of a client.[47] Reasoning should trust in sound moral principles. Doing so will often keep a lawyer and client from considering too seriously the exigencies of a situation. Convenient, challenging, or unusual circumstances do not sway

---

[42] PSALM 48:14 ("For this God is our God for ever and ever; he will be our guide even to the end.").

[43] PROVERBS 16:9 ("In his heart a man plans his course, but the Lord determines his step.").

[44] 1 CORINTHIANS 6:11 ("But you were washed, you were sanctified, you were justified in the name of the Lord Jesus Christ and by the Spirit of our God.").

[45] PSALM 37:23 ("The Lord delights in the way of the man whose steps he has made firm.").

[46] ISAIAH 42:16 ("I will lead the blind by ways they have not known, along unfamiliar parths I will guide them; I will turn the darkness into light before them and make the rough places smooth. These are the things I will do; I will not forsake them.").

[47] PSALM 73:23 ("Yet I am always with you; you hold me by my right hand.").

the faithful lawyer's reasoning. The faithful lawyer encourages a client to keep acknowledging and relying on the faith's moral standards to identify the best course.[48] Faithful reasoning removes seeming obstacles. Sometimes the biggest obstacles are in one's mind, grown dull to the truth in moral reasoning. Faithful reasoning helps the hearer accept the reasoning to grow into the full standard of faith.[49] There is something essentially personified about faithful reasoning, that the reasoning is personal to the client, while also never apart from the lawyer and the reasoning's faith source.[50]

Relationship

It always amused the lawyer how quickly he could discern how opposing counsel would be treating him during the course of a case. Some lawyers instantly mistook the fact that the lawyer represented a certain kind of client in a certain kind of case as if the lawyer would then be a certain kind of lawyer. In fact, though, there was no reason to assume anything about the lawyer. The lawyer had as good a legal education as any lawyer whom he faced. He had handled many different kinds of cases from small to very large, for many different kinds of clients from individual to corporate to government, in many different courts from state to federal at the trial and all appellate levels. He was in a one-lawyer office but had partners in another office and relatively substantial resources. He could be tough or gracious, challenging or accommodating, bold or contrite, and any number of other things depending on the circumstances, although one hopes always honest, competent, and civil. It had taken the lawyer some time to learn the nuances, but he now uniformly tried to treat opposing counsel like he might treat a brother or sister, even if in a tough negotiation for sibling rights.

Yet with some opposing counsel, it continued to be as if he had walked into the first deposition wearing a clown's hat and

---

[48] PROVERBS 3:6 ("In all your ways acknowledge him, and he will make your paths straight.").

[49] 2 CORINTHIANS 3:14, 18 ("But their minds were made dull.... And we, who with unveiled faces all reflect the Lord's glory, are being transformed into his likeness with ever-increasing glory....").

[50] EXODUS 3:14 ("God also said to Moses, 'I am who I am. This is what you are to say to the Israelites: "I am has sent me to you." ' ").

costume, or boots, spurs, and chaps, or diving gear. Some opposing counsel would instantly assume that he somehow perfectly fit a role dictated by the profile of the case and client. In his first medical-malpractice plaintiff's case with a certain medical-malpractice defense lawyer, that lawyer had treated him as if he had horns and a tail. It was not until the case settled that the defense lawyer had treated him as if, just maybe, he was human, despite the lawyer's every effort to show opposing counsel all courtesy that was due her. In his first divorce case with a certain family-law lawyer, that lawyer had tried to bully and boss him as if he had been no better than a grade-school fool was. It was not until the next case with that same lawyer that he began to receive that lawyer's courtesy and respect, even though he had continued to show that lawyer ever-greater courtesy, the more that lawyer mistreated him.

The lawyer came to suspect that the mistreatment was not the product so much of disrespect as it was of fear. No, the lawyer did not scare other lawyers. Yet some lawyers worked out of fear. Some work out of fear that they will lose a case or a client, others out of fear of embarrassment, others out of fear of incompetence. Law careers are demanding and challenging. As soon as a lawyer learns that the lawyer can lose a case or client and that nearly all lawyers sometimes do lose both, the fear of losing dissipates, even if the distaste does not, as it should not. The greatest fear of a lawyer, though, may be that others will regard them, too, as inhuman. Lawyers fear being a caricature of a lawyer rather than a person, and so they become a caricature out of self-protection, to hide their humanity from view even while hiding their view of others' humanity.

Thankfully, though, other opposing lawyers were different. They made no assumptions about the lawyer the first time that they met the lawyer, from the nature of the case. Instead, many of them would politely ask things about the lawyer, like where the lawyer was from, or what court reporters the lawyer liked to use, and other general professional or personal things of common interest. The lawyer would of course initiate and reciprocate the pleasantries. They kept everything professional but were willing to acknowledge the humanity and uniqueness of one another. Occasionally, they argued, but occasionally, they laughed. If the circumstances justified it, such as a full day of depositions with no opportunity to get away for a lunch break, then they might eat a quick sandwich in the deposition room together and relax, at least for a few moments, talking about vacations or family. They might even share a cab to the airport after an out-of-town deposition.

THE FAITHFUL LAWYER

For the lawyers who willingly valued the professional relationship, there was even some opportunity at mentoring. For most of
the lawyer's career, he was on the receiving end of the mentor
relationship, fortunate to litigate against some excellent trial
lawyers and, occasionally, to learn from them with their help. The
lawyer grew to admire and in some instances to emulate these
lawyers, even though technically, they were opponents. One time,
though, the lawyer had a brand new lawyer on the other side of a
difficult case, where he could tell that the new lawyer was in well
over his head and not getting support from his law firm. He kept
trying gentle cautions to the new lawyer who initially resisted but
who eventually took the hints, too late to avoid a large unpaid bill
and frivolous grievance, but appreciative nonetheless. They remain
friendly to this day, their contested case long over, but the
relationship made stronger by their experience of it and, especially,
by the lawyer's willingness to ever-so-gently mentor even his
opposing counsel, when opposing counsel was ready for it.

Faithful lawyers have the skills to form, maintain, and
improve relationships. They seek and value relationships. Lawyers of faith especially have the skill to form and maintain good
client relationships. Lawyers of faith form and maintain good
relationships even with difficult or so-called bad clients. One way
of looking at it is that a faithful lawyer's greatest service is always
to the so-called worst client.[51] Others will criticize faithful lawyers for working among the criminals, ignorant, dishonest, and
poor, thinking that by representing them, lawyers are in some
way attempting to endorse their misconduct or status.[52] Some
think mistakenly that one demonstrates faith by serving only the
morally upright and faithful. The opposite is true, that one
demonstrates faith by forming relationships and keeping company
with those who need effective legal service, particularly that
which the lawyer draws from faith.[53] There is a difference
between representing a bad cause and representing a so-called
bad client.[54] Those clients are often the ones who have the most

[51] MATTHEW 9:10 ("While Jesus was having dinner at Matthew's house,
many tax collectors and 'sinners' came and ate with him and his disciples.").
[52] MATTHEW 9:11 ("When the Pharisees saw this, they asked his disciples,
'Why does your teacher eat with tax collectors and "sinners"?' ").
[53] PROVERBS 31:9 ("defend the rights of the poor and needy").
[54] ECCLESIASTES 8:3 ("Do not stand up for a bad cause....").

128

problems, not the fewest problems.[55] Faith helps lawyers seek out those who most need the service of faith and the transformation that faith brings.[56] The faithful lawyer serves those clients who most benefit by the lawyer's faithful service.[57]

Faithful lawyers also know that their skill depends on more than their role as a representative of a certain client seeking an objective in a certain matter. When a client retains a lawyer, the client also retains the set of wider relationships that the lawyer has developed, maintained, and improved over time in law practice.[58] The persons forming those relationships include the lawyer's partners and associates, law firm staff, judges and court staff, and opposing counsel.[59] Those relationships may even include the client's opposing party, who may have dealt with the lawyer in prior matters. Faithful lawyers know that clients will retain and judge them on the strength of their relationships with others.[60] No client wants a lawyer who does not get along with the judge, whom the judge does not respect. Judges in some measure rely on and even protect the reputation of lawyers whose conduct and character have proven reliable within a community of professionals.[61] For that and other reasons, faithful lawyers maintain right relationships.

Faithful lawyers avoid the kind of attitudes that destroy relationship. Those relationship-destroying attitudes can include righteous anger over misconduct by others.[62] The faithful lawyer avoids the kind of righteous anger that condemns others rather

---

[55] MATTHEW 9:12 ("On hearing this, Jesus said, 'It is not the healthy who need a doctor, but the sick.' ").

[56] MATTHEW 9:13 (" 'For I have not come to call the righteous, but sinners.' ").

[57] MATTHEW 9:12 (" 'It is not the healthy who need a doctor, but the sick.' ").

[58] NUMBERS 16:3 ("The whole community is holy, every one of them... .").

[59] 1 CORINTHIANS 12:24 ("God has combined the members of the body and has given greater honor to the parts that lacked it, so that ... its parts should have equal concern for each other").

[60] NUMBERS 16:2 ("well-known community leaders who had been appointed members of the council").

[61] JEREMIAH 30:20 ("their community will be established before me; I will punish all who oppress them").

[62] EXODUS 34:6 ("slow to anger, abounding in love").

than addresses their actions.[63] Other relationship-destroying attitudes that a faithful lawyer avoids is bitterness over mistreatment
by others, disputing with others solely for the sake of disputing,
and harming the reputation of others with gossip and
exaggeration.[64] Notice that the desire to harm others is the root
of each of these attitudes.[65] Lawyers probably seldom really want
to hurt others, but lawyers, like non-lawyers, can take offense and
see persons as obstacles to things that they want, and determine
to harm others for those wrong reasons.

A faithful lawyer will instead correct others' misconduct[66]
but will do so without getting angry. It is the nature of faith to
take things that persons intend for harm and turn them for good,
like finding the proverbial silver lining in a bad situation.[67] The
faithful lawyer will ignore mistreatment, will find common
ground with opponents, and will protect the reputation of others
whose reputation is vulnerable.[68] The faithful lawyer just tends to
look past another person's faults when it comes to communication
and relationship, which is one reason why those who have
authority like and respect faithful lawyers.[69] Gracious speech is a
way to make and influence friends. Notice how different these
responses are from the usual way of responding to challenges
within relationships. Anger usually begets anger, but the faithful
lawyer responds to anger with kindness.[70] Mistreatment usually
causes more mistreatment, but the faithful lawyer responds to
mistreatment by ignoring it. A vulnerable reputation usually

---

[63] JAMES ("Everyone should be quick to listen, slow to speak and slow to
become angry, for man's anger does not bring about the righteous life that God
desires.").

[64] EPHESIANS 4:31 ("Put away from you all bitterness and wrath and
anger and wrangling and slander…").

[65] EPHESIANS 4:31 ("… together with all malice…").

[66] 2 TIMOTHY 4:2 ("correct, rebuke and encourage").

[67] GENESIS 50:20 (" 'You intended to harm me, but God intended it for
good to accomplish what is now being done, the saving of many lives.' ").

[68] EPHESIANS 4:32 ("… and be kind to one another, tenderhearted,
forgiving one another…").

[69] PROVERBS 22:11 ("He … whose speech is gracious will have the king
for his friend.").

[70] PROVERBS 15:1 ("A gentle answer turns away wrath, but a harsh word
stirs up anger.").

engenders gossip further damaging that reputation, but the faithful lawyer says a good word about the person whose reputation is vulnerable, hoping that challenges will pass for that person.[71]

The faithful lawyer does these things because the lawyer knows that faith has already done the same things for the lawyer.[72] Appreciation for the grace others have shown the lawyer makes the lawyer more willing to show grace toward others. Grace is not a word usually associated with lawyers, but the faithful lawyer actually exhibits much grace toward others. Grace suggests a willingness to think more of a person and be more generous toward them in word and deed than their actions might deserve. The faithful lawyer knows that others have thought more of the lawyer and done more for the lawyer at times than the lawyer has deserved, and so the faithful lawyer exhibits a like kindness.[73] The faithful lawyer knows that faith has shown grace to the lawyer. Faithful lawyers act with grace in this way toward opposing counsel and opposing parties, even when those opponents have not treated the faithful lawyer fairly and have instead abused the professional relationship.[74] A faithful lawyer will even hope for the best for those opponents.[75]

Having the faith to consider the well-being of an opponent does not prevent a lawyer from representing clients in disputed matters. Legal services often involve asserting rights and claims in order to seek remedies in redress. What lawyers of faith do is first to give the opposing party a fair opportunity to make things right without resort to outside enforcement.[76] That practice often means giving reasonable notice making reasonable requests with a fair disclosure of the basis for those requests. When the opposing party does not agree to what justice plainly requires, the

---

[71] 1 PETER 4:8 ("love covers over a multitude of sins").

[72] EPHESIANS 4:32 ("... as God in Christ has forgiven you").

[73] ROMANS 12:13 ("Practice hospitality.").

[74] MATTHEW 5:43 (" 'You have heard that it was said, "You shall love your neighbor and hate your enemy." But I say to you, Love your enemies... .' ").

[75] MATTHEW 5:43 (" '... and pray for those who persecute you... .' ").

[76] MATTHEW 18:15 (" 'If your brother sins against you, go and show him his fault, just between the two of you. If he listens to you, you have won your brother over.").

lawyer of faith will enlist mediators and other reasonable persons to help the lawyer convince the opposing counsel and party.[77] If the opposing party will still not listen, then the lawyer of faith may try to get other members of the opposing party's community, such as expert witnesses whom the opposing party respects, to help change the opposing party's mind.[78] If the opposing party will still not make things right, then the lawyer of faith is free to proceed as the lawyer would against any law breaker.[79] These practices preserve relationships to the greatest extent possible without giving up justice.

So, on the whole, faith admonishes lawyers to be cautious in invoking court proceedings, making every effort to resolve matters first.[80] Lawyers of faith will look for ways to resolve disputes in just ways using the services of wise mediators and counselors.[81] If instead a lawyer rushes to court when the lawyer had the opportunity to resolve the matter with a reasonable opposing counsel, then the lawyer will have already seen defeat.[82] It is funny thing, but a lawyer can quickly spoil a valid claim by asserting it too quickly and aggressively. Graceless and over-reaching actions can easily hide the justice of a claim, turning not only an opposing party but also mediators, judge, and jury against one. Faith especially cautions against taking matters to courts where there is little possibility of justice.[83] Lawyers allow faith to help them discern whether, when, where, and against whom to

---

[77] MATTHEW 18:16 (" 'But if he will not listen, take one or two others along, so that "every matter may be established by the testimony of two or three witnesses." ' ").

[78] MATTHEW 18:17 (" 'If he refuses to listen to them, tell it to the church...' ").

[79] MATTHEW 18:17 (" '...and if he refuses to listen even to the church, treat him as you would a pagan or a tax collector.' ").

[80] MATTHEW 5:40 (" 'If someone wants to sue you and take your tunic, let him have your cloak as well.' ").

[81] 1 CORINTHIANS 6:4-5 (" '[I]f you have disputes about such matters, appoint as judges even men of little account in the church. ... Is it possible that there is nobody among you wise enough to judge a dispute between believers?' ").

[82] 1 CORINTHIANS 6:7 (" 'The very fact that you have lawsuits among you means you have been completely defeated already.' ").

[83] 1 CORINTHIANS 6:1 (" 'If any of you has a dispute with another, dare he take it before the ungodly for judgment instead of before the saints?' ").

initiate legal proceedings. Lawyers seek reconciliation first, when reconciliation is just and possible.[84]

Yet faith does not prohibit lawyers from asserting legal rights in vigorous advocacy in ways that move relationships forward.[85] Sometimes, vigorous advocacy is the best way to restore relationships or make for new relationships. Sometimes, one earns the respect of an adversary first and then finds common ground for relationship. The faithful lawyer gives respect before opposing counsel earns it. Yet sometimes the faithful lawyer sees that the lawyer must earn opposing counsel's respect before gaining it and, with it, relationship. Faith does not prohibit lawyers from participating in court proceedings[86] and initiating court proceedings[87] with and against others.

Indeed, faith requires that lawyers advocate vigorously for justice rather than simply go about acting as if they are above the fray of ordinary life.[88] It would be wrong for a faithful lawyer to ignore justice in order to preserve relationships that the parties have based on injustice. There are right and wrong relationships. It is when a lawyer relieves a helpless person's oppression and gives that person equal footing for relationship with others that the lawyer is doing what faith requires and rewards.[89] It is just that to exercise the greatest skill in preserving and promoting relationship even with opponents, lawyers must ensure that they need to invoke authority before they actually do so. They must also ensure that the authority they invoke is right authority and that the invoking will lead to a fitting outcome. As the saying

---

[84] 2 CORINTHIANS 5:18 ("God... gave us the ministry of reconciliation").

[85] ACTS 22:25 ("As they stretched him out to flog him, Paul said to the centurion standing there, 'Is it legal for you to flog a Roman citizen who hasn't even been found guilty?' "); ACTS 25:11 (" '[I]f the charges against me by these Jews are not true, no one has the right to hand me over to them.' ").

[86] ACTS 25:10 ("Paul answered: 'I am now standing before Caesar's court, where I ought to be tried.' ").

[87] ACTS 25:11 (" 'I appeal to Caesar!' ").

[88] ISAIAH 58:6 (" 'Is not this the kind of fasting I have chosen: to loose the chains of injustice and untie the cords of the yoke, to set the oppressed free and break every yoke?' ").

[89] ISAIAH 58:10 (" '[I]f you spend yourselves in behalf of the hungry and satisfy the needs of the oppressed, then your light will rise in the darkness, and your night will become like the noonday.' ").

goes, discretion can be the better part of valor. The lawyer who begins to rely on the lawyer's string of successes will soon find a downfall.[90]

There is also a distinction between holding others appropriately accountable and seeking undue vengeance.[91] It may be a fine difference, but it remains an important one, based on the faith concept of forgiveness. Faithful lawyers maintain right relationships with clients, opposing counsel, judges, and others. They do so in large part through acts of forgiveness, avoiding revenge.[92] The law itself is forgiving and redemptive. So, too, are faithful lawyers. At one time or another, all lawyers need forgiveness, just as do all clients. Faith teaches that the more we recognize our own need for forgiveness, the more we are able to serve others.[93] While lawyers do appropriately seek redress for their clients, they can still stop short of counseling and pursuing undue vengeance, knowing that justice will suitably avenge wrongs.[94] It can actually be more effective in achieving one's own ends to show kindness rather than harshness to a wrongdoer,[95] if one is only able to keep those ends in sight and avoid the natural tendency to get even.[96] The lawyer who presses a claim so far and hard as to exact every ounce of redress for it will someday be on the receiving end of like vengeance.[97] Better to think of and preserve relationships than to even scores and keep relationships poor and combative.

---

[90] PROVERBS 16:18 ("Pride goes before destruction, a haughty spirit before a fall.").

[91] DEUTERONOMY 32:41 (" 'I will take vengeance on my adversaries and repay those who hate me.' ").

[92] LEVITICUS 19:18 (" 'Do not seek revenge or bear a grudge against one of your people, but love your neighbor as yourself.' ").

[93] LUKE 7:47 ("But whoever has been forgiven little shows only a little love.").

[94] ROMANS 12:19 ("Do not take revenge, my friends, but leave room for God's wrath, for it is written: 'It is mine to avenge; I will repay,' says the Lord.").

[95] ROMANS 12:20 (" 'If your enemy is hungry, feed him; if he is thirsty, give him something to drink. In doing this, you will heap burning coals on his head.' ").

[96] ROMANS 12:21 ("Do not be overcome by evil, but overcome evil with good.").

[97] LUKE 6:37 ("Do not judge, and you will not be judged. Do not condemn, and you will not be condemned. Forgive, and you will be forgiven.").

Counsel

It was a most unusual meeting, the husband coming to the lawyer's office to ask the lawyer to go meet his hospitalized wife. The husband was obviously uncomfortable at even meeting with a lawyer. A drunk driver had badly injured his wife who had an obvious tort claim for the drunk driver's liability insurance. Yet the husband made immediately clear to the lawyer that he wanted no part of the claim. In fact, he made it clear that he wanted no part of meeting with the lawyer except that his wife wanted a lawyer's help and could not get out of the hospital to get it. After listening carefully to the husband and showing a heartfelt concern over the precarious health of the wife, the lawyer dutifully informed the husband about his own rights that the husband was so readily forgoing. No problem, the husband indicated. He still wanted nothing to do with it. The lawyer knew better than to urge or argue. At the husband's request, the lawyer called the wife in the hospital, arranging to visit her the next day. Although the lawyer went on to represent successfully the appreciative wife, the lawyer never again saw the husband.

The lawyer came to realize quickly that lawsuits and legal claims are not for everyone, nor should they be. The lawyer had an office sharer whose elderly neighbors suffered serious injuries in a motor-vehicle accident under circumstances where they would have had substantial claims for liability insurance. The insurer had almost certainly reserved the policy limits for those elderly citizens. Yet they had indicated to the lawyer's office sharer that they had no interest in pursuing claims against anyone. That was where the lawyer and his office sharer properly left it, even though they would have had other counsel to share with the elderly couple if the couple had indicated any willingness to hear it. There is no forcing one's counsel on the unwilling.

The lawyer also realized more and more that while some clients listen to counsel and others do not listen, a lawyer must give the right counsel and then let that counsel have whatever effect it will have. The lawyer recalled another lawyer saying that he had, to no avail, once literally gotten on his knees to beg a certain client to plead guilty so as to avoid a prison sentence that would prevent the client from ever playing with his grandchildren. As much as that lawyer rued the client's ensuing life sentence, it had been the client's informed decision. Right actions must be voluntary. A lawyer does little by trying to force the issue.

The lawyer recalled another prospective client who had simply waited too long to seek the lawyer's help because of the counsel of another professional. When the prospective client finally contacted and met with the lawyer, the lawyer had to explain that limitations periods now barred all claims. The prospective client actually looked relieved about it, despite the lawyer's disappointment for her. The prospective client's doubt about proceeding made the lawyer think that it may have been just as well that she had no option. The lawyer's counsel might have convinced her to do so, but she would have needed to make her own decision, and it looked right then to the lawyer that making decisions was one thing about which the prospective client had no confidence.

The lawyer had the professional and personal satisfaction of seeing other clients be more willing to consider the wisdom of sound counsel. The lawyer found that most clients trust and listen to lawyers. Lawyers are good at reasoning and giving counsel. That is why clients retain them. The lawyer had many clients who had no idea how and whether to proceed until hearing the lawyer's counsel but then promptly agreed and were later happy having done so. The lawyer had other clients who began as doubtful and confused but ended up as trusting, confident, and successful. There were even a few clients who began as doubtful, then developed some confidence during the proceeding, and yet ended up unsuccessful, while still trusting and respectful, given the soundness of the counsel. The lawyer realized that those clients were probably the ones whom he appreciated most, that they had maintained faith in counsel.

The lawyer discovered that sound counsel is a most reliable tool for both the client and lawyer. The lawyer also realized that it is not always the decision that matters or even the decision's outcome. So often, it is the counsel that leads to the decision that is more important than the decision, and the quality of the relationship between lawyer and client. Words of faith and faithful relationship mean more to many clients, especially clients who have few sound counselors, than a lawyer's actions. Long after the legal matter has passed from the client's consciousness, the lawyer's counsel and relationship remain. The lawyer decided to value client counsel and relationship as much as client decision and case outcome. It turned out to be a very good decision.

Faith during law studies and practice also helps law students and lawyers develop and maintain appropriately professional communication and counsel. Faith sets a high standard for good counsel.[98] The law student and lawyer of faith measure counsel not simply by its immediate audience, as if it were confidential, but as if it had the highest of audiences, meaning as if it were fully disclosed and held to account before all authority.[99] Faith indicates that we should speak as if every word were measured by faith, indeed were so sound as to represent faith.[100] It is a very high standard. Against that standard, law students and lawyers of faith always speak nothing other than truth at the time and in the manner they ought to speak.[101] For example, faith requires that we not speak harshly in ways that denigrate others. To do so would be most unlike a lawyer. We must instead always speak to enlighten, guide, and encourage others, thinking about and discerning their individual needs.[102] Doing so sounds more like a lawyer.

Indeed, all of a lawyer's talk, not just the lawyer's counsel, ought to be constructive, not destructive. Destructive words have a damning effect, as if they were piercing the heart of the hearer, while encouraging words heal those kinds of emotional and psychological injuries, which are really faith injuries.[103] Put simply, there is no use to tearing others down,[104] even though it gets to be a common practice within some professional communities. Faith requires that we respond in ways that diminish discord and build harmony where it has the prospect to exist, especially when others speak in unjustified and destructive

---

[98] COLOSSIANS 3:16 ("admonish one another will all wisdom").

[99] PSALMS 19:14 ("May the words of my mouth and the meditation of my heart be pleasing in your sight, O Lord, my Rock and my Redeemer.").

[100] 1 PETER 4:10 ("Whoever speaks must do so as one speaking the very words of God.... .").

[101] PROVERBS 8:6-8 ("I open my lips to speak what is right. My mouth speaks what is true, for my lips detest wickedness. All the words of my mouth are just; none of them is crooked or perverse.").

[102] EPHESIANS 4:29 ("Do not let any unwholesome talk come out of your mouths, but only what is helpful for building others up according to their needs, that it may benefit those who listen.").

[103] PROVERBS 12:18 ("Reckless words pierce like a sword, but the tongue of the wise brings healing.").

[104] PROVERBS 11:12 ("A man who lacks judgment derides his neighbor, but a man of understanding holds his tongue.").

anger.[105] The faithful lawyer hesitates to respond in anger.[106] The faithful lawyer will often have a soft word to turn away the anger of others. Good counsel is often simply to deflect and defuse the harsh words and thoughts of others until the harshness abates, and sound minds can reason.

Good counsel also requires listening as much as speaking. When we cannot speak in constructive manner, then we should not speak but listen, until we understand enough to speak as we should.[107] It is a hard rule to follow because we like to jump in and give our immediate thoughts. Some of us like to hear the sound of our own voice, even when it is not helping our clients. Be assured that the lawyer who just goes on talking and talking without having anything genuinely helpful to say will not be successful.[108] When a lawyer has nothing to say, then it is better for that lawyer not to pretend to give counsel just by talking because loose counsel can destroy a lawyer and client.[109] The faithful lawyer waits for the useless or destructive thoughts to pass and then speaks counsel when, by listening, the lawyer has discerned the right counsel. When others are speaking, we should not interrupt to inject things that we need not say, if we had only listened. If we do interrupt, then we tend to say things that end up sounding foolish and embarrassing.[110]

Instead, what law students and lawyers learn to do is to hold their words until just the right time, keeping their words few while keeping an even temper. When we do so, others judge us

---

[105] PROVERBS 15:1 ("A gentle answer turns away wrath, but a harsh word stirs up anger.").

[106] JAMES 1:19 ("be quick to listen, slow to speak and slow to become angry, for man's anger does not bring about the righteous life that God desires").

[107] JAMES 1:19 ("Everyone should be quick to listen, slow to speak and slow to become angry.").

[108] PROVERBS 10:8 ("a chattering fool comes to ruin").

[109] JAMES 3:6 ("The tongue also is a fire, a world of evil among the parts of the body. It corrupts the whole person, sets the whole course of his life on fire, and is itself set on fire by hell.").

[110] PROVERBS 18:13 ("He who answers before listening—that is his folly and his shame.").

sensible and wise.[111] People learn quickly to avoid a lawyer who talks too much. The lawyer who talks too much will inevitably reveal things that the lawyer should not have. The faithful lawyer never discloses confidential information.[112] You can trust the faithful lawyer with confidences.[113] Another characteristic that makes faithful lawyers so effective is that they hear and receive more from clients and others because of the trust that their character engenders.[114] Hearing and seeing more of situations, the faithful lawyer can give wiser counsel.

The faithful lawyer knows that by holding back destructive words in a dispute, the lawyer can get past the discord to find solutions.[115] Lawyers often find themselves in situations where, in effect, no one is talking, at least not constructively. One of the best ways to get people thinking and talking constructively is for the faithful lawyer simply to allow destructive words to sink in and let the lawyer's non-destructive responses covered over the destruction. The power of sound counsel is that it is often in response to untoward attacks. The content of the counsel may not be as important as the context in which the faithful lawyer gives it. A reasoned word said in response to an unreasoned attack has a more powerful effect than speaking the same reasoned word in other situations.[116] It shows that the participants can get past discord.[117]

When the faithful lawyer speaks in the right way in the right time, it strengthens not only the listener but also the community of which the speaker and listener are a part.[118] It is hard to

---

[111] PROVERBS 17:27 ("A man of knowledge uses words with restraint, and a man of understanding is even-tempered. Even a fool is thought wise if he keeps silent, and discerning if he holds his tongue.").

[112] PROVERBS 29:19 ("A gossip betrays a confidence; so avoid a man who talks too much.").

[113] PROVERBS 25:9 ("do not betray another man's confidence").

[114] 2 CORINTHIANS 8:22 ("our brother ... is zealous, and now even more so because of his great confidence in you").

[115] PROVERBS 26:20 ("Without wood a fire goes out; without gossip a quarrel dies down.").

[116] ECCLESIASTES 10:4 ("calmness can lay great errors to rest").

[117] PROVERBS 15:18 ("a patient man calms a quarrel").

[118] PROVERBS 11:11 ("Through the blessing of the upright a city is exalted, but by the mouth of the wicked it is destroyed.").

remember, but communication between two has an effect on others. If two lawyers fight, then it affects the ability of the community of lawyers to maintain helpful discourse. Members of the community begin to take sides and stir up old differences. By contrast, when two lawyers exercise restraint and get past a difficult situation with sound words and counsel, it strengthens the community of lawyers and helps their clients. Clients depend on the ability of lawyers to speak reasonably with one another. Sound communications also strengthen the law student and lawyer who speak rightly.[119] Sound counsel makes for peace of mind and good reputation, when good reputation has great value for a lawyer.[120]

Sound counsel has its source in faith and the trust, confidence, fitness, and fidelity that faith engenders.[121] Lawyers find that they give more reliable and balanced counsel when they base their counsel on faith.[122] The faithful lawyer is also ready to listen to the counsel of others to become wiser in the lawyer's own counsel.[123] It should not be surprising that listening to sound advice makes one's own advice sound.[124] A client's plans benefit from a faithful lawyer's counsel, indeed, from the advice and counsel not only of lawyers but of many professionals.[125] Yet the faithful lawyer knows that faith counsel is the best counsel. Counsel steeped in the moral principles of faith is the counsel that is most likely to make the client successful. It is at the same time most likely to keep the client's good reputation while also educating the client for benefit in future matters.[126] That is how

---

[119] PROVERBS 13:3 ("He who guards his lips guards his soul, but he who speaks rashly will come to ruin.").

[120] PROVERBS 22:1 ("A good name is more desirable than great riches; to be esteemed is better than silver or gold.").

[121] 2 TIMOTHY 3:16 ("All scripture is God-breathed ...").

[122] 1 KINGS 22:5 (" 'First seek the counsel of the Lord.' ").

[123] PROVERBS 12:15 ("a wise man listens to advice").

[124] PROVERBS 19:20 ("Listen to advice and accept instruction, and in the end you will be wise.").

[125] PROVERBS 15:22 ("Plans fail for lack of counsel, but with many advisers they succeed.").

[126] REVELATION 3:18 (" 'I counsel you to buy from me gold refined in the fire, so you can become rich; and white clothes to wear, so you can cover your shameful nakedness; and salve to put on your eyes, so you can see.' ").

effective sound counsel can be in promoting a client's welfare. Counsel is not simply about the matter at hand but about enlarging the client's overall perspective.

The counsel of a faithful lawyer is especially helpful when a client is making the difficult decision of whether to pursue litigation, with all of its attendant risks and costs.[127] Often, sound counsel involves educating a client to things that the client does not understand or see.[128] Other times, sound counsel involves showing the client something that the client has done wrong in a way that hurts others or hurts the client.[129] Generally, though, counsel involves guiding clients toward decisions, behaviors, and attitudes that are morally right in the sense that they are most fitting to the clients' full circumstances.[130] Sound counsel has as its purpose to help the hearer do the right thing including good works.[131] Faith exhibits faith in doing the right things, not merely in saying the right things.[132] Sound counsel should produce sound action.

Do not underestimate the power of good counsel to benefit the client. When the faithful lawyer counsels within the moral fields of faith, it enlivens the client.[133] Clients draw so much more from sound counsel than just solutions to the immediate matter at hand. Counsel in faith can be far more insightful for the client than ordinary counsel addressed only to the matter at hand.[134] Indeed, faithless counsel is often senseless and even mean-spirited counsel that does the client no good.[135] Faith-filled counsel can reveal the client's deep condition to the client, from which the client can make larger changes outside the immediate matter.[136]

---

[127] PROVERBS 20:18 ("Make plans by seeking advice; if you wage war, obtain guidance.").

[128] 2 TIMOTHY 3:16 ("... and is useful for teaching...").

[129] 2 TIMOTHY 3:16 ("... rebuking, correcting...").

[130] 2 TIMOTHY 3:16 ("... and training in righteousness...").

[131] 2 TIMOTHY 3:17 ("... so that the man of God may be thoroughly equipped for every good work.").

[132] JAMES 2:26 ("so faith without deeds is dead").

[133] HEBREWS 4:12 ("For the word of God is living and active.").

[134] HEBREWS 4:12 ("Sharper than any double-edged sword...").

[135] ROMANS 1:31 ("they are senseless, faithless, heartless").

[136] HEBREWS 4:12 ("it penetrates even to dividing soul and spirit, joints and marrow; ...").

Faith-filled counsel can help the client identify sound criteria for choosing right from wrong, criteria that the client can use repeatedly in other situations.[137] Clients learn much from lawyers. Sound communications and counsel make that learning possible.

Discernment

"Does every lawyer have at least one case from hell?" the lawyer wondered when it was finally over. Like all cases, this one had looked like a clear winner when the lawyer had first met with the client. The lawyer had long ago learned that no case looks as good as the day a lawyer starts it. The bad news, the things about which the client did not know or did not tell you, come later, when the other side begins to tell its side of the story. Yet this case had not just gone a little east and west. It had gone straight south, and way, way beyond the border. The lawyer wondered why he had not timely discerned its problem. He usually exercised good judgment in evaluating cases and clients. Otherwise, he would not have survived in a law practice that depended in large part on contingency-fee cases. The lawyer made a living only because he could sense the justice in cases, and sense it early, before the lawyer and his firm were fully committed to unwise causes. Yet the lawyer knew that he had misjudged this case seriously and, worse, had misjudged this client very, very badly.

The lawyer had often wondered about the source of discernment. He knew some lawyers who had it and others who did not have it. The lawyers who had it were often plaintiff's lawyers, trusting their instincts in contingency-fee cases. The lawyers who did not have it, well, they were not plaintiff's lawyers working on contingency fees, at least not for long. The lawyer was not sure yet what made for discernment. The lawyer thought that experience might have a little to do with it. Yet then again, the lawyer had seen plenty of experienced but undiscerning lawyers and plenty of inexperienced lawyers who exuded discernment. The source instead seemed connected to something more accessible, something that we all share, if we should only care to have access to it. Indeed, the lawyer figured that was in large part the answer. Discernment for lawyers had to do with a lawyer knowing what is most common to all of us. Some legal matters just have a sweet

---

[137] HEBREWS 4:12 ("… it judges the thoughts and attitudes of the heart.").

spot, made sweet because it connects so clearly with something simple, common, and fundamental.

The lawyer recalled one of the first cases that he had tried with his law partner, defending an entity in a case involving several million dollars in claims. The defense had seemed sound from the start and pretty much remained that way right through trial. There had been no settlement offers. On the other side, plaintiff's counsel had either badly misjudged the case or had no discernment, continuing to demand millions and act as if it was a clear winner right down to the moment of the verdict. The lawyer and his partner had only one moment of doubt when the deliberating jury had asked for the plaintiffs' damages charts and a calculator just 20 minutes into their deliberations. Yet 10 minutes later the jury came back with a no-cause verdict, vindicating the lawyer's trust in his law partner's discernment.

The lawyer recalled another sweet-spot case of his own, not to assuage any particular pride but instead just because he was still stinging from defeat in his very, very bad case. The lawyer would not have had to even file the good case except that he received it so late that he had to file to stop the limitations period from running. The opposing party's insurer had instantly suggested mediation, which had promptly led to exactly the generous settlement that the lawyer had hoped for and predicted. The case resolved so swiftly and easily that defense counsel had warned the lawyer not to think that defense counsel would be a pushover for the next case. The speedy resolution briefly made the lawyer feel as if he was pretty discerning, a false pride that the lawyer never would have entertained if he had known anything reliable about discernment.

The lawyer's case from hell soon confirmed that the lawyer was as fallible as anyone was. Before the lawyer even accepted the case, a very wise lawyer had warned the lawyer that he would be in for trouble. The wise lawyer had also warned the lawyer that the wise lawyer would never again have anything to do with opposing counsel, who would make things that miserable on the lawyer. The lawyer figured unwisely that he could manage. All throughout discovery and pretrial, the lawyer felt uneasy as if defense counsel was reeling him in, anticipating his every move and guiding him to just where he did not really want to be. Yet again, the lawyer ignored the warnings, trusting that things would go well at trial. They did not. The trial judge seemed from the outset to be on the other side. Jury draw was a disaster. Defense counsel destroyed each witness on cross-examination so effectively that the lawyer was almost literally looking for the courtroom exit. Every trial lawyer probably knows the feeling but few so intensely as this lawyer felt it. The trial dragged on and on to its obvious no-cause conclusion.

Yet the worst of it was the client who had from the start of trial taken to doing the opposite of whatever the lawyer asked of her. The lawyer's straightforward instructions about courtroom comportment meant nothing to her. The client repeatedly distracted judge and jurors with odd sounds and motions, interrupted the proceedings with incongruous remarks and requests, and so misbehaved in small and large ways that the lawyer obviously had no influence over her. At least, he hoped everyone realized that he had no influence over her because her misconduct utterly embarrassed him. It was not just the loss and the client's antics that had so galled the lawyer. The lawyer had seen nothing change in any way for the client who, within a couple of years, ended up in jail for more serious antics. Discernment, the lawyer decided, may be elusive but worth everything that it takes to get it. There are some things that no lawyer can manage, the lawyer decided. For the rest of his career, he would look to avoid those situations. Courage the lawyer would have. Foolishness he would not.

Lawyers are so valuable to clients and communities not merely because of their counsel but because of their discernment. It is one thing to counsel and advise clients of various means by which they can achieve their objectives. It is quite another thing for lawyers to be discerning regarding the merits of those means and objectives. There is a difference in quality between counsel, in which a lawyer listens to learn the client's objective and then advises how to achieve it, and discernment, in which the lawyer helps the client determine whether the client should pursue the objective and, if so, by what means. Discernment helps the lawyer recognize the hazards to the client and others of the client's proceeding, not merely whether the client is able to proceed. Discernment enables the lawyer to recognize the client's goal and the costs and hazards of proceeding in that and other directions. Discernment helps a lawyer place the lawyer's counsel in the larger contexts that clients may not ordinarily see.[138]

---

[138] DANIEL 1:4 ("Then the king ordered Ashpenaz, chief of his court officials, to bring in some of the Israelites from the royal family and the nobility—young men without any physical defect, handsome, showing aptitude

Faith helps a lawyer discern things more clearly, which gives the lawyer greater knowledge and insight to know what to do that is most helpful to client and others.[139] Faith does so by helping the lawyer perceive the constant moral principles by which all things operate[140] even when those principles are not immediately obvious to others.[141] Faith also exposes the lawyer own intentions, making the lawyer accountable to others.[142] Faith is a key to discernment because faith gives the lawyer something reliable, an external standard, against which to measure counsel. Faith is discerning because faith takes the greatest practical account of circumstances. Faith does not judge by false appearances but by realities.[143] Faith disposes of the myths and fantasies that serve as obstacles to sound judgment. The lawyer who engages in fantasies will quickly find that the lawyer has no clients.[144] Faith makes counsel precise and practical, fitted to both the circumstance in which the lawyer gives counsel and the practical principles that should guide counsel. The faithful lawyer is discerning, meaning insightful, perceptive, and effective in counsel.

The faithful lawyer knows that discernment has both present and future aspects. Discernment's present aspect is to help the lawyer recognize the quality of a person's intentions, for instance, of an opposing party or counsel. Faith teaches the lawyer to look at what those persons produce as an indication of the nature of their intentions.[145] Discernment also helps the lawyer recognize

---

for every kind of learning, well informed, quick to understand, and qualified to serve in the king's palace.").

[139] PHILIPPIANS 1:9-10 ("And this is my prayer: that your love may abound more and more in knowledge and depth of insight, so that you may be able to discern what is best... .").

[140] HEBREWS 6:17-18 ("God wanted to make the unchanging nature of his purpose very clear to the heirs of what was promised ... so that, by two unchangeable things in which it is impossible for God to lie, we ... may be greatly encouraged.").

[141] 2 CORINTHIANS 4:18 ("So we fix our eyes not on what is seen, but on what is unseen. For what is seen is temporary, but what is unseen is eternal.").

[142] PSALM 139:1 ("O Lord, you have searched me and you know me.").

[143] GALATIANS 2:6 ("God does not judge by external appearance... .").

[144] PROVERBS 28:19 ("the one who chases fantasies will have his fill of poverty").

[145] MATTHEW 7:16 (" 'By their fruit you will recognize them.' ").

the quality of a client's motives, intent, and goals, meaning the degree to which they fit the client's circumstances and relationships.[146] As any lawyer knows, clients can entertain lawful goals, meaning goals that the justice system helps parties obtain, but without necessarily having a just basis for them. Just because something is legal and possible does not make it right. Discernment helps the wise lawyer perceive when the basis for lawful action is insufficient. When a lawyer cannot discern the grounds for the client pursuing a certain course and cannot determine whether they are fitting, then discernment helps the lawyer conduct the client's matter in a manner that reveals to the lawyer and client the justice of the client's matter.[147]

Discernment's future aspect is to help the lawyer understand and communicate what the client truly gains and risks by pursuing and achieving the articulated goals, meaning the extent to which the means and goals are worthy of the client and client circumstances. Faith supports and promotes discernment, meaning the ability to see what is good for another in the future.[148] Faith teaches lawyers that justice is a tool for discernment. In that sense, discernment is predictive, the means through which the lawyer sees the client's future in terms of justice. There are some lawful actions that lawyers and clients can take that may outwardly look to be right and usual but that will in the future have such a negative impact that no person of faith can consider them just.[149] In those instances, the faithful lawyer will counsel against the course of action and for a just course.[150]

---

[146] PROVERBS 16:2 ("motives are weighed by the Lord").

[147] 1 KINGS 3:24-28 ("Then the king said, 'Bring me a sword.' So they brought a sword for the king. He then gave an order: 'Cut the living child in two and give half to one and half to the other.' The woman whose son was alive was filled with compassion for her son and said to the king, 'Please, my lord, give her the living baby! Don't kill him!' But the other said, 'Neither I nor you shall have him. Cut him in two!' Then the king gave his ruling: 'Give the living baby to the first woman. Do not kill him; she is his mother.' ").

[148] ROMANS 12:2 ("Then you will be able to test and approve what God's will is—his good, pleasing and perfect will.").

[149] AMOS 5:21 ("I hate, I despise your festivals, and I take no delight in your solemn assemblies.").

[150] AMOS 5:24 ("But let justice roll down like waters, and righteousness like an everflowing stream.").

Some question what justice means, but lawyers of faith recognize that justice often involves fairness to the poor and others who cannot protect and provide for themselves.[151] Sometimes clients wish to pursue actions that are not particularly fair to the poor and others who are unable to protect themselves. Discerning lawyers will help clients see how their actions affect others, particularly those who cannot provide for and protect themselves.[152] Discerning lawyers will not grind the poor for the benefit of wealthy clients because there are few surer ways for the wealthy to bring justice down upon themselves.[153] Faith uses the powerless to inform and correct the powerful.[154] Faithful lawyers seek, promote, and preserve justice.[155] They do so even when, and perhaps especially when, representing clients whose interests seem to conflict with the interests of those who have fewer resources. Lawyers who lack discernment ignore justice, turning the legal system to their own advantage and to the advantage of clients against those persons who most need justice to protect them.[156] Justice systems require lawyers of faith to ensure the proper operation of justice. Faithful lawyers accept their role in discerning what is just and how to preserve and promote a justice system, even while they represent individual clients who are invoking that system.

Discernment leads to effective counsel, that is, counsel that when followed brings right results. Intelligence is one thing, while wisdom is another thing. Some lawyers know lots of law

---

[151] ISAIAH 3:14–15 ("It is you who have devoured the vineyard; the spoil of the poor is in your houses. What do you mean by crushing my people, by grinding the fact of the poor?").

[152] PROVERBS 31:8 ("Speak up for those who cannot speak for themselves, for the rights of all who are destitute.").

[153] PROVERBS 22:22 ("Do not exploit the poor because they are poor and do not crush the needy in court, for the Lord will take up their case and will plunder those who plunder them.").

[154] 1 CORINTHIANS 1:28 ("He chose the lowly things of this world and the despised things—and the things that are not—to nullify the things that are, so that no one may boast before him.").

[155] ISAIAH 1:17 ("seek justice, rescue the oppressed, defend the orphan, plead for the widow").

[156] AMOS 6:12 ("[Y]ou have turned justice into poison and the fruit of righteousness into wormwood.").

but have little sense of how it works for clients. Clients want wise lawyers, not just smart lawyers. Clients want those lawyers who not only know much law but who know what they should do to ensure that law supports them. Many clients have good hearts and want to do the right thing. It is a shame when a lawyer who lacks discernment misleads a client who wants to do the right thing. To the faithful lawyer, wisdom is knowledge applied. The faithful lawyer knows that discernment's root lies in fear of the consequences of wrong action, that is, in fear of not following faith's requirements.[157] The foolish lawyer, one who will not long survive in law practice, does not care about those consequences and lacks the discipline to look forward to them.[158]

The wise lawyer is constantly thinking of faith's require-ments, knowing that one ignores them at great peril. The wise lawyer does not fight the concepts of faith but instead accepts them, so that the lawyer can draw on them for wise counsel.[159] Discernment comes to the wise lawyer through faith concepts, instruction, counsel and actions. The lawyer who grounds think-ing and judging in faith begins to see and understand things that the lawyer did not previously see and understand. Faith gives a lawyer perspective apart from the usual things of the world.[160] Faith enables a lawyer to avoid following the crowd when the crowd heads in the wrong direction.[161] It is that sound faith perspective apart from the usual way of seeing things that leads to discernment. To discern, one must have a foundation from which to evaluate that is different from the foundation on which others are operating. When one swims against the current of accepted thought, drawing on the guidance of faith, one sees the anomalies of that current, how it affects clients and distorts viewpoints.

---

[157] PROVERBS 1:7 ("The fear of the Lord is the beginning of knowledge… .").

[158] PROVERBS 1:7 ("… but fools despise wisdom and discipline.").

[159] PROVERBS 2:1-2 ("My son, if you accept my words and store up my commands within you, turning your ear to wisdom and applying your heart to understanding…").

[160] JOHN 15:19 ("As it is, you do not belong to the world, but I have chosen you out of the world.").

[161] EXODUS 23:2 ("Do not follow the crowd in doing wrong.").

Discernment also involves receiving counsel from others, listening carefully to what other lawyers and professionals think. It is hard to see one's own errors.[162] A faithful lawyer observes others until the lawyer understands how they act. Faith has that quality of helping us see what others are doing.[163] Discernment also makes a lawyer more knowledgeable about how the law works. When you can see things clearly, you understand better how things work.[164] Indeed, when you can see things clearly, you want to know more about how things work.[165] One of the greatest values of discernment, though, is that it makes a lawyer willing to change the lawyer's mind when wrong. A discerning lawyer does not need substantial discipline because a discerning lawyer welcomes correction, always looking for others to correct the lawyer before the lawyer corrects others.[166] It takes only a slight warning for the discerning lawyer to reform quickly the lawyer's ways and thinking.[167] The faithful lawyer does not take offense at correction because the lawyer knows that correction is always difficult when it first occurs but that it quickly gets less difficult and can end up being very positive.[168]

The way to become wise and discerning is to pursue the understanding that comes from faith.[169] People act in predictable ways with predictable motivations. The wise lawyer can discern those predictable ways through the instruction of faith.[170] For these reasons, the faithful lawyer treats discernment as an important tool of law practice, something to acquire at great cost if

---

[162] PSALM 19:12 ("Who can discern his errors?").

[163] PSALM 139:3 ("You discern my going out and my lying down; you are familiar with all my ways.").

[164] PROVERBS 14:6 ("knowledge comes easily to the discerning").

[165] PROVERBS 15:14 ("The discerning heart seeks knowledge. . . .").

[166] MATTHEW 7:5 (" 'You hypocrite, first take the plank out of your own eye, and then you will see clearly to remove the speck from your brother's eye.' ").

[167] PROVERBS 19:25 ("rebuke a discerning man, and he will gain knowledge").

[168] HEBREWS 12:11 ("No discipline seems pleasant at the time, but painful. Later on, however, it produces a harvest of righteousness and peace for those who have been trained by it.").

[169] PROVERBS 2:3 ("and if you call out for insight and cry aloud for understanding").

[170] PROVERBS 23:12 ("Apply your heart to instruction. . . .").

necessary.[171] It is not as if a lawyer can do without discernment, without the ability to see, sense, and predict. The faithful lawyer pursues discernment because discernment has the power to reveal circumstances. It shows us how people think and act, and the consequences of those thoughts and actions. Discernment makes a lawyer able to see with greater clarity and to predict in the way that law practice requires.[172] The forms and truths of faith hold this power of discernment.[173]

The faithful lawyer knows that wisdom makes law practice successful.[174] Wisdom can make a law practice successful even when there are challenges, which there always are.[175] Law practice works for faithful lawyers because faithful lawyers can know things. That is why clients seek lawyers, for the lawyers to discern things about the clients' matters and condition. The things of the world that clients encounter, those things with which they need the help of lawyers, work according to moral principles. Those principles form the foundations on which wisdom and discernment rest.[176] Faithful lawyers know the moral principles and from those principles derive discernment. You hear clients speak trite maxims like, "What goes around comes around." Often, their reasoning is not much more subtle or sophisticated than those trite maxims. The faithful lawyer exercises a far more powerful discernment that moral principles inform and enrich.

At the same time that the lawyer's discernment serves the client, it also serves the lawyer. Discernment will tell the lawyer to say "no" to a client when the means or objective are unlawful or violate conduct rules. What is different about discernment is that it will also tell the lawyer to say "no" to a client even when what

---

[171] PROVERBS 2:4 ("and if you look for it as for silver and search for it as for hidden treasure").

[172] PROVERBS 2:5 ("then you will understand the fear of the Lord and find the knowledge of God.").

[173] PROVERBS 2:6 ("For the Lord gives wisdom, and from his mouth come knowledge and understanding.").

[174] PROVERBS 2:7 ("He holds victory in store for the upright...").

[175] PROVERBS 2:7 ("... he is a shield to those whose walk is blameless, for he guards the course of the just and protects the way of his faithful ones.").

[176] PROVERBS 3:19 ("By wisdom the Lord laid the earth's foundations, by understanding he set the heavens in place... .").

the client proposes is lawful and rule abiding but not wise. The lawyer who wants discernment must make every thought that the lawyer pursues meet the demands of faith.[177] There are times when circumstances will challenge the lawyer of faith including when clients bring problems that seem incapable of resolution. It is especially in those times when faithful lawyers will look to other faithful lawyers,[178] even while they also look to faith.[179] Sometimes another lawyer of faith can supply that which we cannot find on our own.[180]

---

[177] 2 CORINTHIANS 10:5 ("take every thought captive to obey Christ").

[178] DANIEL 2:17 ("Then Daniel returned to his house and explained the matter to his friends... .").

[179] DANIEL 2:18 ("He urged them to plead for mercy from the God of heaven concerning this mystery, so that he and his friends might not be executed with the rest of the wise men of Babylon.").

[180] 1 CORINTHIANS 12:7 ("To each is given the manifestation of the Spirit for the common good.").

Chapter 4

Law Identity

BECOMING A LAWYER OF FAITH

If lawyers require knowledge and skills informed by faith, then they also require a professional identity through which to offer legal services. Lawyers know and do, but they also become. Who a lawyer is can be just as important as what the lawyer knows and does. Identity is a product of knowledge and skills but also of actions and attributes. Faith certainly informs identity. Four moral fields through which a lawyer's identity forms include calling, character, fitness, and responsibility. The lawyer who senses that a law career is a calling develops a more rooted, imaginative, and authoritative identity. Lawyers also form professional character, known by their attributes. Lawyers also must conform their conduct to professional rules, making and keeping themselves fit for service. Conduct rules may seem like they only regulate conduct but if, so, then it is conduct that implicates character. Conduct rules implicate a set of professional attributes like competence, diligence, and disinterestedness that find their source in faith. Lawyers develop out of their calling, character, and fitness a responsibility that completes their professional identity. It takes faith to be an effective lawyer. A lawyer must make knowledge and skills incorporeal and personal, not merely demonstrate that they more or less play by the ethics rules. Lawyer's form and base their professional identity on faith more so than ethics. Examine in detail four moral fields that help a lawyer do so.

Calling

The lawyer was disappointed but not surprised to hear that his friend had left law practice, at least temporarily. His friend had been an effective lawyer. The lawyer had learned just how effective his friend was when he had him on the other side of a couple of cases. His friend was smart, active, insightful, organized, a good writer, and great with clients and witnesses. The lawyer had been so impressed with his skill that the lawyer had invited him to co-counsel a case and then to take another case on referral from the lawyer. His friend had later reciprocated, so that their practices were mutually beneficial to one another. They liked working with one another as much as they had respected one another when on opposite sides. Both lawyers could also handle the unusual case with the difficult client, too, so that they each felt that they played an important role in the local citizenry's access to justice. The lawyer should have been surprised to see his friend leave practice in what would have been mid-career for most other lawyers.

The reason that the lawyer was not surprised that his friend was taking a hiatus from law practice had to do with a few small things that the lawyer had noticed about his friend, just as others (the lawyer later learned) had also noticed. They were the sorts of things that suggest that a person is not quite holding matters together, maybe that the person is in the wrong career at the wrong time and needs to recalibrate. The lawyer had been concerned enough that he spoke with his friend and, separately, with a couple of other acquaintances who would be able to help his friend if necessary. The friend had not shared anything, which was fine with the lawyer, to keep things professional between them. Others, the lawyer learned later, were working with his friend to ensure that he took the right action. That action turned out to be an indefinite hiatus from law practice.

The lawyer spoke to his friend about it. His friend had no clear answer for why he felt it was time to step back from law practice. He admitted that he liked the work and the people. He had just lost something, he felt, on which he could not exactly put his finger. He had no clear plans other than to take some time alone and away from law practice. The lawyer agreed reluctantly with his friend's assessment. It did look like time for his friend to step back and reconnoiter. The lawyer knew that he could no longer refer his friend cases in his friend's current condition. It was a tough and disappointing but necessary decision. The lawyer respected his friend even more for having made it.

The lawyer remembered a law school friend who decided in his last term of law school not to be a lawyer. The two friends reminded the lawyer of one another, that neither seemed called at that moment to be a lawyer. In this case, with his long-time friend now leaving law practice, the lawyer wished his friend well, hoping that he would see his friend again when his friend had regained whatever he had lost that had led him to leave law practice. The lawyer hoped that his friend would return to law practice soon, and he said so to his friend as his friend departed.

After the friend left, the lawyer took a moment to pray for his friend's welfare and guidance. At the same time, the lawyer hoped that the lawyer would not lose his own sense of calling for law practice. Law practice still seemed like being in the game, like it was one of those things one can do that makes life meaningful. The lawyer did not have to win every case to retain that feeling. The lawyer realized again that the sense of calling was not about the status or money. It was more like when two captains pick teams on the playground, and you hope beyond hope that one of them picks you, when the worst thing is for both teams to leave you standing alone on the sidelines. Thinking about that analogy, the lawyer was actually glad that his friend was going to try something different, even if his friend had no clear idea of what he would do. The lawyer hoped that his friend would find something that gave him the rush of being in the game once again. His friend was too skilled to remain on the sidelines. For now, though, the lawyer felt in the game in law practice, and the lawyer hoped that feeling lasted for a lifetime.

Faith teaches law students and lawyers their proper relationship to law practice. Work not only compensates us.[1] It also occupies us[2] and identifies us.[3] To some degree, we take on the qualities of our work, becoming what we do, as if work made us for doing it.[4] Every trade and profession defines its members to some degree. Law does so more than most. People often know lawyers by what we do. You might do any number of other things for a living, and no one would know it. Yet if you are a lawyer,

---

[1] ROMANS 4:4 ("Now when a man works, his wages are not credited to him as a gift, but as an obligation.").

[2] 1 THESSALONIANS 3:8 ("we worked night and day").

[3] 1 CHRONICLES 22:15 ("men skilled in every kind of work").

[4] EPHESIANS 2:10 ("For we are God's workmanship, created in Christ Jesus to do good works, which God prepared in advance for us to do.").

then chances are good that people with whom you have a passing relationship, like your child's teachers, the servers at the lunch counter, or the mail carrier, know it. Lawyers take on an identity as lawyers.

Our relationship with work determines the degree to which work defines us. Whether we sense it or not, we maintain a stance and attitude toward our work. That stance or attitude defines our relationship with our work and the extent to which we take on its identity. We can love or hate work, respect or disrespect it, draw or not draw our esteem from it, and so on. We establish an emotional, psychological, and faith framework within which we relate to work. Once we recognize that we maintain a stance and attitude toward work, and a relationship with it, we have the opportunity to modify that relationship to its best effect. Work need not define us in a way other than the best for those whom we serve through it and for our family members and us. We need only examine our relationship to work and take responsibility for it. When we make explicit our stance and attitude toward work, we take some control over it.[5] We take responsibility for the extent to which and the way in which work defines us.

How should a faithful lawyer regard the work of law practice so as to strike that necessary balance? Faith urges that law students and lawyers consider their law studies, profession, and practice to be faith callings.[6] A calling is a vocation in the best, old-fashioned sense of that word.[7] A calling in its most literal sense is a career that attracts you, reaches out to you, and draws you in toward it until it becomes your vocation. It calls to you. A calling is deeper than a job.[8] Jobs do not call to you. Jobs are perfunctory, fungible. They serve a purpose, usually income, which is a good purpose that we not burden others with providing

---

[5] HEBREWS 4:10 ("anyone who enters God's rest also rests from his own work").

[6] PHILIPPIANS 2:13 ("it is God who works in you to will and to act according to his good purpose").

[7] ROMANS 13:4 ("For he is God's servant to do you good.").

[8] PSALM 42:7 ("Deep calls to deep in the roar of your waterfalls; all your waves and breakers have swept over me.").

for us.[9] We are good models when we work for income even when others might owe and provide income to us.[10] Yet, a calling is more than a job for an income. We might even answer a calling without income.

Anyone can sense a calling.[11] Any job can serve as a calling. A calling need not be something that requires substantial education or even substantial skill, although both education and skill could make a calling more special. Faith plays an integral role in callings.[12] To have a vocation, to participate in work that we see as a calling, is to make that work share in one's faith, so that the work takes on faith's meaning rather than remaining meaningless.[13] A job becomes a calling when we connect our work to things of faith.

The lawyer who gives credence and credit to faith through law studies and practice finds a calling in law practice. Some of us desire to study and practice law simply because we are naturally good at it. Others of us find law studies inherently difficult like Abraham Lincoln found law studies difficult and find the practice of law more or less so. Ability can certainly influence what we discern to be our calling. Yet the natural inclination toward a profession because we enjoy it[14] and it fits our abilities and opportunities[15] is not necessarily the same as a calling. The pleasures of work do not alone imbue it with meaning.[16] When we work solely

---

[9] 1 THESSALONIANS 3:8 ("laboring and toiling so that we would not be a burden to any of you").

[10] 1 THESSALONIANS 3:9 ("We did this, not because we do not have the right to such help, but in order to make ourselves a model for you to follow.").

[11] MATTHEW 9:13 (" 'For I have not come to call the righteous, but sinners.'").

[12] ACTS 13:2 ("[T]he Holy Spirit said, 'Set apart for me Barnabas and Saul for the work to which I have called them.' ").

[13] ISAIAH 41:24 (" 'you are less than nothing, and your works are utterly worthless' ").

[14] ECCLESIASTES 2:1 ("I thought in my heart, 'Come now, I will test you with pleasure to find out what is good.' ").

[15] ECCLESIASTES 2:4 ("I undertook great projects: I built houses for myself and planted vineyards.").

[16] ECCLESIASTES 2:11 ("Yet when I surveyed all that my hands had done and what I had toiled to achieve, everything was meaningless, a chasing after the wind; nothing was gained under the sun.").

out of ease and pleasure, our perceptions of work can change quickly from loving it to hating it.[17] An outstanding law student may find practice daunting, while a student who finds law school challenging may find practice a perfect fit. A calling does not even depend entirely on natural skill fit.[18] Instead, a calling equips us through our perception of faith for tasks that at first seem unnatural.[19] A calling brings us to a place where we feel at home, comfortable, and even honored.[20] That sense of having found a calling is the right relationship to work, the relationship that faith augurs.

In developing a sense of one's calling, it is important to recognize that faith does not benefit from our work, whether we do it more or less skillfully.[21] Faith does not benefit from our work because faith is already complete without it.[22] Faith also does not inhibit work. Instead, faith transforms and supports work as an expression of faith.[23] Faith checks the things that most inhibit work, like the overly aggressive pursuit of money, status, and outward signs of success.[24] Faith supports a lawyer's professional imagination, enabling the lawyer to see possibilities that lead to innovations increasing the scope and effectiveness of the work. Faith invests the work with meaning, helping the lawyer to see work in a positive light, to look forward to work, to work in good physical and mental health rather than in stress and degra-

---

[17] ECCLESIASTES 2:17 ("So I hated life, because the work that is done under the sun was grievous to me.").

[18] EXODUS 4:10 ("Moses said to the Lord, "O Lord, I have never been eloquent.... . I am slow of speech and tongue.' The Lord said to him, '... I will help you speak and will teach you what to say.' ").

[19] EXODUS 4:11 ("The Lord said to him, 'Who gave man his mouth? ... Is it not I, the Lord? Now go; I will help you speak and will teach you what to say.' ").

[20] ROMANS 9:30 ("And those he predestined, he also called; those he called, he also justified; those he justified, he also glorified.").

[21] ISAIAH 66:1 ("Where is the house that you will build for me?").

[22] ROMANS 4:6 ("God credits righteousness apart from works").

[23] MATTHEW 12:11-12 (" 'If any of you has a sheep and it falls into a pit on the Sabbath, will you not take hold of it and lift it out? How much more valuable is a man than a sheep! Therefore, it is lawful to do good on the Sabbath.'").

[24] 1 CORINTHIANS 3:13 ("his work will be shown for what it is"); 1 CORINTHIANS 3:13 ("fire will test the quality of each man's work").

dation.[25] Faith prepares the lawyer for service.[26] In particular, faith prepares lawyers to help their clients and others mature into faith of their own, doing the right work for the right purpose.[27]

While faith invests work with meaning and commitment, faith also helps us recognize that work should not so occupy our minds that we lose sight of faith for faith's sake. Callings do not distort us. A calling becomes a natural fit for a person, making the person well rounded and whole, not solely fit for the work of the calling.[28] Work, especially work that is so engaging intellectually and socially as law practice, has the capacity to occupy us so completely that we lose sight of faith.[29] Some employers, thankfully few, may even intentionally structure the work to keep us distracted from larger commitments that would change our relationship to it.[30] Faith helps us know when it is time to give attention to faith, to devote ourselves fully to it when work would want us to elevate work over faith, to devote ourselves unduly to work rather than to faith expressed through work.[31] A calling is not a mission of self-destruction. It is not an excuse to ignore other things including other relationships outside of work.

Faith, in other words, helps us keep a balance to work. We do not make an idol of work, allowing it to destroy us. Lawyers of faith can better take the difficulties of work because they have

---

[25] PROVERBS 3:7-8 ("Do not be wise in your own eyes; fear the Lord and shun evil. This will bring health to your body and nourishment to your bones.").

[26] EPHESIANS 4:12 ("to prepare God's people for works of service").

[27] EPHESIANS 4:12-13 ("so that the body of Christ may be built up until we all reach unity in the faith and in the knowledge of the Son of God and become mature, attaining to the whole measure of the fullness of Christ").

[28] EPHESIANS 4:1 ("live a life worthy of the calling you have received").

[29] LUKE 10:39-40 ("... Mary ... sat at the Lord's feet listening to what he said. But Martha was distracted by all the preparations that had to be made. She came to him and asked, 'Lord, don't you care that my sister has left me to do the work by myself? Tell her to help me!'").

[30] EXODUS 5:7-9 ("That same day Pharaoh gave this order to the slave drivers and foremen in charge of the people... [,] '... They are lazy; that is why they are crying out, "Let us go and sacrifice to our God." Make the work harder for the men so that they keep working and pay no attention to lies.' ").

[31] LUKE 10:41-42 (" 'Martha, Martha,' the Lord answered, 'you are worried and upset about many things, but only one thing is needed. Mary has chosen what is better, and it will not be taken away from her.'").

faith's countervailing balance. Lawyers of faith hold onto faith in a way that keeps work from taking faith from them, enabling them to keep work in its proper perspective as an expression of faith, not a substitute for it. The lawyer who sees law practice as a calling knows that putting aside the work for appropriate respite preserves the calling. The faithful lawyer knows that the work must maintain its meaning to be effective. The faithful lawyer knows that to treat work as an idol, as if it had more significance than the faith that enlivens it, is to destroy the meaning of the work and to destroy the lawyer.

Faith also helps lawyers understand what their relationship is to the problems and projects of the world that make up the content of law practice. Law practice is practical. It deals with everyday problems and projects, and many different kinds of them. Some law students and lawyers struggle over what their legal specialty should be. Faith urges us to relax in faith, let faith be our calling, and let faith guide us to work that faith has fitted us to do for faith's sake.[32] That work is always the right work, even when it leads us to challenging places.[33] Faith relieves us of the sense that we have to find just the right niche in order to feel called. Callings develop around places of effective service.

Faith also helps law students and lawyers participate in the problems and projects of the world while not being too much of that world. Lawyers obviously deal with practical matters. Law practice is not at all abstract. Yet lawyers cannot rely fully and solely on the content of their practice to give it meaning. The world's problems and projects do not give lawyers the answers. Indeed, they often suggest false solutions and commitments that would eventually prove completely unsatisfactory.[34] What lawyers of faith do is to carry the meanings of faith into the world's problems as a solution to them and into the world's projects as a

---

[32] MATTHEW 10:39 (" 'Whoever finds his life will lose it, and whoever loses his life for my sake will find it.'").

[33] EPHESIANS 4:1 ("As a prisoner for the Lord, I urge you to live a life worthy of the calling you have received.").

[34] 1 JOHN 2:15-16 ("Do not love the world or the things in the world. The love of the Father is not in those who love the world; for all that is in the world ... comes not from the Father but from the world.").

guide for them.[35] Doing so helps the lawyer manage law practice as a calling, not getting so engrossed in the work itself as to miss its larger aspects. It also helps the lawyer treat law practice as an endeavor that expects more from the lawyer than simply a job, that law practice has a higher standard.[36] That law practice sets a higher standard for us may be the greatest value of its calling. The faithful lawyer seeks earnestly to maintain a law practice worthy of a lawyer's calling.

Character

The lawyer did a slight double take when he saw the mediator enter the waiting room. Apparently, the other waiting lawyers had also noticed. The forty-something mediator looked like he had aged 30 years. What little was left of his hair was wispy white. His face was sallow and frame gaunt. The mediator wore his usual suit and tie, but now the collar of his white shirt hung loosely about his chicken-skinny neck. For a moment, the lawyer thought that maybe this person was someone else, maybe even the mediator's father. The lawyer knew the mediator as a pillar of the local professional community, a name partner in one of the area's two or three leading mid-size firms, and a professional troubleshooter. The mediator was the kind of lawyer to whom everyone turned when there was a serious problem within the professional community requiring serious attention, like a misbehaving judge or other irregularity at the courthouse.

Despite his degraded appearance, the mediator had the same genial, outward-looking demeanor that had made him so effective as a lawyer and mediator. Sensing the shock that his appearance had caused to the waiting lawyers, the mediator quickly addressed the point so that they could get on with the mediation. Yes, the mediator had cancer, and yes, he was probably going to die within the next few months, the mediator explained, "but what are you going to do?" the mediator said in an almost offhand manner. "I figured that I may as well end it doing what I should rather than feeling sorry for myself." A couple of the older lawyers inquired

---

[35] MATTHEW 5:15-16 ("You are the light of the world.... . [L]et your light shine before others, so that they may see your good works and give glory to [God] in heaven.").

[36] EPHESIANS 4:1 ("As a prisoner for the Lord, then, I urge you to live a life worthy of the calling you have received.").

about treatments and then about, well, planning, asking how the mediator's wife and kids were doing. That is when it got a little rough. The mediator admitted that family was the hard part but added that he and his wife had taken some time off until she had told him it was time to get back to work. Everyone chuckled at the mediator's humor, but eyes had already glistened. The mediator excused himself to the restroom while the waiting lawyers filed too silently into the mediation room.

The mediator died just a week later, much sooner than the lawyer and others had expected. The death shook the lawyer and other members of the professional community. The lawyer had seen other lawyers deal with death before, but this death was different. Usually, the death was of a client or relative of a client, making it the subject of a professional matter rather than a disconcerting sideshow. This death was one of their own, and not just anyone. It kicked a pillar out of the whole construction. There was not much hullabaloo about the mediator's death, the lawyer noticed. Sentiment is not a prevalent professional value. Lawyers are not always the best at admitting loss, even when it is so great a loss as that of an in-his-prime comrade trial lawyer. Yet the mediator's death definitely lingered for a long, long time within the lawyer's professional community.

Over the ensuing years, as the lawyer traveled about the state and country and came to know other professional communities, the lawyer recognized that every local bar has its lawyers of strong character. The lawyer also came slowly to discern some of what may make for that character. It began with experience. New lawyers can certainly have the potential for great character, but character is something tried and true, not potential. Persevering repeatedly through deep challenges tests the fabric of one's professional identity, revealing the small flaws for correction. It also makes the fabric stronger. Lawyers whom challenges have tested learn to rely less on themselves and increasingly on the best attributes of a lawyer. The lawyer knew other lawyers who were characters of a different kind, who had retreated into personal idiosyncrasy. The lawyer of true character does not retreat but remains accountable to something outside of the lawyer, the lawyer decided.

The lawyer also decided that he had found in his own law practice a thing of great value, that he had a law partner of character. So many times, the lawyer had seen his law partner do the right thing at the right time for the right person in the right matter, as if providence had made those moments to test, shape, and demonstrate his law partner's character. "Everything is a test," the lawyer remembered the saying going. Well, if so, then his law partner was passing the tests and getting better for it. It was no wonder that his law partner attracted people like bees to honey. His law partner's character and the way that he felt that he had personally benefited from it made the lawyer realize that if there were any advice that he would give a new lawyer, then it would be to find and work with a lawyer of strong character.

The faithful lawyer has character. Character can mean many things, but one of the primary things it means is for others to know that a certain lawyer has an elevated or purified, perhaps noble, quality.[37] Lawyers draw character from many qualities, a principal one of which is integrity.[38] To have integrity means that a lawyer is the same inside in what the lawyer thinks and intends as outside in what the lawyer says and does for the benefit of client, profession, and community. To have integrity is to be transparent rather than secretive about one's character and motives, and to have those motives be the right motives, not the wrong motives.[39] It would not be integrity if a lawyer were transparently selfish, for instance. The faithful lawyer is transparent in the lawyer's motivation to promote the ends and identity of faith.[40] Lawyers of character have consistent motives, words, and actions. That consistency, and the fact that the lawyer's motives are always for the best, make the lawyer of character reliable for everyone's good in all circumstances. Clients and communities turn to lawyers of character in times of challenge because of that consistency and motive.

Faith plays a critical role in developing character. Character develops when a lawyer is consistently pursuing faith, attempting to make faith active in the lawyer's life and service, and finding professional identity in faith.[41] One cannot consistently build and maintain integrity by pursuing one's own ends. One's own ends

---

[37] RUTH 3:11 ("All my fellow townsmen know that you are a woman of noble character.").

[38] PROVERBS 10:9 ("The man of integrity walks securely.... .").

[39] LUKE 11:44 (" 'You are like unmarked graves which people walk on without knowing it.'").

[40] 1 CORINTHIANS 10:31 ("whatever you do, do it all for the glory of God").

[41] ACTS 17:28 ("For in him we live and move and have our being.").

inevitably clash with the interests of others, when people rightly judge lawyers by their willingness to help others rather than merely help themselves.[42] Dividing one's self in that manner between what one wants to pursue selfishly on the inside and what one wants others to see one pursuing on the outside is what makes for a lack of integrity. If a lawyer is often thinking about the lawyer's own welfare on the inside but wanting to look like the lawyer cares about and serves others on the outside, then the lawyer's mind, words, and actions are inconsistent, which is a lack of integrity. That inconsistency destroys character. One must find something consistent to pursue, inside and outside, that will work as a professional commitment. That pursuit is faith.

Faith works so well to build a lawyer's character because faith is not something outside, distant, and abstract. Faith is not even so much something that a lawyer can meticulously observe, like a practice.[43] If it were, then we would inevitably manipulate and distort it. Faith is different from formalism, from playing by the rules but having rule-breaking intentions.[44] If lawyers could pursue faith simply by engaging in prescribed practices, then lawyers could practice faith outside without really carrying it inside. Faith would then not help us with character and particularly with integrity. Faith would be just another convenient formula to achieve our own ends, leaving us without character and integrity.

Instead, though, we must carry faith within us,[45] so that faith makes us consistent on the inside and outside, while knowing that we do not control faith. For faithful lawyers, there is no fooling others into thinking that we have character when we do not. The pursuit of faith makes for that consistency. Faith encourages and allows us to aim for a kind of perfection that would simply not be possible without it.[46] Of course, we do not achieve perfection,[47]

---

[42] PHILIPPIANS 2:4 ("Each of you should look not only to your own interests, but also to the interests of others.").

[43] LUKE 17:21 (" 'The kingdom of God does not come with your careful observation...'").

[44] 2 CORINTHIANS 3:6 ("the letter kills, but the Spirit gives life").

[45] LUKE 17:21 (" '...nor will people say, "Here it is," or "There it is," because the kingdom of God is within you.'").

[46] 2 CORINTHIANS 13:11 ("Aim for perfection....").

but with faith we can legitimately aim for it because faith is generous and complete.[48] That is why faith is so effective at developing character. Faith forms character not when a lawyer pursues the lawyer's own character but when the lawyer pursues and reveres faith.[49] The faithful lawyer gives up trying to seem to be anything other than faithful, and the result is increasing character as the lawyer takes on the character of faith.[50] Some have no interest in pursuing perfection and instead take pride in their faults. That comfort with their own wrongs hides faith from them.[51]

Lawyers develop character by persevering through challenges, relying on hope and ultimately on faith.[52] We all know that overcoming challenges is what builds character, particularly when the challenges require faith. Overcoming a challenge by cheating or faking something certainly does not build character. It is when we rely on faith, on doing the right things even when it is not evident that those things will alone overcome the challenge, that we build character. Relying on faith in those situations and persevering in ways that build character are unusual but valuable skills for a lawyer. Relying on faith in those situations is a bit like looking toward something that you know is there but that you cannot see clearly.[53]

Faithful lawyers also build good character by seeking faithful company, knowing that the attitudes of others can affect our own attitudes toward faith and our own character.[54] By keeping faith, lawyers find other lawyers who also keep faith, forming a kind of professional support system.[55] Lawyers are particularly careful in choosing partners and associates, knowing that faith builds faith, and character builds character.[56] The law firm that has several

---

[47] ROMANS 3:23 ("for all have sinned and fall short of the glory of God ...").

[48] ROMANS 3:24 ("...and are justified freely by his grace").

[49] 2 CORINTHIANS 7:1 ("perfecting holiness out of reverence for God").

[50] LEVITICUS 11:44 ("be holy because I am holy").

[51] ISAIAH 59:2 ("your sins have hidden his face from you").

[52] ROMANS 5:4 ("suffering produces perseverance; perseverance, character; and character, hope").

[53] HEBREWS 11:27 ("he persevered because he saw him who is invisible").

[54] 1 CORINTHIANS 15:33 (" 'Bad company corrupts good character.'").

[55] 1 JOHN 1:7 ("if we walk in the light, as he is in the light, we have fellowship with one another").

[56] PROVERBS 12:26 ("A righteous man is cautious in friendship").

lawyers of character tends to support the development of other lawyers of character. That is because those other lawyers learn to rely on right action even when it is not apparent that right action will suffice. In other words, they rely on faith.

The faithful lawyer's character includes humility.[57] To be humble is to recognize how little value there is in one's own person and actions, that is, not to deceive one.[58] The lawyer of faith avoids arrogance, preferring to be duly concerned with the lawyer's own condition and circumstance.[59] The faithful lawyer knows that to be arrogant is to run the risk of being humbled.[60] The faithful lawyer does not let the desire to look good be the lawyer's motivation in anything. There is no selfish ambition in the faithful lawyer, for that lawyer knows that nothing the lawyer does out of the desire to look good is good.[61] Doing things to look good is the opposite of showing good character. Lawyers do not earn good character by show. The good things that the faithful lawyer does that others do not see develop good character. The faithful lawyer especially avoids that worst kind of ingrained, inward-looking pride, which is vanity or conceit about the good quality of one's self.[62]

The faithful lawyer does not assume that the law is always on the lawyer's side, which would be the height of pride.[63] The faithful lawyer instead recognizes that the law stands apart and

---

[57] 1 PETER 3:4 ("Instead, it should be that of your inner self, the unfading beauty of a gentle and quiet spirit, which is of great worth in God's sight."); 1 PETER 5:5 ("clothe yourselves with humility").

[58] GALATIANS 6:3 ("If anyone thinks he is something when he is nothing, he deceives himself.").

[59] ROMANS 11:20 ("Do not be arrogant, but be afraid.").

[60] MATTHEW 23:12 ("For whoever exalts himself will be humbled, and whoever humbles himself will be exalted.").

[61] ISAIAH 64:6 ("all our righteous acts are like filthy rags").

[62] PHILIPPIANS 2:3 ("Do nothing out of selfish ambition or vain conceit...").

[63] JOSHUA 5:13-14 ("Now when Joshua was near Jericho, he looked up and saw a man standing in front of him with a drawn sword in his hand. Joshua went up to him and asked, 'Are you for us or for our enemies?' 'Neither,' he replied, 'but as commander of the army of the Lord I have now come.'").

that the lawyer must pursue it through humble faith.[64] The faithful lawyer is constantly thinking that others are better than the lawyer is. In that way, the faithful lawyer pushes conceit aside.[65] In a way, faith requires that we consider ourselves nothing, certainly not the judge of our own merit, and instead to think of ourselves simply as servants would think of themselves, which is that we are to serve others.[66] Thinking of the welfare of others has the effect of lifting us up in the eyes of others,[67] perhaps as pride would have had us lifted up through ourselves. Let others take note of your good character, while taking no note of your own.

Character protects the faithful lawyer in times of challenge, especially when others think that the faithful lawyer is to blame for something in exercising the authority of a lawyer.[68] Faith protects the lawyer, just as much as it protects non-lawyers who exercise and rely on faith.[69] The justice issues of law practice where the lawyer must stand firm under challenge by opponents and others can make a lawyer feel alone, as if it is the lawyer against the world. When a lawyer stands in faith, the lawyer does not stand alone but instead invokes the presence and authority of all those who stand together in faith.[70] The faithful lawyer may look alone but is not alone, and the faithful lawyer knows it. That kind of courage to stand on right word and action when it appears that one stands alone is a special aspect of faith.

---

[64] JOSHUA 5:14 ("Then Joshua fell facedown to the ground in reverence, and asked him, 'What message does my Lord have for his servant?'").

[65] PHILIPPIANS 2:3 ("... but in humility consider others better than yourselves.").

[66] PHILIPPIANS 2:5-6 ("Your attitude should be the same as that of Christ Jesus: Who, being in very nature God, did not consider equality with God something to be grasped, but made himself nothing, taking the very nature of a servant, being made in human likeness.").

[67] PHILIPPIANS 2:9 ("Therefore God exalted him to the highest place and gave him the name that is above every name... .").

[68] DANIEL 6:4 ("At this, the administrators and satraps tried to find grounds for charges against Daniel in his conduct of government affairs, but they were unable to do so. They could find no corruption in him, because he was trustworthy and neither corrupt nor negligent.").

[69] PSALM 37:28 ("For the Lord loves the just and will not forsake his faithful ones. They will be protected forever... .").

[70] 2 KINGS 6:16 (" 'Don't be afraid,' the prophet answered. 'Those who are with us are more than those who are with them.'").

Character in times of challenge makes the faithful lawyer stronger, giving the faithful lawyer courage out of knowing that the lawyer can and should rely on faith for strength.[71] The faithful lawyer knows that strength and courage are matters of commitment and command, more so than attributes or responses.[72] It is not as if either you have courage or you do not. Rather, it is that either you exercise courage or you do not. Character in times of challenge begins with trust, that is, with the faithful lawyer having acted in a manner consistent with the obligations of the lawyer's office.[73] It also includes basic honesty. Yet it also includes simple devotion to duty in a way that the standard of care requires, for the lawyer not to be careless with the matters entrusted to the lawyer.[74]

The faithful lawyer remains constant in good times and bad, under challenge and when successful.[75] Character helps make the faithful lawyer content in just the way that a lawyer should be content, which is in all circumstance, not just good circumstance.[76] Law practice, particularly contingency-fee practice, can be feast or famine. Every law practice has its good times and bad. Every lawyer sometimes feels flush and sometimes feels wanting.[77] The faithful lawyer develops the character that it takes to remain balanced, to feel at peace in both situations.[78] Character borne of faith helps a lawyer continue through the hard times,

---

[71] PSALM 27:14 ("Wait for the Lord; be strong and take heart and wait for the Lord.").

[72] JOSHUA 1:9 (" 'Have I not commanded you? Be strong and courageous. Do not be terrified; do not be discouraged, for the Lord your God will be with you wherever you go.'").

[73] DANIEL 6:4 ("They could find no corruption in him, because he was trustworthy...").

[74] DANIEL 6:4 ("... and neither corrupt nor negligent.").

[75] JOB 1:21 ("The Lord gave, and the Lord has taken away; blessed be the name of the Lord.").

[76] PHILIPPIANS 4:11 ("... I have learned to be content whatever the circumstances").

[77] PHILIPPIANS 4:12 ("I know what it is to be in need, and I know what it is to have plenty.").

[78] PHILIPPIANS 4:12 ("I have learned the secret of being content in any and every situation, whether well fed or hungry, whether living in plenty or in want.").

knowing that faith is what gives the lawyer strength.[79] When a lawyer develops a strong relationship with faith, it is as if faith continually replenishes the lawyer every time that circumstances draw on the lawyer.[80] Faith is reviving. Indeed, the character of a faithful lawyer not only replenishes the lawyer but also feeds the needs of the lawyer's clients and others around the lawyer.[81] With that replenishment, faith also gives lawyers courage.[82] Faith makes lawyers braver. Faith helps lawyers see things more clearly and not be so concerned about being wrong in their actions and judgments.[83]

Faithful character also ensures that the lawyer receives what the lawyer needs for law practice.[84] We all have desires. When a lawyer desires the right things, the lawyer tends to receive them.[85] Good character tends to bring the prosperity that any lawyer desires by helping the lawyer pursue faith.[86] Bad character destroys reputations and, with it, destroys fortunes.[87] Good character leads lawyers to pursue the right things first, and then prosperity and all that the faithful lawyer desires follow.[88] Faithful lawyers pursue character first, rather than trusting in the security of money or other things, knowing that good character brings continual prosperity.[89] You can see it repeatedly that a

---

[79] PHILIPPIANS 4:13 ("I can do everything through him who gives me strength.").

[80] JOHN 4:14 (" 'But whoever drinks the water I give him will never thirst. Indeed, the water I give him will become in him a spring of water welling up to eternal life.'").

[81] JOHN 7:38 (" 'Whoever believes in me, as the Scripture has said, streams of living water will flow from within him.'").

[82] GENESIS 26:24 ("Do not be afraid, for I am with you. . . .").

[83] PSALM 27:1 ("The Lord is my light and my salvation—whom shall I fear?").

[84] PSALM 34:10 ("those who seek the Lord lack no good thing").

[85] PROVERBS 10:24 ("what the righteous desire will be granted").

[86] PSALM 107:9 ("he satisfies the thirsty and fills the hungry with good things").

[87] PROVERBS 13:21 ("Misfortune pursues the sinner, but prosperity is the reward of the righteous.").

[88] MATTHEW 6:33 (" 'But seek first his kingdom and his righteousness, and all these things will be given to you as well.'").

[89] PROVERBS 11:28 ("Whoever trusts in his riches will fall, but the righteous will thrive like a green leaf.").

lawyer of good character simply continues to receive what the lawyer needs over time, even when circumstances would indicate hard times for others.[90] The good work that comes from good character has its way of producing good rewards,[91] even while that same good character protects the lawyer from hard times.[92]

Fitness

"You know, I did what I could," the old counsel was telling the lawyer seated at his table at the bar association luncheon, "but I guess nothing was going to stop him." The old counsel was speaking with regret about a trial lawyer in another firm whose law license the attorney discipline board had finally revoked for misconduct relating to drug abuse and convictions. A lawyers assistance program had assigned the old counsel to the trial lawyer as a sort of professional big brother. It would be the trial lawyer's last chance to reform after shaky attempts at rehabilitation. The trial lawyer had not reformed. One last drug conviction followed, leaving the discipline board no choice but to revoke the trial lawyer's license. The revocation would have painful to all the lawyers at the luncheon had it been any lawyer, but those who knew him said that this trial lawyer had been the best ever. The trial lawyer had wasted enormous talent.

The lawyer knew of other lawyers whom the attorney discipline board had disbarred as unfit to practice law. Each one was a most curious case, taking the license of a lawyer who from the outside seemed to have things going just right—status, opportunity, reputation, support. One was a well-to-do transactional lawyer who, just into the third decade of a highly successful career, simply started taking for personal use huge sums of client money. The lawyer remembered a close friend of the transactional lawyer saying that he was one of the first to discover what the transactional lawyer had done. The friend asked the transactional lawyer about it, why he had done it, but the transactional lawyer had no explanation. The transactional lawyer's misconduct,

---

[90] PSALM 58:11 ("Then men will say, 'Surely the righteous still are rewarded....'").

[91] ISAIAH 3:10 ("Tell the righteous it will be well with them, for they will enjoy the fruit of their deeds.").

[92] PSALM 5:12 ("For surely, O Lord, you bless the righteous; you surround them with your favor as with a shield.").

for which the criminal-justice system convicted and imprisoned him and bar officials disbarred him, mystified the friend and other lawyers in the local bar. It was not drugs or alcohol. What was it?

Then there was the local bar leader who successfully quit drinking when he realized that he had a problem. Yet the bar leader soon exchanged his drinking problem for a gambling problem that led to his embezzling client funds. Prison is a long fall from grace for a bar leader. The lawyer met the former bar leader a couple of times when the former bar leader spoke to other lawyers and law students about the perils of addiction, as part of his post-release rehabilitation. The former bar leader had some insight into his fall. Prison, he explained, gives you time for reflection. The former bar leader felt that beginning in law school, he had never quite got himself grounded in the way that he needed, so that he first picked up an old family habit and later exchanged it for his personal addiction. The lawyer learned from this disbarred former bar leader that grounding was very, very important, even for very, very successful lawyers.

Fitness, the lawyer decided firmly, depended on having that grounding. Each of these three lawyers' experiences proved it to the lawyer, although it was something that he would have learned from his own experience without that evidence. Every decent lawyer soon learns that you cannot practice law with an empty soul. It is not only drugs, money, and gambling that tempt unfitness. It is also power, authority, and status. To avoid temptations, addictions, and abuses, you must have some sort of roadmap, the lawyer had learned. You cannot practice law in a vacuum, as if it were somehow neutral. Law practice forces a lawyer to choose. It forces lawyers to define their commitments. Even if you do resist temptations and corruption, then you must still find the will and energy to keep on practicing, without depression or psychosis stealing your fitness.

The lawyer knew that there are plenty of natural enemies attacking one's capability. Greed, arrogance, pride, insensitivity, jealousy, and appetite were among them, but there were always others to discover. The lawyer felt that researching, naming, and keeping a close eye on those enemies would be wise practices. It is good to have friends but better to know your enemies. Law practice trains a lawyer to be diligent, resourceful, analytic, and descriptive. The lawyer started a small library on the enemies of his fitness. One might still catch him. Anything is possible. Yet none was going to sneak up on him.

Admission to a bar and licensure for law practice require both character and fitness. Fitness implies something different from character. One can have good character but not be particularly fit for law practice. Character implicates the question of one's moral qualities like honesty, meaning that one will not lie, cheat, and steal one's way through law practice. By contrast, fitness does not involve qualities as much as it involves abilities. The question of fitness has more to do with whether one is mentally and emotionally able to act as a lawyer. A person can have great character, meaning that the person is entirely trustworthy, but still not be fit for law practice because the lawyer could not meet its mental and emotional challenges. When in the rare case a lawyer suffers from a mental or emotional breakdown and must withdraw from law practice, we do not say that the lawyer has bad character. Rather, we say that the lawyer is not currently fit for law practice.

Lawyers tend to treat questions of fitness as involving primarily medical questions of physical and mental condition. For example, they tend to ask whether a lawyer has suffered from mental illness, the illness interferes with the lawyer's work, and treatment by medication or other therapeutic regimens will alleviate the interfering symptoms sufficiently for the lawyer to continue law practice. Diagnoses like severe schizophrenia and paranoia may indicate unfitness to practice law, depending on the psychoses' manifestation and the effect of treatment. There can even be physical conditions that interfere with law practice, like the onset of severe pneumonia, cancers, heart failure, and other conditions the effect and treatment of which can keep a lawyer from practicing or can limit the lawyer's practice.

One would think that ordinarily, faith has not much to do with a lawyer's fitness to practice law. There can be, nevertheless, a faith dimension to fitness. Although the level of our challenges certainly varies, and some physical, mental, and emotional conditions determine unfitness without respect to faith, at some level everyone faces physical and mental challenges in the practice of law at one time or in one form or another.[93] Fitness, at least at its early stages, often becomes a matter of how a lawyer responds to

---

[93] ROMANS 6:19 ("you are weak in your natural selves").

those challenges. The lawyer who ignores early symptoms of potentially debilitating conditions invites unfitness. The lawyer who does not treat the lawyer's physical condition as something to which the lawyer must attend in order to maintain an effective law practice invites unfitness. That is where faith comes in, urging that we consider carefully our physical condition, treating our health as precious to faith in that faith lives in and works through it.[94] Faith tells us to watch what we put into our bodies.[95] Faith urges an extraordinary commitment to a lawyer's physical well being, to ensure an effective work of faith.[96]

You hear and see it in practice that a certain lawyer continues down a path that appears to other lawyers like it is inviting unfitness. It may be a combination of so-called lifestyle choices. It may begin with over-eating or other inattention to healthy diet, and the failure or refusal to exercise. The lifestyle choices may include chain smoking or other excessive use of tobacco products. It may include substance abuse like excessive drinking or the use of illicit drugs. Or the choice threatening unfitness may simply be the failure or refusal to attend to a developing condition like diabetes, liver disease, or coronary artery disease. Some lawyers refuse to have annual physical examinations or do other routine things to address their fitness. After counseling clients to do things right, those lawyers fail to do right by themselves, falling into habits that compromise their ability to serve.[97]

In those instances, faith can be a critical ingredient to the fitness required for law practice. Fitness means that law practice requires that a lawyer must do things in fitting ways.[98] Faith helps make and keep a lawyer fit in several ways. First and probably most importantly, faith encourages a lawyer to take care of

---

[94] 1 CORINTHIANS 6:19 ("Do you not know that your body is a temple of the Holy Spirit, who is in you, whom you have received from God?").

[95] JUDE 8 ("these dreamers pollute their own bodies").

[96] 1 THESSALONIANS 4:4 ("each of you should learn to control his own body in a way that is holy and honorable").

[97] 1 CORINTHIANS 9:27 ("I beat my body and make it my slave so that after I have preached to others, I myself will not be disqualified for the prize.").

[98] 1 CORINTHIANS 14:40 ("everything should be done in a fitting and orderly way").

the lawyer's own diet, exercise, and habits.[99] Faith also strengthens a lawyer when the lawyer feels no natural strength.[100] The weak moments when a lawyer is tired and frustrated are when a lawyer might do things, like ignore or take shortcuts in work or health that could mislead the lawyer into being unfit. Faith steadies a lawyer in those moments so that the lawyer can draw and regain strength. Fitness is not entirely a matter of saying no to bad habits. It is also having a positive frame of mind that gives a lawyer cause for good personal habits. Faith is always stronger than the lawyer is strong, meaning that a lawyer can rely on faith for fitness.

Faith is also a way for a lawyer to identify and resist those things that would make the lawyer unfit in a weak moment.[101] Resistance is in part a matter of commitment but also in part a matter of discernment, seeing what it is that one should resist.[102] Without faith, it is harder for the lawyer to see the challenges and to avoid those challenges when the lawyer's defenses are down. What faith does in those moments when the temptations to unfitness are most near is to help the lawyer see that the challenges are not so much physical and mental as they are moral and attitudinal, meaning matters of faith.[103] Lawyers can be in different respects physically and mentally less able and yet be fit lawyers. Physical or mental weakness is not the primary barrier to law practice. After all, lawyers find all kinds of accommodations in order to keep practicing when they face physical, mental, and emotional challenges. The real barrier is the unfitness that preys upon weakness when a lawyer does not fortify weakness with faith.[104] It is when the lawyer fails to seek appropriate

[99] DANIEL 1:8 ("Daniel resolved not to defile himself with the royal food and wine... .").

[100] EPHESIANS 6:10 ("Finally, be strong in the Lord and in his mighty power.").

[101] EPHESIANS 6:11 ("Put on the full armor of God so that you can take your stand against the devil's schemes.").

[102] JAMES 4:7 ('Resist the devil, and he will flee... .").

[103] EPHESIANS 6:12 ("For our struggle is not against flesh and blood, but against the rulers, against the authorities, against the powers of this dark world and against the spiritual forces of evil in the heavenly realms.").

[104] 2 CORINTHIANS 12:9 ("My grace is sufficient for you, for my power is made perfect in weakness.").

accommodations in faith that a physical or mental challenge can become unfitness for law practice.[105] The faithful lawyer knows that weakness is not the real challenge, but rather, that the real challenge is the lack of faith. The faithful lawyer actually welcomes weakness and the challenges that come with it as an opportunity to demonstrate faith.[106]

Faith helps the lawyer resist acts that would constitute or contribute to unfitness, by drawing strength, protection, and discernment from faith. The faithful lawyer pursues the full dimensions of faith even in the face of, and especially in the face of, physical and mental challenges. Faith in its fullest dimensions prepares a lawyer not merely for the ordinary day-to-day work but for the most difficult of professional challenges.[107] It helps the lawyer remain rooted and committed to effective law practice. Even when there is really nothing more that a lawyer can do to demonstrate the lawyer's fitness, and the challenge persists in a way that the lawyer does not control or necessarily even understand, faith helps the lawyer to be able to continue in law practice.[108]

Faith aids fitness in part because of its truth dimension. The lawyer who has spoken and stood by the truth finds the strength and demonstrates the fitness to continue.[109] When others see the lawyer who has a physical or mental challenge still speaking truth, they are less concerned about the lawyer's fitness. Faith also aids fitness by helping the lawyer continue to take the actions that the circumstances require, so that others cannot criticize the lawyer's fitness by pointing to wrong actions.[110] When others who see the lawyer face physical and mental challenges while still taking the right actions notwithstanding those challenges, then

---

[105] 2 CORINTHIANS 12:9 ("Therefore I will boast all the more gladly about my weaknesses, so that Christ's power may rest on me.").

[106] 2 CORINTHIANS 12:10 ("That is why, for Christ's sake, I delight in weaknesses, in insults, in hardships, in persecutions, in difficulties. For when I am weak, then I am strong.").

[107] EPHESIANS 6:13 ("Therefore put on the full armor of God, so that when the day of evil comes, you may be able to stand your ground ... .").

[108] EPHESIANS 6:13 ("... and after you have done everything, to stand.").

[109] EPHESIANS 6:14 ("Stand firm then, with the belt of truth buckled around your waist...").

[110] EPHESIANS 6:14 ("... with the breastplate of righteousness in place ...").

they continue to have confidence in the lawyer's fitness. Faith especially keeps the lawyer fit by making the lawyer ready to take the right action at the right moment, when standing still and ignoring things would demonstrate a lawyer's unfitness.[111] Faith engenders action when a lack of faith might lead to inaction demonstrating unfitness. Faith keeps a lawyer prepared, when lack of preparation is often the first and sometimes the critical last indication of unfitness.[112]

In faith's fullest sense, it acts like something of a shield for a lawyer when the lawyer's other circumstances weaken the lawyer, making the lawyer vulnerable to things that might lead to charges of unfitness.[113] Faith has a way of dampening those charges, in a sense, of putting out fires that might harm the lawyer's abilities and reputation.[114] Faith also protects the lawyer's mind and intentions, not just the lawyer's actions and reputation.[115] Faith keeps the lawyer thinking along the right lines, so that negative thoughts do not become unfit words and actions. Faith keeps the lawyer speaking in the right way to others, and by thinking and speaking in the right way, leads the lawyer to right actions fitting the circumstances.[116] The words that a lawyer speaks have their own power to influence the lawyer, even while they reveal the lawyer's good or bad intentions.[117]

The faithful lawyer keeps reaching out to the words and forms of faith in the most challenging of personal circumstances, when poor health, finances, relationships, and other personal matters might make the lawyer do something that would prove the lawyer unfit for law practice. The faithful lawyer turns toward faith in those circumstances, asking faith to provide what the

---

[111] EPHESIANS 6:15 ("... and with your feet fitted with the readiness that comes from the gospel of peace.").

[112] 2 TIMOTHY 4:2 ("be prepared in season and out of season").

[113] EPHESIANS 6:16 ("In addition to all this, take up the shield of faith...").

[114] EPHESIANS 6:16 ("... with which you can extinguish all the flaming arrows of the evil one.").

[115] EPHESIANS 6:17 ("Take the helmet of salvation ...").

[116] EPHESIANS 6:17 ("... and the sword of the Spirit, which is the word of God.").

[117] PROVERBS 10:32 ("The lips of the righteous know what is fitting, but the mouth of the wicked only what is perverse.").

lawyer needs in order to keep practicing effectively.[118] The practice of law is a privilege that no lawyer should have to lose, when by relying on faith the lawyer might maintain the lawyer's fitness. Faith aids fitness. The faithful lawyer will call on faith throughout the lawyer's law career in times of physical, mental, and emotional challenge when unfitness threatens.

Responsibility

The lawyer had not expected the judge's reaction. Neither had opposing counsel. The two of them had gotten along well throughout the case, maybe because they had several prior cases together and had grown to respect one another. They had joked and made small talk while they waited for the trial judge to enter the courtroom for the pretrial conference on the record, as was the practice in this federal court. The clerk entered to announce the judge's entry, saying ceremoniously, "All rise," even though only the lawyer and opposing counsel were present, and both were already standing at counsel table. The trial judge entered, looking more stern and irritated than usual. The lawyer noticed the judge's irritation immediately, thinking, "This does not look good." Peeking at opposing counsel, the lawyer saw that he, too, had noticed the judge's stern demeanor and was looking more than usually nervous.

The trial judge quickly made evident the source of his displeasure. The lawyer and opposing counsel had taken too lightly their job of drafting the proposed joint pretrial order. They thought that they had good reason to give the order short shrift. After all, it was a bench trial. The lawyer and opposing counsel each knew what the other planned and trusted one another that there would be no surprises. They were both highly experienced trial lawyers who had been before the trial judge on several other cases. The trial judge had already decided cross-motions for summary judgment and so was familiar with the case. The lawyer and opposing counsel would have no disputes over pleadings, law, or evidence. They had made reasonable efforts to resolve the case without trial. Under these circumstances, there seemed little need to give the proposed joint pretrial order its usual full treatment. Brevity would save both sides time and expense without prejudicing anyone.

---

[118] EPHESIANS 6:18 ("And pray in the Spirit on all occasions with all kinds of prayers and requests.").

Yet in drafting the proposed joint pretrial order and submitting it to the trial judge just before the pretrial conference, the two lawyers had miscalculated the trial judge's willingness to accept an order that was less detailed and articulate than the usual order. They had completed each section of the proposed joint pretrial order and agreed to it, but they had apparently not adequately informed the trial judge in the manner of the usual order. To demonstrate to the lawyer and opposing counsel their irresponsibility, the trial judge went through the proposed joint pretrial order line by line, ridiculing their joint work with questions like, "What does this mean?" "What does that mean?" "How am I supposed to know?" The trial judge treated the lawyer and opposing counsel like first-term law students, challenging each minor premise and assumption of their sorry joint work.

The trial judge finally reached the end of the order. He indicated that the lawyer and opposing counsel were to resubmit a revised order, adding that he was disappointed in the lawyer and opposing counsel from whom he expected better. He then rose brusquely, turned around, and walked out the small door in the huge wall behind the bench. The court reporter and clerk gathered their papers without looking at the lawyer or opposing counsel, knowing that to do so would wrongly either invite some reaction or further embarrass the lawyer and opposing counsel. They need not have worried. The lawyer and opposing counsel were far too professional to have acknowledged their chastisement to court staff and put court staff in an awkward position. The court reporter and clerk filed out. The lawyer and opposing counsel gathered their own papers, saying nothing to one another until they were in the hallway where courtroom microphones would not pick up their discussion. Neither felt like talking. They knew better than to say anything, anyway. The lawyer smiled wryly at opposing counsel and said, "I guess I'll send you a revised order." Opposing counsel gave an equally painful smile, nodding silently.

The lawyer had learned some time ago what it meant to be responsible, including not to whine about appropriate chastisement. In fact, it had been federal trial judges who had done more than anyone else to teach him that lesson. They have a way of doing that to lawyers. Oddly, another federal trial judge had chastised the lawyer and a different opposing counsel once before over another proposed joint pretrial order that the trial judge had felt was too detailed. In that case, the lawyer and opposing counsel had disagreed about many things. Opposing counsel had put her many objections into her parts of the proposed joint pretrial order. The lawyer had put his many responses into his parts of the proposed joint pretrial order. Their contentious efforts made for a long proposed order, but the lawyer had supposed that it was to work that way.

The trial judge had firmly disabused both the lawyer and opposing counsel of that senseless notion. Again, the lawyer knew when the judge entered the courtroom that they were in trouble. Opposing counsel, though, had missed the signs. In the hallway before the pretrial conference, opposing counsel had told the lawyer that she had never met the judge before and only heard about his legendary willingness to dress down lawyers. The lawyer knew all about it from prior cases. As the pretrial conference got started with the judge asking first one side and then the other side warm-up questions, the lawyer noticed that opposing counsel had begun not to rise fully and stand erect behind counsel table with each answer. "Mistake," thought the lawyer, "she's in for it." Sure enough, the first time that opposing counsel did a sort of half-rise that only lifted her seat out of the chair at counsel table but left her hands on the chair's arms, the judge launched into a tirade against disrespectful lawyers. The lawyer felt bad for opposing counsel who, though an experienced managing partner of a statewide law firm of over 100 lawyers, blushed and hung her head at the judge's five-minute tongue lashing. In the hallway after the pretrial conference, opposing counsel offered promptly to arbitrate the case.

The lawyer had seen the same federal trial judge's effect on other lawyers. One was a criminal defense counsel whom the lawyer had seen many times in state-court practice. Criminal defense counsel was a jovial former police officer who was ordinarily very confident and at ease in courtrooms, where he had spent much of his professional life. The lawyer happened to run into him outside of the federal trial judge's courtroom one day, where the two of them had briefly discussed the judge's toughness on lawyers. They entered the courtroom together, sitting in the gallery until the judge called the criminal defense counsel's matter. The lawyer noticed that the criminal defense counsel's eyes were twice their usual size as he approached the lectern. There were no fireworks that day, but the lawyer noted that the criminal defense counsel's pants legs were shaking as he stood at the lectern. The lawyer decided not to tease the criminal defense counsel about it later.

The lawyer remembered that at one time the lawyer would have been indignant at a trial judge's chastisement. The lawyer had learned, though, that chastisement was not necessarily a bad thing. It has a way of making a lawyer more responsible. The lawyer had begun to realize that the judges who were willing to hold him to higher standards had taught him more than other judges had. It took a while, but he learned not to take their criticism personally, even when they made it personal. The lawyer learned to think, prepare, evaluate, and then stand firm under pressure without any unnecessary pride or arrogance.

The best example came when the same federal trial judge had excoriated the lawyer in motions in limine the day before a major civil-rights trial. The judge had said personal things disparaging the lawyer's competence and fitness when the lawyer was confident that he had full factual and legal support for his positions. He had been fully responsible to the law and trial judge. The lawyer was right. Two weeks later the trial ended with a jury verdict in favor of the lawyer's clients. The judge was suddenly gracious, inviting the lawyer and opposing counsel into chambers for the first time, where he complimented the lawyer and opposing counsel on their preparation, cooperation, and professionalism. The lawyer was glad then for the many small lessons that federal trial judges had taught him about responsibility.

Faith during law studies also helps law students and lawyers develop and demonstrate responsibility. When it comes to professional comportment, law students and lawyers do not blame others. We rightly accept responsibility for our actions and their consequences.[119] We also rightly do not use the misconduct of others to shield ourselves. The shortcuts of others will burden faithful lawyers who nonetheless rightly do not complain of it or blame those others.[120] Lawyers avoid even quiet blaming.[121] Instead, lawyers of faith tend to look past the burdens that others place on them. They resist judging the actions of others when those actions are in some ways like the lawyers' own actions.[122] It is often unfair to judge another without having been in their place. You never quite know the good that they may actually be doing by acting in a way that you do not understand, or the unseen challenges that they may be facing that would explain

---

[119] HEBREWS 13:7 ("Consider the outcome of their way of life....").
[120] PHILIPPIANS 2:14 ("Do everything without complaining....").
[121] JAMES 5:9 ("Don't grumble against each other....").
[122] MATTHEW 7:1-2 ("Do not judge, or you too will be judged. For in the same way you judge others, you will be judged, and with the measure you use, it will be measured to you.").

their behavior.[123] Better to judge yourself first. The faithful lawyer sees the lawyer's own responsibility first and by doing so avoids others blaming the lawyer.

You have probably noticed that events soon hold everyone to account.[124] There is no avoiding judgment.[125] Thus, it is far better to take responsibility than to have others place it on you. When the faithful lawyer takes responsibility, the lawyer manages bad situations better. A bad situation can affect a lawyer adversely, but when the faithful lawyer takes responsibility for it, others respect the lawyer's responsibility. People expect people to blame others when things go wrong. They do not expect people to accept responsibility. The faithful lawyer distinguishes the lawyer's conduct by accepting and even calling for the lawyer's own responsibility.[126] When a lawyer refuses to take responsibility and others have to place it on the lawyer, the lawyer comes out far worse than the underlying condition itself would have made the lawyer. It is as if the lawyer has now engaged in two wrongs, the underlying situation plus the refusal to take responsibility for it. It is far better to accept responsibility and come out even or ahead than to reject responsibility and come out two behind.[127]

When things go wrong, faithful lawyers take broader responsibility, including sometimes for things of which they were not the primary cause. The faithful lawyer will accept supervisory responsibility.[128] A lawyer of faith knows that responsibility lies not only for the lawyer's own actions but also on occasion for review and remediation of others' actions.[129] Responsibility

---

[123] ROMANS 14:4 ("Who are you to judge someone else's servant? To his own master he stands or falls. And he will stand, for the Lord is able to make him stand.").

[124] DEUTERONOMY (" 'If anyone does not listen to my words that the prophet speaks in my name, I myself will call him to account.' ").

[125] ECCLESIASTES 3:15 ("Whatever is has already been, and what will be has been before; and God will call the past to account.").

[126] JOSHUA 22:23 (" 'may the Lord himself call us to account' ").

[127] 1 SAMUEL 25:23-24 ("When Abigail saw David, she ... fell at his feet and said: 'My lord, let the blame be on me alone.' ").

[128] EZEKIEL 3:17 (" 'I have made you a watchman' ").

[129] EZEKIEL 3:18 (" 'When I say to a wicked man, "You will surely die," and you do not warn him or speak out to dissuade him from his evil ways in

involves accepting account not only for one's own actions and welfare but also for others for whom we should be caring.[130] The lawyer who rejects the lawyer's responsibility for a client will lose the privilege of practicing law.[131] A faithful lawyer accepts responsibility for the actions of team members and subordinate lawyers and staff.[132] In that way, a lawyer of faith shows leadership, defuses situations of divisive blaming, and gives others the opportunity to acknowledge their own wrongs. By taking responsibility, the faithful lawyer shows others the way to take responsibility for their own situations. The faithful lawyer builds teams by taking responsibility for the actions of subordinate team members. Taking responsibility is a powerful opportunity, especially when the responsibility has to do with wrongs.[133]

At the same time, the faithful lawyer does not take credit for good things that were the result of others' actions. The faithful lawyer is quick to give credit where credit is due.[134] Responsibility has to do with accepting blame for bad situations, not with taking credit for good ones. The faithful lawyer knows that responsibility is more powerful than credit. It can do more for a lawyer to take responsibility for wrongs, and then to make the wrongs right, than for a lawyer to take credit for good outcomes for which the lawyer was only partly responsible or not responsible. To take credit when credit is not due is to deprive others of that credit and to weaken the lawyer in the eyes of others, while also weakening the bonds of the team that produced that good

---

order to save his life, that wicked man will die for his sin, and I will hold you accountable for his blood.' ").

[130] EZEKIEL 34:8-9 (" '[B]ecause my shepherds ... cared for themselves rather than for my flock, ... I am against the shepherds and will hold them accountable for my flock.' ").

[131] EZEKIEL 34:8-9 (" 'I will remove them from tending the flock so that the shepherds can no longer feed themselves.' ").

[132] EZEKIEL 3:19 (" 'But if you do warn the wicked man and he does not turn from his wickedness or from his evil ways, he will die for his sin; but you will have saved yourself.' ").

[133] EPHESIANS 5:15 ("Be very careful, then, how you live—not as unwise but as wise, making the most of every opportunity, because the days are evil.").

[134] ESTHER 2:22 ("Queen Esther ... reported it to the king, giving credit to Mordecai.").

outcome.[135] Lawyers of faith are quick to take responsibility for wrongs and quick to give credit for rights, while slow to take credit for rights and slow to assign responsibility for wrongs.

The faithful lawyer knows that faith holds each one accountable,[136] and not just for major wrongs, because little wrongs are just as often our undoing.[137] The faithful lawyer knows that the lawyer is responsible for every word and action, an exacting standard that leaves no room for shirking responsibility.[138] Words have a powerful effect when it comes to evaluating conduct and assigning fault. By taking responsibility in word and deed, the faithful lawyer actually finds the lawyer receiving less, not more, blame.[139] The faithful lawyer understands that there is a powerful sense of judgment in the justice system and beyond, and acts in ways responsible to that judgment. The faithful lawyer accepts accountability and behaves accordingly, expecting that others will measure the lawyer's performance.[140] Lawyers of faith welcome accountability because they expect and prepare for accountability. The faithful lawyer knows that when someone holds the lawyer accountable, the person respects the lawyer enough to expect something from the lawyer. The only lawyers who escape accountability are those from whom no one expects anything. To be a lawyer from whom no one expects anything is no position to envy.

The faithful lawyer remains accountable even for those things that the lawyer knows others will never discover.[141] In those confidential areas where no one else has access, some

---

[135] LEVITICUS 7:18 ("It will not be credited to the one who offered it, for it is impure... .").

[136] 2 THESSALONIANS 1:8 ("He will punish those who do not know God and do not obey the gospel of our Lord Jesus.").

[137] SONG OF SONGS 2:15 ("Catch for us the ... little foxes that ruin the vineyards... .").

[138] MATTHEW 12:36 ("But I tell you that men will have to give account on the day of judgment for every careless word they have spoken.").

[139] MATTHEW 12:37 ("For by your words you will be acquitted, and by your words you will be condemned.").

[140] ROMANS 14:12 ("So then, each of us will give an account of himself to God.").

[141] HEBREWS 4:13 ("Nothing in all creation is hidden from God's sight. Everything is uncovered and laid bare before the eyes of him to whom we must give account.").

persons scheme as if no one will ever know their schemes. Yet the faithful lawyer never uses the lawyer's ability to conceal a wrong to justify the lawyer's misconduct.[142] The faithful lawyer acts the same accountable way with confidences as the lawyer acts with those things that the lawyer knows circumstances will eventually reveal. In that manner, the faithful lawyer receives less blame because the lawyer is always acting accountably rather than making erring judgments about where the lawyer will and will not be accountable.

Lawyers of faith also recognize that they are responsible to their clients when their clients do wrong for lack of the lawyer's warning. Faithful lawyers warn their clients to keep their clients from doing wrong.[143] Lawyers owe their clients warnings, especially against the kind of immoral action that exposes clients to liability and judgment.[144] Lawyers do not just give their own opinions. They give clients fair notice of what the law and morality require. Clients suffer when lawyers fail to give them due warning of what is right and wrong, and of the consequences of their wrongs. Lawyers know that the law will hold the lawyers accountable if the lawyers do not warn their clients.[145] Faithful lawyers remain responsible to their clients.

Just as much as responsibility is a critical professional attribute, so, too, irresponsibility and blaming destroy the service and reputation of lawyers. It is human nature to blame others. Doing so comes naturally to us.[146] When we do something wrong, the first thing that we do is to look for others who either made us do it or who also did it, to justify our own misconduct. Blaming others is a bad way to go about things when we are the

---

[142] ISAIAH 29:15 ("Woe to those who go to great depths to hide their plans from the Lord, who do their work in darkness and think, 'Who sees us? Who will know?'").

[143] EZEKIEL 33:3 ("he sees the sword coming against the land and blows the trumpet to warn the people").

[144] EZEKIEL 33:7 ("'hear the word I speak and give them warning from me'").

[145] EZEKIEL 33:6 ("But if the watchman sees the sword coming and does not blow the trumpet to warn the people and the sword comes and takes the life of one of them, ... I will hold the watchman accountable for his blood.").

[146] GENESIS 3:12 ("The man said, 'The woman you put here with me—she gave me some fruit from the tree, and I ate it.").

responsible ones. It only creates more wrongs, revealing our own flawed character while also drawing others into our own wrongs.

Not only do we blame others, but also we reject the moral standards that prove our misconduct. When everything crashes down around us because of our own wrongs, we blame and challenge the standards as if the standards are wrong.[147] That is when things get preposterous, when a lawyer blames the law and its moral standards for the lawyer's own wrong.[148] A lawyer does not make the moral standards by which everyone judges lawyers and others.[149] You can see how destructive irresponsibility is and how easily we fall into it. Lawyers must resist the tendency to blame others for our own wrongs. A faithful lawyer is responsible and accountable.

---

[147] PROVERBS 19:3 ("A man's own folly ruins his life, yet his heart rages against the Lord.").

[148] ISAIAH 29:16 ("You turn things upside down, as if the potter were thought to be like the clay!").

[149] ISAIAH 29:16 ("Shall what is formed say to him who formed it, 'He did not make me'? Can the pot say of the potter, 'He knows nothing'?").

Chapter 5

Law Practice

THE DEMONSTRATION OF FAITH

If faith informs law studies and the formation of a lawyer through knowledge, skills, and identity, then faith also informs law practice. Faith informs law practice through the moral fields of service, stewardship, diligence, and charity. At its root, law practice involves serving clients, community, profession, family, friends, and others. Lawyers must have a right understanding of service. Service requires stewardship of the resources necessary for law practice. Service is not possible without stewardship. Law practice also depends on a high degree of diligence, another field that faith informs. Finally, law practice itself benefits by the charity that a lawyer offers, often through pro-bono service and its influences. This chapter explores those faith fields.

Yet before examining in detail the faith that law practice requires, recognize that law practice brings a lawyer into contact with clients and others who do not share a lawyer's faith. Indeed, law practice is in large part a matter of communicating to clients and others how the moral fields of law work, meaning helping them understand, trust in, and rely on articles of faith. To be effective at law practice, lawyers must know what clients and others believe, not just what they must come to understand of the law and its moral equivalents. We are better lawyers when we can modify our counsel to act on the worldviews held by our clients and others. When we fail to recognize what others believe, meaning the basis for how they will hear, incorporate, and act on our counsel, then we fail to serve those clients effectively. Faith includes right relationship to others,[1] not solely right relationship to faith's author.[2] Worldviews matter. What effective lawyers do is develop the capacity to recognize worldviews in clients, judges, opposing counsel, and others, and adapt their advice, arguments, and actions to draw on the strengths and remediate the weaknesses of those worldviews when they are inconsistent with the moral fields within which human experience operates.

Service

"Now, did I get everything correct?" the worker's compensation counsel asked the client. The client, the comp lawyer, and the lawyer who was handling the client's products-liability claim had just spent an hour evaluating the client's comp claim. The lawyer had brought comp counsel in to handle the comp claim, as had been the lawyer's practice. At the end of the hour, comp counsel had dictated a summary of the tasks that comp counsel and his legal assistant would be doing to move the client's comp claim forward. Comp counsel had periodically paused during the dictation to ask the client to confirm or clarify certain information. When comp counsel was done, he had what would become a transcribed memorandum of everything that the client had agreed and expected, which comp counsel would promptly send to the client. It was a most impressive and efficient service, one of the reasons why the lawyer always called on this comp counsel.

The lawyer knew that law practice is all about service. Over the years, the lawyer had observed many different lawyers handling matters in many different ways. Many of the practices that the lawyer had the privilege to observe were exceedingly respectful services to the clients. Repeatedly, the lawyer had thought that he was doing everything that he reasonably could to keep client matters moving forward and keep clients informed, when he would observe another lawyer doing something extraordinarily more effective and special. The lawyer adopted a few of those practices but also knew that each lawyer must serve in the way that they know best. Other lawyers were doing some things that

---

[1] JOHN 13:34 (" 'A new command I give you: Love one another. As I have loved you, so you must love one another.' ").

[2] HEBREWS 12:2 ("Let us fix our eyes on Jesus, the author and perfecter of our faith.").

the lawyer could not have done. Probably, the lawyer was doing some things that other lawyers could not do.

The lawyer enjoyed many things about law practice, but service had become the major one. The lawyer liked the intellectual challenges, the variety of matters, the clients' different personalities, the professional community, the working conditions, and the compensation. It was not those things, though, that made the lawyer jump out of bed every workday morning. It was the opportunity, even the need, to serve others. The lawyer knew that it sounded corny, but there was something essentially satisfying about constant, direct, simple, and effective acts of service. The lawyer had many times heard the truism that law is a service profession. The lawyer believed it and liked it.

The lawyer celebrated that law practice was a good place for service, even if it was not by any means the only service profession. When the lawyer picked up fresh meat or fish at the meat counter on the rare occasions that the lawyer shopped for groceries, he relished watching the butcher's small services. The butcher would let the customer point out which filet, would place it on the scale and respectfully ask the customer if it was the right weight, and then would carefully double-wrap it, mark the package, hand it gently over the counter, and ask if there was anything else, over and over, all day long. The lawyer appreciated the many people from whom he received service each day, whether dry cleaners, gas-station cashiers, bank tellers, and restaurant servers, or in law practice, then secretaries, legal assistants, court clerks, and even judges. The lawyer took solace in believing that his legal service was not particularly original or altruistic but instead simply reciprocating for service provided by others.

One of the lawyer's favorite times for service was when a case settled. The uncertainty and any contentiousness were over, but there was still the matter of effectuating the settlement and seeing that the client received the money. The lawyer knew that in his personal-injury practice, time was of the essence for most of his clients. There were bills to pay, and the collectors were not going to wait for a dilatory lawyer. To speed the process, the lawyer would have the client's settlement statement ready at any gathering where there was a chance of settlement. If the case settled, then the lawyer would have the client approve the disbursements and acknowledge the net proceeds immediately. The lawyer would also immediately send defense counsel the proposed dismissal. If defense counsel did not promptly send a proposed release, then the lawyer would have the client sign one of the lawyer's own releases and send it to defense counsel. Some *defense counsel probably assumed that the urgency was the client's greed or lawyer's greed, though it was not. It was simply thoughtful, efficient, respectful, and satisfying service.*

The care that faith has us show for others turns itself into service to those others.[3] Fundamentally, law is a service profession. What that means is that lawyers are to help whom they are most able and where they are most able. The faithful lawyer knows that the greatest lawyer is the one who serves most and best.[4] Look at the stories of great lawyers, and you will see that it is not so much that they found greatness within them but that they found clients and causes to serve. Effective service to those who have the greatest need is the surest way to distinguish you as a lawyer, proving again that law is a service profession. The care to which the faithful lawyer commits in faith causes the lawyer to serve.[5]

Faith lends an important positive and normative dimension to serving others. Service does not mean to work solely or primarily to please another. People pleasing can become a desperate and distorting pursuit, unhealthy for both the pleaser and the pleased. Lawyers are not people-pleasers. They are far from it, being too wise for others to manipulate them in that manner. Rather, service means to do right for others in a manner that is good for them while reflecting well on faith.[6] The service must honor faith. If it does not, and if it only pleases the client or others, then it will not be authentically beneficial for the client and is not the kind of act that a faithful lawyer would pursue. Service has a purpose and purity about it that goes beyond the client to touch on and honor faith.

There are many kinds of legal service. Some law students and lawyers have great concern over what kind of law they should practice, choosing the best specialty field based on lifestyle

---

[3] 1 PETER 4:8 ("Each one should use whatever gift he has received to serve others, faithfully administering God's grace in its various forms.").

[4] MATTHEW 23:11 ("The greatest among you will be your servant.").

[5] 1 THESSALONIANS 1:3 ("your work produced by faith, your labor prompted by love, and your endurance inspired by hope").

[6] 1 THESSALONIANS 2:4 ("We are not trying to please men but God, who tests our hearts.").

criteria like hours, status, promotion, and compensation.[7] It makes sense to prepare responsibly for viable practice areas, but to choose law practice based on personal criteria is to miss the best sense of the profession. You should balance your own desires for your career with the needs of clients for your service. A lawyer of faith will serve those persons whom the lawyer encounters in the needs that those persons have, where the lawyer is most capable of helping.[8] The faithful lawyer does the work at hand[9] and does it passionately no matter what that work may seem to merit in the eyes of other lawyers.[10] There may be practice areas in which the faithful lawyer would like to participate, but the lawyer will still serve those who come to the lawyer with real needs for immediate legal service, even if that service means that the lawyer must do something that the lawyer would prefer not to do. Law practice is not so much about choosing what you think is best for you. It is a lot about doing what you know is best for others.

Indeed, the faithful lawyer may go to great lengths to meet the real needs of troubled clients.[11] The faithful lawyer sees need and, along with it, sees imaginative and effective ways to serve needs. The faithful lawyer will serve the client in need and enlist others also to do so. In appropriate instances, the faithful lawyer

---

[7] LUKE 10:25-32 ("On one occasion an expert in the law stood up to test Jesus. 'Teacher,' he asked, 'what must I do to inherit eternal life?' 'What is written in the Law?' he replied. ... ' "Love your neighbor as yourself." ' 'You have answered correctly,' Jesus replied. 'Do this and you will live.' But he wanted to justify himself, so he asked Jesus, 'And who is my neighbor?' In reply Jesus said: 'A man was going down from Jerusalem to Jericho, when he fell into the hands of robbers. They stripped him of his clothes, beat him and went away, leaving him half dead. A priest happened to be going down the same road, and when he saw the man, he passed by on the other side. So too, a Levite, when he came to the place and saw him, passed by on the other side.' ").

[8] LUKE 10:33-34 ("But a Samaritan, as he traveled, came where the man was; and when he saw him, he took pity on him. He went to him and bandaged his wounds, pouring on oil and wine.").

[9] ECCLESIASTES 9:10 ("Whatever your hand finds to do, do it with all your might... .").

[10] 1 THESSALONIANS 5:12 ("to respect those who work hard among you").

[11] LUKE 10:34 ("Then he put the man on his own donkey, took him to an inn and took care of him."). The next day he took out two silver coins and gave them to the innkeeper. 'Look after him,' he said, 'and when I return, I will reimburse you for any extra expense you may have.'").

may even extend the client relationship over time while also enlisting the help of others to ensure that the client gets the best service and makes the best improvement possible.[12] It is not about getting matters behind you, turning over a clientele. It is about building lasting relationships through effective service. The faithful lawyer knows that the lawyer's best marketing is the satisfaction of well-served clients.

Some think that the way to get success and acclaim is to get others to serve you. They see many people serving the rich and famous, and they see the powerful continually gaining more power to make others do things for them, rather than the powerful doing things for the people.[13] As a result, they think that for a lawyer to be successful, the lawyer must get others to serve the lawyer. Some lawyers want to join firms that provide them with their every need especially for meaningful work and high compensation. They then begin to want law firm staff to do things that they should do for themselves, other lawyers to do their work for them, and finally clients to meet their needs, whether for meaningful assignments, larger compensation, or respect and appreciation. Some lawyers try to build practice around their own needs.

The faithful lawyer knows that the way to success and acclaim is the opposite, that is, to serve others, not to get them to serve you.[14] The faithful lawyer will join a firm that needs the lawyer's service and then will ensure that the firm and its clients, lawyers, and staff receive what they need from the lawyer. The faithful lawyer thinks about the needs of everyone associated with the firm, especially those unappreciated but essential staff members like secretaries, clerks, and bookkeepers. Law firm managing partners actually care a lot about how a lawyer treats law firm staff. The faithful lawyer treats them well. Faith teaches

---

[12] LUKE 10:35 ("The next day he took out two silver coins and gave them to the innkeeper. 'Look after him,' he said, 'and when I return, I will reimburse you for any extra expense you may have.'").

[13] MARK 10:42 ("You know that among the Gentiles those whom they recognize as their rulers lord it over them, and their great ones are tyrants over them.").

[14] MARK 10:43 ("But it is not so among you; but whoever wishes to become great among you must be your servant...").

that to be the greatest lawyer, you would have to be the best at serving all.[15] That service may include those to whom you might not think that you owe anything in particular. Watch, though, and you will see how considerate lawyers of faith can be to law firm staff.

Service does have a sacrificial quality to it, even though there are very few who really like to sacrifice.[16] We all would like others to sacrifice for us but are seldom willing to give up things that we want for the benefit of others. Faith, though, shows us how to serve even to the point of giving up things to others that one desires for one's self.[17] One way in which we do that is to serve those who cannot give us anything in particular back, like recognition, appreciation, or sometimes compensation. Some of the most sacrificial service is service that does the right things for others when there is no apparent return to one's self. It may even be an ordinary thing like reviewing and completing some simple paperwork that does not really draw on one's technical skills as a lawyer. Those small thankless tasks can add up to meaningful service. Faith teaches lawyers that the way to gain success and even acclaim is to serve those who are least able to give that acclaim. These small things add up to a law practice of real substance.

Service can actually take many different forms, depending on our particular gifts and callings. It is not as if all lawyers do the same things equally well and for the same individuals. Rather, we each serve differently, but our service is equally effective and valuable to those whom we serve.[18] We should not look down on the service of others. Instead, we should each use consistently whatever education and experience we have to do the best for

---

[15] MARK 10:44 ("...and whoever wishes to be first among you must be slave to all.").

[16] JOHN 15:13 ("Greater love has no one than this, that he lay down his life for his friends.").

[17] MARK 10:45 (" 'For the Son of Man came not to be served but to serve, and to give his life as a ransom for many.'").

[18] 1 CORINTHIANS 12:4–7 ("There are different kinds of gifts, but the same Spirit. There are different kinds of service, but the same Lord. There are different kinds of working, but the same God works all of them in all men.").

others, recognizing that service is effective in many forms.[19] When we serve others, especially those who are least able to care for themselves, then we are serving someone greater. Some would say that in those times, we are serving the greatest.[20] It is odd, but serving a pauper can become like serving a king, only better, because when one serves a king one can expect a present return, while when serving a pauper one knows that the return is in the future.

We should especially be helping those who share the same commitments that we share in serving.[21] Helping a helper, meaning serving someone who serves others, has something especially satisfying about it. When we provide legal services to clients who share our commitment to service, it is as if we multiply our own service through them. Imagine helping someone so that the person can resume or continue to help many others. That kind of service to servants makes serving so much more effective. There are times when we tire of serving, but in those times, we remember that we are earning a reward for our service that is greater than we can presently see or imagine, if we just keep serving.[22] Service is a bit like placing money in an interest-earning account, when it is better to place money in than to take money out.

Basing our law practice on service may sound like it will constrain and confine us, but actually, it is exactly in that kind of well-intentioned service that lawyers find the greatest freedom.[23] Faith brings freedom.[24] Lawyers find liberty in the truths of faith.[25] Faith fosters a set of conditions within the mind and

---

[19] 1 PETER 4:10 ("Each one should use whatever gift he has received to serve others, faithfully administering God's grace in its various forms.").

[20] MATTHEW 25:40 ("I tell you the truth, whatever you did for one of the least of these brothers of mine, you did for me.").

[21] GALATIANS 6:10 ("As we have opportunity, let us do good to all people, especially to those who belong to the family of believers.").

[22] GALATIANS 6:9 ("Let us not become weary in doing good, for at the proper time we will reap a harvest if we do not give up.").

[23] GALATIANS 5:13 ("You, my brothers, were called to be free. But do not use your freedom to indulge the sinful nature; rather, serve one another in love.").

[24] PSALM 146:7 ("The Lord sets prisoners free....").

[25] JOHN 8:32 (" 'If you hold to my teaching, you are really my disciples. Then you will know the truth, and the truth will set you free.'").

through the actions of the lawyer of faith such that the lawyer faces no constraint.[26] It is when we pursue our own good rather than the good of others that law practice most confines us. One supposes that it is not a bad thing to want to be a famous lawyer, but in the odd way of things, seeking fame would be one of the worst ways to go about getting fame. We should instead make it our goal to stay out of the limelight while we do earnestly those things which come to us, and which we can do with what we have on hand.[27] Attend any awards ceremony that recognizes lawyers, and you will see the proof of it. The lawyers who rise to acclaim are those who do the small service consistently to the best of their abilities for the sake of those for whom they do it, not themselves. At award ceremonies, you tend to meet humble lawyers, those lawyers who have made it their career to serve quietly.[28]

Those lawyers who serve others so well receive not only acclaim but also blessing. Faith enables generous giving.[29] Indeed, faith makes a lawyer pleased to give rather than to give grudgingly.[30] The more that a faithful lawyer gives, the more that the lawyer receives, in that oddly indirect way in which we best pursue those blessings.[31] Lawyers who pursue their own gain directly run the risk of becoming selfish and greedy, and knowing it, while giving satisfies and pleases the lawyer's conscience.[32] Lawyers who pursue effectively others' gain receive their own gain without those risks of selfish actions.[33] What those lawyers receive back fits what they give and yet is more than they had

---

[26] 2 CORINTHIANS 3:17 ("Now the Lord is the Spirit, and where the Spirit of the Lord is, there is freedom.").

[27] 1 THESSALONIANS 4:11 ("Make it your ambition to lead a quiet life, to mind your own business and to work with your hands....").

[28] PROVERBS 25:6 ("Do not exalt yourself in the king's presence, and do not claim a place among great men....").

[29] 2 CORINTHIANS 8:3-4 ("they gave as much as they were able, and even beyond their ability ... they urgently pleaded with us for the privilege of sharing in this service").

[30] 2 CORINTHIANS 9:7 ("for God loves a cheerful giver").

[31] LUKE 6:38 ("Give, and it will be given to you.").

[32] ACTS 20:35 (" 'It is better to give than to receive.'").

[33] 1 PETER 5:2 ("not greedy for money, but eager to serve").

anticipated receiving.[34] What the giving lawyer receives back may be far beyond what the lawyer might have imagined, indeed so much that the lawyer really has no room for all of it.[35] It is the nature of giving through service to bring back more to the giver. Examine the best and most successful lawyers, and you will often see that they are the lawyers who give the most of themselves and, by doing so, give the best service.[36] The faithful lawyer knows that service is the key to law practice and that law is a service profession.

With all of that said on behalf of faithful service, the faithful lawyer knows that as much as the lawyer's service may help another, it is not as if the lawyer or lawyer's service is so incredibly special. Serving is a humble act in which the faithful lawyer lowers the lawyer's own self in effect to a position beneath the client. Serving can also humble a lawyer. It is not as if service is such a grand thing. It is actually often mundane. Service is itself modest. The faithful lawyer keeps service in the proper perspective, knowing that anything the lawyer does is really quite ordinary, especially when compared to the grand and special things of faith.[37] The faithful lawyer also knows that service rendered without the kind of caring that makes it service in faith is really doing nothing for a client.[38] The faithful lawyer cares for the client according to the truths of faith when serving. In this manner, the faithful lawyer keeps the right attitude toward service.

---

[34] LUKE 6:38 ("A good measure, pressed down, shaken together and running over, will be poured into your lap. For with the measure you use, it will be measured to you").

[35] MALACHI 3:10 (" 'Test me in this,' says the Lord Almighty, 'and see if I will not throw open the floodgates of heaven and pour out so much blessing that you will not have room enough for it.'").

[36] MATTHEW 20:27 ("whoever wants to become great among you must be your servant, and whoever wants to be first must be your slave").

[37] ISAIAH 64:6 ("all our righteous acts are like filthy rags").

[38] 1 CORINTHIANS 13:3 ("If I give all I possess to the poor and surrender my body to the flames, but have not love, I gain nothing.").

Stewardship

For the thousandth time, the lawyer made the last time-keeping entry in the computer software, closed the laptop computer's lid, and pushed back his chair to reflect momentarily on another day's work. The lawyer never really grew tired of time keeping, like many other lawyers professed to do. The lawyer had certainly read the many condemnations of hourly billing. He understood much of the criticism, particularly in the perverse incentive hourly billing created for taking longer to do an hourly client's work. Yet what he did not understand or at least that with which he did not agree was the complaint that hourly billing was a slave master making a lawyer's work unpleasant. Nor, at root, did he really agree that hourly billing created the wrong incentives.

Instead, what the lawyer had found over the years was that time-keeping was an excellent tool for managing his activities properly. The lawyer liked that his law firm had, for a time, published at the end of each month the hours that each lawyer in the firm was working. The information gave him a clearer sense of the firm's expectations and of his own measure in meeting them. The lawyer could adjust accordingly, backing off a bit if it looked like he was doing more than what the collective record of the lawyers demonstrated was wise, or kicking it up a notch if he was doing less than his part. As much as the lawyer enjoyed law practice, the lawyer wanted to lead a healthy and balanced life. As much as the lawyer enjoyed time off for family, the lawyer wanted to make a responsible contribution to the firm that supported it financially. Time-keeping helped him do both things, and the lawyer liked that assistance.

Independent of what the firm expected, the lawyer liked that he knew how much time he was working and where he was spending that time. The lawyer handled both hourly and contingency-fee cases, keeping track of his time and activities for both kinds of cases. The time records for hourly matters helped the lawyer keep the work in its proper financial perspective. There was always more that you could do on any matter. You could always improve the quality or appearance of the work product. The firm's and client's expectations for a certain-sized bill helped the lawyer determine when a project was complete. If the task was to take no more than about 10 hours, then that information gave the lawyer a sense of the level of work to produce. If the lawyer could produce a better work within that same 10 hours than the firm and client expected, then there would be more credit to the lawyer. The lawyer appreciated that incentive to work more efficiently and wisely.

THE FAITHFUL LAWYER

The lawyer's time-keeping records on contingency-fee cases were equally helpful. The firm kept track of that time just in case the court awarded fees by statute or under sanction. Then, contemporaneous time records would be necessary to substantiate the fee request. Yet fee awards happened relatively rarely. What was more helpful was that the lawyer could use the expected fee that a case would generate to estimate an appropriate number of hours to spend on the case and to adjust activities accordingly. It was not a lock-step system. Some small cases warranted large hours, and some large cases warranted small hours. Yet generally, the larger cases warranted larger hours and smaller cases smaller hours. Contingency-fee lawyers must manage their time responsibly. It was good that the lawyer had a way of tracking how much time he had expended on a contingency-fee case at any stage of the proceedings, so that he could manage his time and caseload in a way that kept the staff and rent paid, and the lights on. At the end of a contingency-fee case, the lawyer could readily calculate his effective hourly rate to ensure that he was choosing cases that would keep the practice open. Why not act responsibly?

In the larger scheme of things, the lawyer felt that those who worked in other trades and professions had like accountability measures. The grocer, plumber, and tailor all have their margins. Every private commercial venture does. The lawyer did not begrudge any of them a profit, nor did he think that he was due a profit without earning it. If the lawyer's work had merit, then the client would pay the bill, or the lawyer's client would receive compensation out of which to pay a contingency fee. Ask the elderly. They will tell you that time is the most precious commodity for a lawyer, a client, or any person leading any life. To be a true steward, why not measure and justify at least the professional part of it by tenths of an hour?

Faith also helps law students and lawyers learn the role of money and our relationship to it in law practice. Lawyers earn income through many different fields of law using different skills in different practice settings. In the main, then, lawyers earn, as others earn, by doing the right work.[39] There is no great secret to financial success in law practice. Notice, though, that lawyers do not earn by pursuing money directly. Chasing money does not work. The client who sees the client's lawyer chasing after the

---

[39] 1 CORINTHIANS 3:8 ("The man who plants and the man who waters have one purpose, and each will be rewarded according to his own labors.").

client's money will quickly find a new lawyer. When clients see that we only care for money and not for them or their causes, then they know that they are not getting our service. The faithful lawyer must show a different attitude toward money than to pursue it for its own sake, if the lawyer wants to have clients.

Faith shows us that pursuing money for money's own sake simply wears us out rather than making us rich in the manner that we desire and need to be rich.[40] It is true about money that once you have the desire for it, you can never have enough. What we really should desire are some of the things that money represents only imperfectly but faith represents perfectly, like provision and security, and also competence and honor.[41] Knowing the futility of chasing money helps us show restraint when we feel the desire to do so.[42] It also helps us redirect our desire to the things that we should pursue like the well-being of others. Our desire should not be for riches or, for that matter, for poverty, but to have what we need each day so that we can continue in law practice. In that way, we avoid both the distraction of riches and the temptation to lie, cheat, and steal to avoid poverty.[43] The first big step toward stewardship is to know what amount of money is enough, which is what one needs that day to continue in service.

Many lawyers are financially successful, some even extraordinarily so. Yet there are successes, and then there are successes. Successes won without faith can be false and fleeting, while successes earned through faith are authentic and durable.[44] The kind of success that comes to a lawyer through faithful service is the most trustworthy success. You do not have to be false and flashy to be financially successful as a lawyer. Lawyers can find great financial success simply through humble and faithful ser-

---

[40] PROVERBS 23:4 ("Do not wear yourself out to get rich....").

[41] 2 CORINTHIANS 3:5 ("our competence comes from God").

[42] PROVERBS 23:4 ("have the wisdom to show restraint").

[43] PROVERBS 30:8 ("[G]ive me neither poverty nor riches, but give me only my daily bread. Otherwise, I may have too much and disown you and say, 'Who is the Lord?' Or I may become poor and steal, and so dishonor the name of my God.' ").

[44] PROVERBS 15:6 ("The house of the righteous contains great treasure, but the income of the wicked brings them trouble.").

vice.[45] Clients are not dumb. A law degree is not a license to print money. Faithful service, not luck or greed, make a lawyer's service reliably profitable.[46] There is no surer way to succeed financially than always to act according to the dictates of faith, consistently and carefully.[47] That is what you will find faithful lawyers doing, taking great care to do things right.

Stewardship is the faith concept through which the faithful lawyer learns these truths about money. A steward is one who holds and uses money or other resources for the benefit of others. To be a good steward is to keep money and property in a condition fit to benefit others. The faithful lawyer treats the law firm's financial and technical resources as a resource owned by another for the lawyer to use for the best effect of others. The faithful lawyer treats the lawyer's own finances and property in the same way, as if the lawyer held that property in trust to use for the greatest effect for the benefit of others. It is remarkable how quickly the rich turn poor and the poor rich, and how quickly we each pass on, leaving what we thought was our property to others. The faithful lawyer knows that all property is really something that we hold only temporarily before it passes on to others. The faithful lawyer is a steward of every resource.

The faithful lawyer also knows that time is the lawyer's greatest resource. The faithful lawyer treats time as the lawyer would treat other resources, as a wise steward. To treat time as would a wise steward means to think about how best to apply it for the benefit of others. You will not see lawyers of faith wasting time. Once time is gone, it is gone. You can never get it back. The faithful lawyer treats each moment as a precious resource, knowing that once the moment passes, the lawyer is accountable for what remains from it. Keeping that sense of time as a resource for which one is accountable as a steward helps to invest law practice

---

[45] PROVERBS 22:4 ("Humility and the fear of the Lord bring wealth and honor and life.").

[46] DEUTERONOMY 30:9 ("Then the Lord your God will make you most prosperous in all the work of your hands....").

[47] DEUTERONOMY 28:13 ("If you pay attention to the commands of the Lord your God that I give you this day and carefully follow them, you will always be at the top, never at the bottom.").

with appropriate urgency, meaning, and richness. Each moment is its own exchange.

Those faithful lawyers who are financially successful know not to boast about being rich. Instead, the faithful lawyer takes greater satisfaction in knowing justice.[48] It would be wrong to deny completely that doing well financially is something in which one can take some pleasure. Yet those lawyers who do well financially are glad not so much that they are rich but that they have done the right things in the right ways, and riches followed.[49] The faithful lawyer accepts wealth not so much as a reward but instead as an indication of having done rewarding things resulting in riches. The faithful lawyer keeps looking to do those things, knowing that effective service is its own reward, and that the riches that sometimes come from effective service are an additional blessing.

The faithful lawyer also knows that riches are uncertain. The faithful lawyer takes no security in riches but instead takes security in faith.[50] The faithful lawyer continues to do good acts of service and then uses any wealth that results to give generously to persons in need and to good causes.[51] To be a steward of wealth is to know that it can provide for one's self while also helping others. The faithful lawyer will use wealth to make connections that lead to additional opportunities for service, knowing that generosity brings its own profit.[52] Wealth is not something to hoard but to share in ways that help others while equipping others for service. By using wealth like a steward would use wealth, to expand the lawyer's productive and beneficial influence,

---

[48] JEREMIAH 9:23 (" 'Let not ... the rich man boast about his riches, but let him who boasts boast about this: that he understands and knows me, that I am the Lord, who exercises kindness, justice and righteousness on earth, for in these I delight... .' ").

[49] PSALM 119:14 ("I rejoice in following your statutes as one rejoices in great riches.").

[50] 1 TIMOTHY 6:17 ("Command those who are rich in this present world not to be arrogant nor to put their hope in wealth, which is so uncertain, but to put their hope in God, who richly provides us with everything for our enjoyment.").

[51] 1 TIMOTHY 6:18 ("Command them to do good, to be rich in good deeds, and to be generous and willing to share.").

[52] PSALM 112:5 ("Good will come to him who is generous... .").

lawyers of faith prepare themselves for a reward where it really counts in the future, when they can most benefit from it.[53]

In the end, faith teaches law students and lawyers that money is not the end. Dying rich is certainly no gain and probably instead a loss. It does not leave us any better off to die surrounded by wealth that we could have used for others.[54] In the worst of times, money really offers us no protection. You cannot take money with you beyond the grave—that much is certain.[55] Money and the kind of things that you acquire with money just do not endure.[56] Indeed, chasing riches while in law practice leads us away from doing the things that would make us better off in life and when dying.[57] Life is for pursuing faith, not money. It would be better to be poor while making many rich than to be rich while making many poor. That is what it means to be a steward, to hold things in ways that make others benefit, even though we could treat those things as our own. Stewardship is a powerful faith concept.

Faith teaches us that we need that power when it comes to money. Money has a powerfully deceptive way about it. We often think that everything would be better if we only had more money—that money solves all problems. Yet the opposite is often the case, that more money only brings more problems. One can actually have nothing and yet, in a way, possess everything.[58] It is especially the one who is rich and yet chooses poverty so that others may become rich, who does the most for everyone while

---

[53] 1 TIMOTHY 6:19 ("In this way they will lay up treasure for themselves as a firm foundation for the coming age, so that they may take hold of the life that is truly life.").

[54] MATTHEW 19:23 ("Then Jesus said to his disciples, 'I tell you the truth, it is hard for a rich man to enter the kingdom of heaven.'").

[55] ISAIAH 10:3 ("What will you do on the day of reckoning, when disaster comes from afar? To whom will you run for help? Where will you leave your riches?").

[56] PROVERBS 27:24 ("for riches do not endure forever").

[57] MATTHEW 19:23 (" 'Again, I tell you, it is easier for a camel to go through the eye of a needle than for a rich man to enter the kingdom of God.'").

[58] 2 CORINTHIANS 6:10 ("poor, yet making many rich; having nothing, and yet possessing everything").

having the most for one's self.[59] The pursuit of faith in law practice and throughout life brings us to the place of fulfillment and rest we all seek, not the pursuit of money. Rich lawyer and poor lawyer alike can reach that place only through faith and not with the substitute of money.[60] Treat money, time, and other resources as a steward would treat another's property, and you will find your law practice the better for it.

Diligence

The uneasy task loomed. The lawyer's stomach turned slightly each time he thought of it while he continued to do other work. The lawyer soon realized that he was putting off the task, delaying it when he should be starting it. The lawyer recognized what he was doing as the dreaded "p" word: procrastination. Then a thought occurred to the lawyer. Maybe the lawyer was just circling and stalking the task like a hungry lion, while using the other work as a distraction to soften up the task. The lawyer let out a chuckle at the thought, put aside the other work, and had at it. As usual, the lawyer made immediate progress on what he thought would be a difficult project with ambiguous criteria and an unclear objective. The lawyer had the project nearly done within half the time he had estimated for it. The lawyer checked the clock: quitting time. Nah, the lawyer thought. Just finish it. Ten minutes later, the lawyer had finished the work. The lawyer headed home relieved and satisfied, ready to enjoy the evening more than he would have if the project had remained untouched until the morning.

The lawyer knew other lawyers who procrastinated. He had co-counseled cases with several other lawyers, some of whom were marvelously efficient. One counsel in particular so impressed the lawyer that he tried to work with him any time that he could. That counsel was the only lawyer with whom he had worked who would volunteer for a task, start it, and complete it more quickly and consistently than the lawyer. Other lawyers never volunteered, declined to accept tasks when asked, could not seem to get started

---

[59] 2 CORINTHIANS 8:9 ("For you know the grace of our Lord Jesus Christ, that though he was rich, yet for your sakes he became poor, so that you through his poverty might become rich.").

[60] MATTHEW 25-26 ("When the disciples heard this, they were greatly astonished and asked, 'Who then can be saved?' Jesus looked at them and said, 'With man this is impossible, but with God all things are possible.'").

on tasks, requested frequent extensions, and could not seem to let go of completed work. One whom the lawyer discovered to be a procrastinator suffered client grievance and malpractice suit. The lawyer learned to avoid those lawyers, who seemed like malpractice traps.

The lawyer was not a procrastinator and never would be, he had long ago decided. The lawyer had learned that every task delayed grows larger in the mind. Every task delayed invites another higher-priority task arising during the delay, compounding the stress from the delayed task with other delayed tasks. It was like logs jamming up in a river. The lawyer decided to keep the logs flowing. He decided to start every task as early as he could rather than work against deadlines. He determined to finish every task as efficiently as he could, notwithstanding the due date. The practice often enabled the lawyer to hold completed work, let his mind mull the subject, and return to improve the completed work before its due date. It was surprising how often the practice led to significant improvements in the work. The lawyer also found that he rarely needed to request extensions, when requesting extensions was a common practice especially among the appellate lawyers with whom the lawyer worked.

Early in his career, the lawyer had briefly entertained the thought that the more work he did, the more work there would be to do, that work generates work so that there was no use in being particularly efficient or productive about it. The lawyer briefly entertained the thought, promoted by many, that he had to learn to say "no" to avoid being constantly over-burdened. Yet in time, the lawyer had instead discovered a natural limit to the tasks and productivity that others will expect of a lawyer. The lawyer never figured out exactly how it worked, but staying productively on task seemed to keep the lawyer with just the right constant work flow. Perhaps it was that others knew and respected when the lawyer was occupied. That was certainly true with trials that they tended to keep you out of the way and beyond the reach of others.

In any case, the lawyer found that he was able to say "yes" often and "no" rarely, making him very satisfyingly productive. The satisfaction came in several ways. A happy clientele was one of them. The lawyer never had a client file a grievance against him, when grievances were relatively common in his practice area. No client sued the lawyer for malpractice despite his being in a high-risk field. Compensation was another satisfaction. Bonuses were frequent. The firm's bookkeeper would even hint to the lawyer's wife when they chatted that the lawyer more than pulled his fair share in the firm—job security. In the end, though, the lawyer *knew that diligence was a matter of professional survival and satisfaction. Law practice was too challenging to be anything less than diligent about it. Law practice was too rewarding when a lawyer was diligent, the lawyer decided.*

Faith during law studies and law practice helps law students and lawyers develop and demonstrate diligence. To be diligent means to attend to appropriate tasks to their natural completion.[61] We should do what we should until we finish that which is for us to do.[62] Law studies and practice require constant timely work including a high degree of organization and discipline. Law practice is certainly complex. Cases and other client matters each have their own unique schedules on which the lawyer must complete specific tasks. Getting everything done requires constant attention to those schedules and to the work that will meet them.[63] Diligence is frankly a key to law practice. Diligent lawyers are simply more successful. They get things done, when getting things done is a large part of law practice. Diligent lawyers make for more satisfied clients. They also breathe easier. There are so many reasons for a lawyer to be diligent in law practice.

Faith helps us remain diligent because it calls us to stay on top of things, watching for developments.[64] When the faithful lawyer sees a development of consequence, the lawyer discerns diligently the relevant task to be always prepared.[65] Faith urges that we are accountable at all times.[66] Faith is attentive and makes us attentive, though which we gain greater understanding.[67] Faith is also caring and makes us caring. Attention and caring lead to active labor on behalf of clients. Faith also makes us better at what we do, meaning that we do tasks more quickly. As we labor faithfully over law studies and practice, our understanding and

---

[61] REVELATION 22:11 ("let him who does right continue to do right").

[62] HEBREWS 6:11 ("show this same diligence to the very end").

[63] JOSHUA 8:4 (" 'Listen carefully. ... All of you be on the alert.'").

[64] MARK 13:33 ("Be on guard! Be alert!").

[65] ROMANS 8:9 ("You, however, are controlled not by the sinful nature but by the Spirit, if the Spirit of God lives in you.").

[66] MARK 13:33 (" 'Be on guard! Be alert! You do not know when that time will come.'").

[67] PROVERBS 4:1 ("Listen, my son, to a father's instruction: pay attention and gain understanding.").

skills grow, while those who do not labor faithfully fall behind.[68] We find that tasks are easier, and their ease makes us more willing to pursue them. The more attentive and caring we are, the better at law practice we are, and the more we want to pursue it. Diligence through faith has a way of making practice better.

The mental and emotional side of being a lawyer also gets better when we are diligent through faith in our law practice. When we are consistently prepared, we have no need to be ashamed of how we perform and can instead expect approval.[69] Diligence in preparation makes for better performance, while better performance makes for approval. The faithful lawyer then gives credit to faith for that performance, so that faith continues to serve the lawyer. The lawyer does not think how diligent the lawyer is but thinks how well faith serves the lawyer. The faithful lawyer draws strength for diligent service not so much from the lawyer but from faith. The faithful lawyer knows that doing the right work for faith's sake will bring the strength that the lawyer needs and will leave the credit for the work to faith rather than to the lawyer, which is important.[70] We do not serve to bring attention to ourselves but to the work of faith.

Sometimes, it seems like no one appreciates our work. That kind of feeling can be discouraging and lead to a lack of diligence, as if it did not matter that we do our work. Yet the standard we should set for our work is always to do our best, as if our work was for one whom we value and trust more than anyone else whom we value and trust.[71] What we should try each day is to do quietly the small things that are within our reach without involving ourselves unfairly in the affairs of others.[72] By doing for ourselves and with diligence our law-practice tasks, without

---

[68] 1 THESSALONIANS 5:6 ("So then, let us not be like others, who are asleep, but let us be alert and self-controlled.").

[69] 2 TIMOTHY 2:15 ("Do your best to present yourself to God as one approved, a workman who does not need to be ashamed and who correctly handles the word of truth.").

[70] 1 PETER 4:11 ("If anyone serves, he should do it with the strength God provides, so that in all things God may be praised through Jesus Christ.").

[71] COLOSSIANS 3:17 ("Whatever you do, whether in word or deed, do it all in the name of the Lord Jesus, giving thanks to God the Father through him.").

[72] ISAIAH 30:15 ("in quietness and trust is your strength").

thinking that someone else can or should do them for us, we avoid burdening others with having to do those things for us, while also winning their respect.[73] People begin to take notice of how we quietly go about finishing our work. We also set an example for others, which helps strengthen the organization within which we work.[74] Just when we think that no one was noticing how diligently we work, we realize that others do notice.

Faithful work also earns us refreshing rest.[75] It is a funny thing, but just when we think that there is no end to work and that we will never get any rest, when we apply ourselves to the work at hand, we suddenly find refreshing breathers in the work.[76] Faithful work has its natural breaks. It is not as hard as you may think to work in faith.[77] When a lawyer completes one task, there is often a wait before the next task on the same project. Diligent work does make for natural interludes, when faith strengthens the lawyer again for the work.[78] It is when a lawyer fails to work diligently that the work piles up and the lawyer gets hopelessly behind. Diligence makes for hope and rest. Lack of diligence makes for unending burden and labor. It is also often true that a task done promptly saves other work, while a task done only after undue delay requires more work than it would have if the lawyer had done it promptly. Diligence is efficient. Sloth is not. Take it unduly easy, and you will quickly lose what little extra you have and find yourself in need of the basics.[79]

Perhaps most of all, by working diligently at our law practice, we provide for ourselves and our families, and in so pro-

---

[73] 1 THESSALONIANS 4:11-12 ("Make it your ambition to lead a quiet life, to mind your own business and to work with your hands, just as we told you, so that your daily life may win the respect of outsiders and so that you will not be dependent on anybody.").

[74] 2 THESSALONIANS 3:7 ("You yourselves know how you ought to follow our example. We were not idle when we were with you....").

[75] ECCLESIASTES 5:12 ("The sleep of a laborer is sweet....").

[76] 2 CORINTHIANS 4:16 ("we are being renewed day by day").

[77] MATTHEW 11:30 (" 'For my yoke is easy and my burden is light.' ").

[78] HEBREWS 13:21 ("...Jesus [will] ... equip you with everything good for doing his will...").

[79] PROVERBS 6:10-11 ("A little sleep, a little slumber, a little folding of the hands to rest—and poverty will come on you like a bandit and scarcity like an armed man.").

viding, confirm our faith.[80] Let us face it: compensated work is satisfying. To be able to bring a paycheck home is satisfying. It confirms all that we do to earn the paycheck. Diligent work brings financial reward, whether it is hourly work, which has a natural reward for hours worked, or contingency-fee work, where the reward comes because the work is prompt and effective. When diligence produces its financial reward, a lawyer wants to be more diligent. Because of this natural reward for effort, the more diligent a lawyer is, the more diligent a lawyer wants to be. Diligence has such a natural reward that it confirms one's faith in diligence.

Some of our problems in law studies and practice are due to laziness, meaning when we take it easy when we should be doing the work. Sometimes, we just do not do what is within our reach, instead just taking it easy.[81] The problem in doing so with law studies is that the less we work at it, the more we begin to think that we know what we do not know.[82] Law studies are unusual in that respect that the more one works at them, the more one realizes how much there is to know. That realization helps a lawyer. While lawyers should know as much as they can, lawyers should also know how little that they know. It is a dangerous thing for a lawyer to be complacent with law knowledge, thinking that the lawyer knows much when the lawyer knows little. Clients can easily be hurt that way.

Law practice is the same way, that the less one works at it, the less one realizes how much there is to do in order to do it right. From the outside, law practice can look easy. You just show up for trial, right? Actually, though, when one works diligently at law practice, one quickly sees how much there is to do to be well prepared in anything, whether it is for a trial or in another client matter. So another danger of failing to work diligently is that the

---

[80] 1 TIMOTHY 5:8 ("If anyone does not provide for his relatives, and especially for his immediate family ,he has denied the faith and is worse than an unbeliever.").

[81] PROVERBS 10:5 ("He who gathers crops in summer is a wise son, but he who sleeps during harvest is a disgraceful son."); PROVERBS 20:34 ("A little sleep, a little slumber, a little folding of the hands to rest—and poverty will come on you like a bandit and scarcity like an armed man.").

[82] PROVERBS 26:16 ("The sluggard is wiser in his own eyes than seven men who answer discreetly.").

lawyer leaves things undone that the lawyer does not even realize the lawyer should have done. Some tasks have more to them than meets the eye. Diligent work prevents those embarrassing surprises. It also prevents a lawyer from burdening others with the lawyer's undone work and the lawyer's own needs. The diligent lawyer provides for the lawyer's own needs so that others do not have to provide for the lawyer in the lawyer's stead by doing the lawyer's undone work.[83] The faithful lawyer works diligently while avoiding those who do not.[84]

Diligence also has an aspect of doing the right work, not just any work. Sometimes we go off on our own tangents, doing things that really make no sense to the objective at hand, when we should be exercising better judgment and being wise about our time and work.[85] Other times, our challenges are in just talking about doing the work rather than actually doing it, when talk does not help and work does.[86] The more we work at it, the more we know how little we know without that work. For that reason, we should avoid liking and pursuing that sense of ease, for it tends to sneak up on us and rob us of our diligence. It is simple. Wise work is the most consistent thing that we can do to ensure that we have what we need and that we provide others with what they need. We earn what we are due.[87] We should do everything as if we do it for the most important client whom we hope most to

---

[83] 2 THESSALONIANS 3:7-8 ("We were not idle when we were with you, nor did we eat anyone's food without paying for it. On the contrary, we worked night and day, laboring and toiling so that we would not be a burden to any of you.").

[84] 2 THESSALONIANS 3:6 ("stay away from every brother who is idle").

[85] PROVERBS 12:11 ("He who works his land will have abundant food, but he who chases fantasies lacks judgment.").

[86] PROVERBS 14:23 ("All hard work brings a profit, but mere talk leads only to poverty.").

[87] PROVERBS 20:4 ("A sluggard does not plow in season; so at harvest time he looks but finds nothing."); PROVERBS 20:13 ("Do not love sleep or you will grow poor; stay awake and you will have food to spare.").

impress.[88] With diligence coming from faith, a lawyer never tires of doing the right thing for clients.[89]

The faithful lawyer exercises one other kind of diligence, and that is diligence in the study and exercise of faith to improve the lawyer's law skills and practice. Lawyers should investigate and study faith as part of their diligent practice, participating in faith community, letting faith strengthen their skills and attitude toward law practice.[90] Lawyers should not neglect their education and the skills that they have but should work to improve both, particularly through study of things that strengthens their faith.[91] The lawyer who devotes earnest effort to hone the lawyer's education and skills shows everyone that the lawyer is improving.[92] It is impressive when one who is already a skilled lawyer continues to work to improve their skills. Faith makes us want to do that, to continue to improve, which is an important part of diligence.

Charity

The lawyer had never been more appreciative of pro bono. Nearing the end of his law career, the lawyer had taken a new job that meant he was no longer practicing law full time. The lawyer missed law practice. He missed the bombardment of telephone calls, faxes, emails, regular mail, and office visits that gave work such constant high energy. The lawyer missed the office staff, missed overhearing them joke gaily with the couriers and office suppliers, and groan about tasks and clients with one another. The lawyer missed dealing with other lawyers in that constant you've-got-something-I-want tension that colored every interaction with interest and purpose. He missed the legal matters that placed the lawyer in the middle of the thick stream of commerce and society

---

[88] COLOSSIANS 3:23 ("Whatever you do, work at it with all your heart, as working for the Lord, not for men.... It is the Lord Christ you are serving.").

[89] 2 THESSALONIANS 3:13 ("And as for you, brothers, never tire of doing what is right.").

[90] 1 TIMOTHY 4:13 ("Until I come, devote yourself to the public reading of Scripture, to preaching and teaching.").

[91] 1 TIMOTHY 4:14("Do not neglect your gift....").

[92] 1 TIMOTHY 4:15 ("Be diligent in these matters; give yourself wholly to them, so that everyone may see your progress.").

where he daily dealt with the essential stuff of life. Law practice will never let you feel as if life is passing you by while you stand on its banks. Instead, law practice makes you feel as if life is sweeping you along, soaking you in its experience.

Yet most of all, the lawyer missed the clients. The lawyer missed the service to the clients, missed doing things that mattered to help others. He missed the clients' emotion including their anger, tears, frustration, and confusion. The lawyer missed the clients' perseverance, the constantly hopeful way in which they met the greatest challenges of life like job loss, business collapse, partnership dissolution, bankruptcy, foreclosure, divorce, incarceration, serious illness, severe injury, disability, and death. The lawyer missed the clients' joy, the constantly appreciative way in which they accepted the blessings of life including childbirth, adoption, graduation, marriage, home purchases, business start-ups, and transferring wealth from generation to generation.

Pro-bono service made up for some of what the lawyer missed of law practice. The lawyer's new job enabled him to continue some modest pro-bono service so long as he did not take matters that required court appearances and other matters that might interfere with his new work commitments and schedule. The lawyer could still go to pro-bono service sites in a cultural center, soup kitchen, and homeless shelter to consult with pro-bono clients. The lawyer had to restrict the work mostly to intake, evaluation, and consultation. He might rarely do a little research, make a telephone call, or write a letter for a pro-bono client. Yet nearly all of what the lawyer did was just sit and talk with client after pro-bono client, sorting their legal problems from their health or social problems, helping them articulate obtainable objectives, and connecting them with other legal or community resources.

The pro-bono work meant so much to the lawyer. It forced the lawyer to think, read, write, investigate, and talk about law as a resource and solution for common problems. The pro-bono work made law real and authentic rather than abstract and intellectual. The pro-bono work expanded the lawyer's skills and kept his knowledge current. The pro-bono work informed the lawyer of community health and needs. It also showed the lawyer how the community was meeting those needs. It introduced him to a warm and vital community of social-service providers including not only social workers and nonprofit administrators but also other lawyers doing pro bono. Of course, the lawyer hoped and believed that the pro-bono service helped the clients, which was the most important and satisfying product. The lawyer realized that those things that meant so much to him from pro-bono work were *simply the blessings of charity, proving once again that it is so much better to give than to receive charity.*

Faith also leads us to charity in law practice. Charity is an old-fashioned word that many of us no longer appreciate. It sounds odd in a professional setting in any case. Yet charity still makes sense. Charity suggests giving money or offering service to those who most need it, without expectation of return. In the professional setting, lawyers tend to think of charity as pro-bono service. Charity makes us step outside of the usual transactional realm in which lawyers operate, where every legal service depends on payment or some other form of consideration in a bargained-for exchange. Charity helps us take law practice into a different realm, where the economy is not so clearly monetary, but where the things that the lawyer receives have a different kind of value.[93] There is still an exchange of sorts, but the exchange instead becomes one of money or service to the person in need, for that person's appreciation, or failing appreciation, for the satisfaction of having met a need. No one can take that kind of reward from you, not even time itself.

In faith's terms, charity is more powerful than the monetary economy in which lawyers and others typically operate. When we help one who is unable to pay for it, it is as if we serve someone larger who looks out for the poor, in effect making a loan that comes back to us later with interest.[94] You have to appreciate the unusual but powerful ways in which charity rewards those who give it. Lawyers of faith make it a point to reach out with compassion to those who cannot afford their services and do not have a lawyer's advantages.[95] Lawyers of faith particularly reach out to those who are most broken by life and least successful, meaning those who cannot help the lawyer. By doing so, those lawyers create an account of sorts for themselves on which they will draw

---

[93] LUKE 12:33 (" 'Sell your possessions and give to the poor. Provide purses for yourselves that will not wear out, a treasure in heaven that will not be exhausted, where no thief comes near and no moth destroys.' ").

[94] PROVERBS 19:17 ("He who is kind to the poor lends to the Lord, and he will reward him for what he has done.").

[95] COLOSSIANS 3:12 ("clothe yourselves with compassion").

when drawing will be most satisfying and meaningful.⁹⁶ Just
when the faithful lawyer most needs encouragement, the charity
that the lawyer has done will provide it.

The faithful lawyer also knows that it is not always immediately obvious who those persons most in need are. Sometimes, a
lawyer must just take a chance on it, trusting that what seems like
a real need in fact is one. That kind of spontaneous charity can
lead to the greatest kinds of rewards.⁹⁷ We do not plan all charity.
A lot of it just happens. The faithful lawyer is always ready to
offer charity when the occasion suddenly arises. Another way that
the opportunity for a lawyer to provide charity can arise suddenly
when you least expect it is among those who are nearby in your
community but without family or other social support, and most
alone in their needs for service.⁹⁸ It may be someone you see every
day who most needs your charity. The faithful lawyer is on the
watch for those charitable opportunities, too.

As odd as it may seem, a lawyer's charity also has a way of
inoculating the lawyer from harm when the lawyer faces trouble
and assisting the lawyer in the lawyer's own time of need.⁹⁹ It is
hard to explain how that happens, but the lawyer who helps
others when they cannot give back adequately for the lawyer's
help generates a kind of goodwill on which the lawyer then draws
in the lawyer's own times of need. We all have times of need, even
successful lawyers. Yet why, after all, should anyone help the
lawyer in need when the lawyer failed to help others in need when

---

⁹⁶ LUKE 14:13-14 (" 'But when you give a banquet, invite the poor, the
crippled, the lame, the blind, and you will be blessed. Although they cannot
repay you, you will be repaid at the resurrection of the righteous.' ").

⁹⁷ ECCLESIASTES 11:1 ("Cast your bread upon the waters, for after many
days you will find it again.").

⁹⁸ DEUTERONOMY 14:29 (serve so that "the aliens, the fatherless and the
widows who live in your towns may come and eat and be satisfied, and so that
the Lord your God may bless you ion all the work of your hands").

⁹⁹ PSALM 41:1-2 ("Blessed is he who has regard for the weak; the Lord
delivers him in times of trouble. The Lord will protect him and preserve his
life; he will bless him in the land and not surrender him to the desire of his
foes.").

the lawyer was able?[100] There is a natural justice to things including especially those things of generosity and charity.

Lawyers of faith do not do charitable works for the return. The faithful lawyer acts without expectation of return but receives an unexpected and well-deserved return in any case.[101] In that mysterious power that giving has, the more that we give as lawyers, the more that we receive in the practice of law, and the things that we receive tend even to outweigh what we give in both quantity and quality.[102] That is truly unusual about giving, that we receive back things that are worth more than we give. It is so easy for a lawyer to give a little legal service. It often does not cost the lawyer much to do so. Yet the lawyer who does so in a charitable manner receives back gratitude, satisfaction, and respect that the lawyer could not have purchased for any amount of money. In the end, by performing pro-bono service and giving in other ways through law practice, the faithful lawyer ends up lacking nothing at all.[103]

There are important considerations to the way that we give through our law practices. For one, we should not give grudgingly as if it were a distasteful duty to give. We should treat pro-bono service and other charitable works as a joy and privilege, not a burden.[104] In addition, we should not tell everyone what we are doing, bragging about our pro-bono service.[105] Yet it is right that others see the charity that you perform. It is good to be a model

---

[100] LUKE 6:38 (" 'For with the measure you use, it will be measured to you.' ").

[101] PROVERBS 22:9 ("A generous man will himself be blessed, for he shares his food with the poor.").

[102] LUKE 6:38 (" 'Give, and it will be given to you. A good measure, pressed down, shaken together and running over, will be poured into your lap.' ").

[103] PROVERBS 28:27 ("He who gives to the poor will lack nothing, but he who closes his eyes to them receives many curses.").

[104] 2 CORINTHIANS 9:7 ("Each man should give what he has decided in his heart to give, not reluctantly or under compulsion, for God loves a cheerful giver.").

[105] EPHESIANS 2:9 ("For it is by grace that you have been saved, through faith—and this not from yourselves, it is the gift of God—not by works, so that no one can boast.").

in your law practice.[106] Doing so can encourage other lawyers to do their own pro-bono service, while also encouraging them in developing their own faith out of which pro-bono service grows.[107] Studies show that persons of faith give substantially more money and time to others, which is not surprising, because charity is a work of faith. It is hard for a person without faith to give a reason for doing charity. Yet to do pro bono for the attention that it brings you is to do it the wrong way, for a present reward rather than because it is the right thing to do.[108] Save your reward for when it counts, from whom it counts. People who see you bragging about it will only think less of you anyway.

In our law practices, we should also give both freely and generously, with ease and abundance when it comes to those who are unable to provide for themselves and so need our legal service. We should not take shortcuts in pro bono but give the same legal service that we would give to a paying client, or better service, as if we were serving the most special client of all.[109] In this way, we find ourselves receiving more than ever and at the same time not growing weary but instead letting charitable work refresh us.[110] Generosity of this kind blesses not only those of us who exercise it but also our families including our children. There are few better ways to gain the respect of your children than to give generously to others, in confidence that they receive a similar

---

[106] 1 PETER 2:12 ("Live such good lives among the pagans that, though they accuse you of doing wrong, they may see your good deeds and glorify God on the day he visits us.").

[107] TITUS 2:7 ("In everything set them an example... .").

[108] MATTHEW 6:1-4 (" 'Be careful not to do your "acts of righteousness" before men, to be seen by them. If you do, you will have no reward from your Father in heaven. So when you give to the needy, do not announce it ... to be honored by men. ... But when you give to the needy, do not let your left hand know what your right hand is doing, so that your giving may be in secret. Then your Father, who sees what is done in secret, will reward you.' ").

[109] MATTHEW 25:40 (" 'The King will reply, "I tell you the truth, whatever you did for one of the least of these brothers of mine, you did for me." ' ").

[110] PROVERBS 11:24-25 ("One man gives freely, yet gains even more; another withholds unduly, but comes to poverty. A generous man will prosper; he who refreshes others will himself be refreshed.").

benefit to what you do by giving.[111] Your family shares in your charitable giving and service. They certainly share in the respect that it engenders.

Giving has its effect not just on you, the lawyer who does pro bono in law practice, and on your family, but also on the community in which you give. When you give consistently and generously, and serve specific legal needs in a community that has its legal issues, then your giving tends to help others see the need to give likewise. Pick a community where your giving will make a difference. Your giving can change the community for the better far beyond what you might expect from your individual service. Charity, even in small ways, can change communities.[112] Giving changes communities not just because it reduces the need but also because it influences and changes the givers.

The opposite is also true, that the lack of charity can adversely affect whole communities. Those, like lawyers, who have the capacity to be generous but instead hold onto their wealth and take security in it become arrogant. In becoming arrogant, they adversely affect the whole welfare of the community.[113] The rich often set the tone for a community. People look up to them and emulate them, even when they should not. When the rich, including lawyers, fail to give often and generously, others will do likewise, and the community suffers. There is no holding on to riches, thinking that riches alone will satisfy you. A lawyer can be rich and successful in every way except charity, and yet lack everything worthwhile.[114]

---

[111] PSALM 37:25-26 ("... I have never seen the righteous forsaken or their children begging bread. They are always generous and lend freely; their children will be blessed.").

[112] ISAIAH 58:10 ("And if you spend yourselves on behalf of the hungry and satisfy the needs of the oppressed, then your light will rise in the darkness, and your night will become like the noonday.").

[113] 1 TIMOTHY 6:17-18 ("Command those who are rich in this present world not to be arrogant nor to put their hope in wealth, which is so uncertain, but to put their hope in God, who richly provides us with everything for our enjoyment. Command them to do good, to be rich in good deeds, and to be generous and willing to share.").

[114] MARK 10:21 ("Jesus looked at him and loved him. 'One thing you lack,' he said. 'Go, sell everything you have and give to the poor, and you will have treasure in heaven. Then com, follow me.' ").

Charity, meaning primarily pro-bono service, also has the effect of preserving and enlarging the skills of a lawyer. There are many different kinds of legal needs. Pro-bono clients tend not to come to lawyers with the particular needs that lawyers are most comfortable in serving. Lawyers tend to specialize, when need has no specialty. So when providing pro-bono service, lawyers find themselves doing a variety of basic legal services that they learned in law school and can readily master but that they have not done in some time or ever. By doing pro bono, lawyers develop new skills or recover old skills, including skills with which they can serve their own family.[115] As their skills expand to meet common legal needs of common individuals, they become masterful lawyers satisfied in what they do, rather than unhappy legal specialists whose overly narrow and technical skills fail to serve those most in need of service. It is those lawyers whom the community knows and respects,[116] and whom no circumstance or enemy can trouble. Indeed, opponents seem to serve solely to show the power of justice served by the faithful lawyer.[117] Charity enlarges the skills and professional life of a lawyer, even though its purpose is to serve others.

---

[115] ISAIAH 58:7 ("Is it not to share your food with the hungry and to provide the poor wanderer with shelter—when you see the naked, to clothe him, and not to turn away from your own flesh and blood?").

[116] ISAIAH 58:8 ("Then your light will break forth like the dawn, and your healing will quickly appear; then your righteousness will go before you, and the glory of the Lord will be your rear guard.").

[117] EXODUS 9:16 ("I have raised you up for this very purpose, that I might show you my power and that my name might be proclaimed in all the earth.").

Conclusion

FAITHFUL PROFESSIONALS

The foregoing chapters should have shown that the constructs of faith are enough unlike secular constructs, and yet so grounded in the real, that they would have to inform law studies and law practice. This post-modern, secular, technological age is a good time for faith to inform law students and lawyers. Faith constructs add a sorely lacking meta-narrative, one that is so ancient[1] as to be timeless,[2] while also broad, deep, and fully profound.[3] Faith constructs encourage constant professional development across a wide range of fields and skills, while nurturing a sensitive, whole, and creative person through reflective practices maintained around explicit intentions. Faith lends social and historical context to individual and corporate concerns, while promoting one's engagement with those concerns. It also helps the professional join theory to purposeful action, providing service with its theoretical foundation and theory with its practical expression.

---

[1] ISAIAH 43:13 (" 'You are my witnesses,' declares the Lord, 'that I am God. Yes, and from ancient days I am he."); DANIEL 7:9 ("the Ancient of Days took his seat").

[2] PSALM 119:160 ("all your righteous laws are eternal").

[3] PSALM 139:17 ("How precious to me are your thoughts, O God! How vast is the sum of them!").

At its most fundamental level, faith involves belief in, trust of, and obedience to the divine.[4] The faithful lawyer acts under the same conduct rules as the secular lawyer but with different intentions and motivations. The faithful lawyer acts not merely to please others or so that others would know that the lawyer has followed the law.[5] The faithful lawyer acts also to come closer to and please the lawgiver.[6] The faithful lawyer sees beyond the actions that the law requires, to the way that those actions reflect the character of the lawgiver,[7] a character that the faithful lawyer then pursues and claims as the lawyer's own.[8] Identity with faith guides and motivates the faithful lawyer in professional practice, even when the laws and rules do not.[9]

Faith's differences to the lawyer can be profound. Faith sees the individual as corrupt, in need of the redeeming quality of faith,[10] while secularity sees the individual as good, needing only freedom from faith, law, and lawyers. Faith sees the individual mind as subjective and deceitful,[11] in need of transcendent truth, while secularity sees the individual mind as constructing truth in a world where there are no independent meanings. Faith sees the self as broken, in need of transformation,[12] while secularity sees the self as injured, in need of therapy. Faith sees our need for

---

[4] HEBREWS 11:6 ("And without faith it is impossible to please God, because anyone who comes to him must believe that he exists and that he rewards those who earnestly seek him.").

[5] GALATIANS 1:10 ("Am I now trying to win the approval of men, or of God? Or am I trying to please men? If I were still trying to please men, I would not be a servant of Christ.").

[6] GALATIANS 6:8 ("the one who sows to please the Spirit, from the Spirit will reap eternal life").

[7] ISAIAH 33:22 ("the Lord is our judge, the Lord is our Lawgiver").

[8] GENESIS 9:6 ("for in the image of God has God made man"); 2 CORINTHIANS 3:18 ("And we ... are being transformed into his likeness with ever-increasing glory, which comes from the Lord, who is the Spirit.").

[9] 1 CORINTHIANS 13:1 ("And these three remain: faith, hope and love. But the greatest of these is love.").

[10] ROMANS 3:23 ("for all have sinned and fall short of the glory of God, and are justified freely by his grace through the redemption that came by Christ Jesus").

[11] JEREMIAH 17:9 ("The heart is deceitful above all things, and beyond cure.").

[12] MARK 10:18 (" 'No one is good—except God alone.' ").

redemption and its possibility,[13] while secularity sees nothing wrong to redeem and nothing as redeemer. Faith sees responsibility as resting with us,[14] while secularity sees responsibility as resting with others. Faith sees love as owed to one another,[15] while secularity sees love as owed to the self. Faith sees the self as something to humble,[16] while secularity wants the self exalted. These differences are just some of the differences between faith and the popular way of thinking about things, which seems so attractive.

Faith calls law students and lawyers to stand on faith apart from secularity.[17] Faith does not call lawyers to abandon our profession. Lawyers could quit the practice of law to pursue faith, but we do not because our faith calls us to it. Nor does faith work against lawyers in our profession. We could cut off our faith apart from our profession, but we do not because faith permeates and enriches practice. Faith is not in tension with our profession. We do not struggle between the forms of our faith and norms of our profession because our faith vitalizes our practice. Law students and lawyers of faith allow faith to transform and redeem their law studies and law practice.[18] We integrate faith with study and practice, allowing faith to work through our profession. This guide should have shown how faith in law studies leads to hope that leads to service in practice, the greatest being service. Law studies and practice are activities of faith. They generate hope

---

[13] MARK 10:26-27 (" 'Who then can be saved?' Jesus looked at them and said, 'With man this is impossible, but not with God; all things are possible with God.' ").

[14] EZEKIEL 14:20 ("They would save only themselves by their righteousness."); 1 TIMOTHY 4:16 ("Watch your life and doctrine closely. Persevere in them, because if you do, you will save both yourself and your hearers.").

[15] 2 JOHN 1:5 ("I ask that we love one another.").

[16] LUKE 14:11 (" 'For everyone who exalts himself will be humbled, and he who humbles himself will be exalted.' ").

[17] LEVITICUS 11:45 ("be holy, because I am holy"); 1 PETER 1:15 ("just as he who called you is holy, so be holy in all you do").

[18] JOHN 10:10 (" 'I have come that they may have life, and have it to the full.' ").

that we might flourish in peace, order, and prosperity.[19] With that hope, we begin to trust that we can care for one another, law professors for students, and lawyers for clients, friends and strangers, in deeply meaningful service.

A lawyer sees the need for faith in the lawyer's own moral claims and failings, and the moral claims and failings of clients. A lawyer finds in faith the redemption and transformation that both lawyer and client need. Belief, obedience, honesty, and trust flow from that transformation. The lawyer finds in the law faith's forms of love, covenant, provision, and community. The lawyer invokes those aspects of law through skillful reason, relationship, counsel, and discernment. As the lawyer does so, the lawyer develops an identity based on the law's calling, and the character, fitness, and responsibility of a lawyer. By grounding the lawyer's knowledge, skill, and identity in faith, the lawyer is able to practice with service, stewardship, diligence, and charity. These 24 moral fields of faith addressed in the 24 sections of this book form a reliable foundation for law studies and law practice.

Yet, faith has much more to say to a lawyer. The 24 sections of the six chapters of this guide only suggest a little of what faith holds for the lawyer who is willing to pursue faith. Although this guide has over one thousand footnotes, it barely touches on the detail and authority that one finds in faith. Its statements are the barest gloss on powerful subjects that one could explore so much more deeply.[20] There is much more for the faithful lawyer to learn and explore in the realm of faith. That realm is rich beyond any lawyer's imagination,[21] rich in just the way that will serve a faithful lawyer. This guide should only stimulate your pursuit of faith within law studies and practice, to explore faith's connections to the work of a lawyer. Listen to faith speak on the subjects you encounter in law studies and practice. Faith is the greatest companion you could find for law studies and practice. Faith will serve you well.

---

[19] GALATIANS 5:22 ("But the fruit of the Spirit is love, joy, peace, patience, kindness, goodness, faithfulness, gentleness and self control.").

[20] EPHESIANS 2:7 ("the incomparable riches of his grace").

[21] EPHESIANS 3:8 ("the unsearchable riches of Christ").

CONCLUSION

Serve faith well, too. The paradigm shift that faith asks of a lawyer is not to evaluate faith based on how it serves the lawyer but to evaluate the lawyer on how the lawyer serves faith. In the largest scheme of things, faith creates a lawyer, every lawyer,[22] to please faith,[23] not to please the lawyer's own self. It is not so much a question of having a satisfying and meaningful career. The question is instead having a career that satisfies faith. There is no kinder friend and master than faith, and none more rewarding.[24] It is truly odd, but when you make that last shift in paradigm to please faith rather than have faith please you, then satisfaction and meaning are readily available. We get what we want only by going at it indirectly.

In the end, law studies and practice will lead you to much better things that we all seek, so long as you seek in faith.[25] As a vocation, law practice is only part of a life, although like any vocation an important part. The challenge with both vocation and life is to connect them with something larger in human history. The challenge is to connect one's personal history with human history. Faith makes that connection. It does so because the history of humankind is a faith history. In its broadest sense, history involves ontology, teleology, and eschatology—origin, purpose, and an ending—just as a single life involves the same. Faith defines origin, purpose, and ending for humankind broadly and any individual specifically. Make your law practice part of the story of humankind, rich in justice, eternal, and divine.

The lawyer realized with regret that his new job meant that he had effectively retired from full-time law practice. At first, the lawyer thought that he might at any moment return to full-time law practice, although that possibility grew more and more remote as the months and then years went by. The lawyer still helped his former law partner from time to time. He also continued with pro-bono work. Through bar meetings and events, the lawyer also kept

---

[22] GENESIS 1:27 ("So God created man in his own image, in the image of God he created him; mal and female he created them.").

[23] 1 THESSALONIANS 4:1 ("live in order to please God"); JOHN 5:30 ("I seek not to please myself but him who sent me.").

[24] 1 CORINTHIANS 15:53 ("cloth[ing]... the mortal with immortality").

[25] HEBREWS 10:1 ("The law is only a shadow of the good things that are coming—not the realities themselves.").

up his contacts with many of the lawyers and judges with whom he had once had matters. To the lawyer's disappointment, though, the full-time practice of law receded in the rear-view mirror quickly. The lawyer found distractions but not substitutes. Increasingly, he looked with envy at his professional acquaintances who remained in practice. The lawyer recognized more and more the feeling of loss and disconnection that other retired lawyers had once conveyed to him when he had been actively practicing.

On rare occasions during the lawyer's retirement, something would cause the lawyer to look back wondering if law practice had allowed the lawyer to do anything meaningful. To yearn must be our condition. Then one day he rediscovered a manila folder stuffed with client thank-you cards among a few of the old master files he had once kept in his office credenza. The lawyer remembered having decided at some point later in his career to start keeping client thank-you notes in the folder. He remembered that he would read a client thank-you note quickly, reach back to the drawer of his credenza, and toss the note in the folder. Maybe it had been a cautionary action, just in case a client later complained, or maybe it had been a lawyer's equivalent of keeping your child's crayon drawings. Now, in retirement, it did not matter. There was the stuffed folder of client thank-you notes, each one its own record of something meaningful.

The lawyer knew what meaning to draw from those notes, and it was not that the lawyer was anything special. Clients are kind. They are generous and appreciative. Most every lawyer could have a desk drawer full of client thank-you notes, if they cared to save them. Clients trust, respect and admire their lawyer, even if not so much the other side's lawyer. What clients really respect, though, are the kinds of things that faithful lawyers exhibit. They respect charity, truth, and reason. They respect diligence, character, and fitness. Clients expect to see in their lawyer responsibility, stewardship, and service. Faith is the root of all those characteristics that clients need from and laud in their lawyers, the retired lawyer decided.

The lawyer flipped briefly through a few more thank-you notes, then closed the folder and slid it back among the other folders in his credenza to head home for the day. The day was the day before the day that lawyers and non-lawyers alike take off near the end of the year to celebrate faith. The lawyer and his family would spend an hour late that evening in a house of faith, celebrating with other members. The lawyer was one of several members chosen to read a few verses that evening, each reading describing another stage in faith's entry into the world. The lawyer already knew well the verses that the lawyer was to read. They were among the few that he had memorized some time ago. As he and his family drove to the house of faith, he recited them repeatedly, even though he would have the book of faith in front of him as he read that evening.

When the lawyer's turn came between carols, he stepped to the lectern and began his reading, letting his eyes close to concentrate more fully on each word of faith. As he did so, the words seemed to catch fire and shine with their own light, bringing even more glitter to the celebratory evening. The reading was over too soon for the lawyer, who opened his eyes and returned disappointed to his seat with his family. On their way out of the house of faith that evening, a friend stopped the lawyer to thank him for reading with such care and feeling, surprising the lawyer who had thought that only he had felt the fire of the words of faith as he had read them. Another person who overheard the friend's gratitude laughed and interjected, "Yeah, but what do you expect? He's a lawyer."

The lawyer knew the person intended the jibe to be lightly denigrating in that way that people think and speak of lawyers. Yet the lawyer just smiled and shrugged at it, thinking that it was not such a bad way to be known after all, as a lawyer who speaks words of faith with fire. He hugged his wife as they headed out the door into the chill winter night. They would need to get their daughter to bed so that they could finish the wrapping. It was going to be a special day tomorrow for the retired lawyer, more special than he had expected now that he knew that he was still filled with faith's words of fire, even if he had left the law practice that had let him see those words of faith show their charitable service to others.

Afterword

THE FAITHFUL LAWYER'S CODE

1.0 ACTIONS

1.1 Serving. Do justice. Matthew 23:23; Luke 11:42. Lay down your life for your friend. John 15:13. Be a servant. Matthew 20:26. Be ready to serve. Luke 12:35. Serve others. Luke 22:26. Serve all. Mark 9:35. Wash one another's feet. John 13:14. Feed the hungry. Matthew 25:35. Invite in the stranger. Matthew 25:35. Invite in the poor, crippled, and blind. Luke 14:13. Clothe the naked. Matthew 25:35. Look after the sick. Matthew 25:36. Put your hands on sick people. Mark 16:18. Heal the sick. Matthew 10:8; Luke 10:9. Visit the prisoner. Matthew 25:36. Do as Jesus did for you. John 13:15.

1.2 Persevering. Lift your head in troubles. Luke 21:28. Do not worry about tomorrow. Matthew 6:34. Do not worry about your life. Luke 12:22. Do not worry how to defend yourself. Luke 21:4. Do not let your heart be troubled. John 14:27. Do not be afraid. Mark 5:36; John 14:27. Do not fear men. Matthew 10:28. Take courage. Matthew 14:27. Stand firm. Luke 21:19. Stand firm to the end. Matthew 24:15. Persevere producing a crop. Luke 8:15.

1.3 Earning. Do not serve money. Matthew 6:24; Luke 16:13. Do not store up for yourself. Luke 12:21. Store up treasure in heaven. Matthew 6:20. Put money to work. Luke 19:13. Be trustworthy with little. Luke 16:10. Pay your taxes. Luke 20:25. Guard against greed. Luke 12:15. Lend without expecting it back. Luke 6:35. Tithe. Matthew 23:23. Bring out good things. Luke 6:45. Bear fruit. Luke 13:9; John 15:2. Do not work for food that spoils. John 6:27. Work for food that endures. John 6:27.

1.4 Succeeding. Do not seek praise from men. John 5:44. Do not love praise from men. John 12:43. Do not love the important seats. Luke 11:43. Do not take the place of honor. Luke 14:8. Take the lowest place. Luke 14:10. Do not exalt yourself. Luke 18:14. Humble yourself. Matthew 23:12; Luke 14:11, 18:14. Say "I am unworthy" when only doing your duty. Luke 17:10. Hunger for righteousness. Matthew 5:6. Let your light shine. Matthew 5:16.

1.5 Giving. Give. Luke 6:38. Do not steal. Luke 18:20. Use wealth to gain friends. Luke 16:9. Give out of your poverty. Mark 12:44; Luke 21:4. Give in secret. Matthew 6:4. Give freely. Matthew 10:8. Give to the believer. Matthew 10:42. Sell what you have. Luke 18:22. Sell your possessions and give to the poor. Matthew 19:21; Luke 12:33. Give what you have to the poor. Luke 11:41. Give to the poor. Luke 18:22. Give to the one who asks. Matthew 5:42. Give to everyone who asks. Luke 6:30. Use gifts. Matthew 25:21.

1.6 Receiving. Do not set your heart on food and drink. Luke 12:29. Do not worry about eating and drinking. Matthew 6:25. Do not worry about what to eat. Luke 12:22. Eat what is set before you. Luke 10:8. Fast without showing it. Matthew 6:17. Hunger. Luke 6:21. Do not worry about what to wear. Matthew 6:25; Luke 12:22. Report what good you see and hear. Luke 7:22.

1.7 Learning. Let no one deceive you. Matthew 24:4. Do not claim that you can see. John 9:41. Clear your eyes. Luke 6:42. See with your eyes. Matthew 13:16; John 12:40. Hear with your ears. Matthew 13:16. Understand with your heart. John 12:40. Interpret the times. Luke 12:56. Let go of the traditions of men. Mark 7:8. Gain knowledge. Luke 11:52. Consider carefully what you hear. Mark 4:24. Be careful of your heart. Luke 21:34. Watch for teachers who bear no fruit. Matthew 7:15. Guard against men. Matthew 10:17. Guard against the Pharisees' teaching. Matthew 16:12. Beware of those who teach rules for show. Luke 20:46. Do not look for the living among the dead. Luke 24:5. Leave blind guides. Matthew 15:14. Understand the word. Matthew 13:23. Retain the word. Luke 8:15.

1.8 Teaching. Tell how much God has done for you. Luke 8:39. Tell how the Lord has had mercy on you. Mark 5:19. Proclaim God's kingdom. Luke 9:60. Be fishers of men. Mark 1:17. Catch men. Luke 5:10. Acknowledge Jesus before men. Matthew 10:32. Teach others to obey Jesus. Matthew 28:20. Do not teach others to break the commandments. Matthew 5:19. Preach the gospel to all. Mark 16:15. Tell others of Jesus's resurrection. Luke 24:9. Talk with others about Jesus. Luke 24:15. Tell what Jesus has done for you. Luke 24:35. Explain the scriptures. Luke 24:27. Speak the word with authority. Luke 7:7.

1.9 Speaking. Speak what Jesus tells you. Matthew 10:27. Speak just what you are taught. John 8:28. Do not speak on your own. John 7:16. Speak no careless words. Matthew 12:36. Stop wailing. Luke 8:52. Speak faith over problems. Matthew 17:21. Do not swear an oath. Matthew 5:34. Let your yes be yes and your no be no. Matthew 5:37. Do not justify yourself to men. Luke 16:14.

1.10 Judging. Do not judge. Matthew 7:1; Luke 6:27. Do not judge by human standards. John 8:15. Stop judging by appearances. John 7:24. Make right judgments. John 7:24. Do not condemn. Luke 6:37. Show a sinning brother his fault. Matthew 18:15. Rebuke a brother who sins. Luke 17:3.

1.11 Sinning. Be clean inside. Matthew 23:26. Do not entertain evil thoughts. Matthew 9:4. Do no evil. Matthew 7:23. Stop sinning. John 5:14. Cut off your hand if it causes you to sin. Matthew 18:7. Leave your life of sin. John 8:11. Do not do the devil's desires. John 8:44. Do not consent to wrong action. Luke 23:51. Do not walk by night. John 11:9. Do not look at another in lust. Matthew 5:28. Do not murder. Luke 18:20. See your own sin before showing others theirs. Matthew 7:5. Choose what is better. Luke 10:42. Do not break the commandments. Matthew 5:19. Obey the commandments. Matthew 19:17. Let go of the traditions of men. Mark 7:8. Understand the word. Matthew 13:23. Cleanse the sinner. Matthew 10:8. Drive out demons. Matthew 10:8.

1.12 Believing. Believe the gospel. Mark 11:15. Do not doubt. Matthew 14:31, 21:21. Do not doubt Jesus's resurrection. Luke 24:38. Believe when others tell of Jesus's resurrection. Luke 24:11. Believe the prophets. Luke 24:25. Stop doubting and believe. John 20:27. Have faith. Matthew 17:20.

1.13 Praying. Pray always. Luke 31:36. Watch always. Luke 21:36. Watch and pray. Matthew 26:41. Do not sleep but wake and pray. Luke 22:46. Pray in secret. Matthew 6:6. Do not pray babbling. Matthew 6:7. Do not pray for the world. John 17:9. Pray for those who mistreat you. Luke 6:28. Pray forgiveness of others. Luke 23:34. Pray "God have mercy on me." Luke 18:13. Pray that Jesus remembers you. Luke 23:43. Ask Jesus for healing. John 4:49. Pray not to be tempted. Luke 22:39. Pray as Jesus taught you. Matthew 6:9. Persist in prayer to God. Luke 18:5. Ask. John 16:24. Ask, seek, and knock. Matthew 7:7; Luke 11:9. Ask in Jesus's name. John 14:13. Believe Jesus is able. Matthew 9:28.

2.0 PERSONS

2.1 Yourself. Lose your life. Luke 9:24, 17:33. Do not love your life. John 12:25. Hate your life. Luke 14:26; John 12:25. Do not seek to please yourself. John 5:30. Deny yourself. Matthew 16:24; Luke 9:23. Do nothing on your own. John 8:28. Give up everything. Luke 14:33. Take your cross. Matthew 10:38; Mark 8:34; Luke 9:23. Carry your cross. Luke 14:27. Enter by the gate. John 10:1. Enter by the narrow door. Luke 13:24. Do not look back. Luke 9:62. Change. Matthew 4:17, 18:3. Turn. John 12:40. Repent. Luke 13:5. Repent under preaching. Luke 11:32. Repent and believe the gospel. Mark 1:15. Be perfect. Matthew 5:48. Walk in the light. John 12:35. Doubt your own righteousness. Luke 18:9. Weep. Luke 6:21. Weep for yourself. Luke 23:28. Guard against hypocrisy. Luke 12:1.

2.2 Others. Stay with the worthy. Matthew 10:11. Stay in church praising God. Luke 24:53. Receive prophets and the righteous. Matthew 10:41. Come together in Jesus's name. Matthew 18:19. Try hard to settle matters. Luke 12:58. Settle quickly with your adversary. Matthew. 5:25. Be a peacemaker. Matthew 5:9. Love one another. John 15:17. Love much. Luke 7:47. Do to others as you would have them do to you. Luke 6:31. Forgive. Luke 6:37. Forgive another's sins. John 20:23. Do not be angry with your brother. Matthew 5:22. Strengthen your brothers. Luke 22:32. Reconcile with your brother. Matthew 5:24. Love your neighbor as yourself. Luke 10:27. Do not burden others. Luke 11:46. Love one another. John 13:34.

2.3 *Family.* Be united to your wife. Mark 10:7. Be faithful to your wife. Luke 18:20. Do not commit adultery. Luke 18:20. Do not separate what God joins. Matthew 19:6. Honor your father and mother. Matthew 15:4; Mark 7:10; Luke 18:20. Love Jesus more than family. Matthew 10:37. Leave home and family for God. Luke 18:29. Tell your family how much the Lord has done for you. Mark 5:19. Do not call any man "father." Matthew 23:9.

2.4 *Children.* Welcome little children. Matthew 18:5. Welcome little children in Jesus's name. Luke 9:48. Do not look down on little children. Matthew 18:19. Do not cause a child to sin. Matthew 18:6. Do not hinder children's faith. Matthew 19:14. Humble yourself like a little child. Matthew 18:4. Become like little children. Matthew 18:3. Be like the youngest. Luke 22:26.

2.5 *God.* Seek God's Kingdom. Matthew 6:33; Luke 12:31. Have in mind God's things. Matthew 16:17; Mark 8:25. Do not test God. Matthew 4:7; Luke 4:12. Serve God only. Matthew 4:10; Luke 4:8. Do the will of God. John 4:34. Give God your fruits. Luke 20:10. Belong to God. John 8:47. Commit your spirit to God. Luke 23:45. Recognize God's coming to you. Luke 19:44. Receive God like a child. Luke 18:17. Love God with everything. Luke 10:27. Praise God for healing. Luke 17:18. Obtain God's praise. John 5:44. Love praise from God. John 12:43. Ask God to send you. Matthew 9:38. Hear what God says. John 8:47. Put God's word into practice. Luke 8:21. Do what God says. Matthew 21:29. Do what pleases God. John 8:29. Obey the word of God. Luke 11:28. Do God's work. John 9:4. Show God's work in your life. John 9:3. Just believe. Mark 5:36. Hold to God's commands. Mark 7:8.

2.6 *Jesus.* Believe in Jesus. Luke 22:67; John 6:29, 11:26. Know Jesus. John 8:19, 14:7. Respect Jesus. Luke 20:13. Accept Jesus. John 3:43. Come to Jesus. Matthew 11:28; John 6:35. Love Jesus. John 14:21. Feed on Jesus. John 6:57. Eat and drink Jesus. John 6:54. Confess Jesus as God's son. Matthew

16:17; Luke 22:70. Do not deny Jesus. Luke 22:61. Acknowledge Jesus before men. Luke 12:8. Follow Jesus. Matthew 4:19; Mark 8:34; Luke 18:22; John 8:12, 12:26, 21:19. Praise Jesus. Luke 19:38. Honor Jesus. John 5:23. Work for Jesus's honor. John 7:16. Remain in Jesus. John 15:4. Remain in Jesus's love. John 15:9. Watch for Jesus's coming. Luke 12:37. Do not be deceived about Jesus's coming. Luke 21:8. Watch for Jesus's return. Matthew 24:42. Listen to Jesus. John 8:37. Listen to Jesus's voice. John 10:16. Listen carefully to Jesus. Luke 9:44. Answer Jesus. Luke 22:68. Remember what Jesus told you. Luke 24:6. Build on Jesus's words. Matthew 7:24. Hold to Jesus's teaching. John 8:31. Do not reject Jesus's words. John 12:48. Keep Jesus's words. John 8:50, 12:47. Take Jesus's yoke. Matthew 11:29. Come to Jesus for rest. Mark 6:31. Urge Jesus to stay with you. Luke 24:29. Recall Jesus's death. Matthew 26:36. Lose your life for Jesus. Matthew 16:25; Mark 8:35. Accept anyone Jesus sends. John 13:20. Stand by Jesus in trials. Luke 22:28. Serve Jesus. John 12:26. Do what Jesus says. Luke 6:46; John 15:14. Do what Jesus did. John 14:12. Do the work Jesus gives you. John 6:27. Feed Jesus's sheep. John 21:17.

2.7 The Holy Spirit. Receive the Holy Spirit. John 20:22. Stay in the Spirit. Matthew 25:4. Abide until you have power. Luke 24:49. Never speak against the Holy Spirit. Matthew 12:32.

2.8 Enemies. Bless those who curse you. Luke 6:28. Rejoice over insults. Matthew 5:12. Do not resist an evil person. Matthew 5:38. Love your enemies. Matthew 5:44; Luke 6:27. Do good to your enemies. Luke 6:35. Do good to those who hate you. Luke 6:27. Forgive those who sin against you. Matthew 6:14. Forgive your brother. Matthew 18:22. Have mercy. Matthew 5:7. Be merciful. Matthew 23:23; Luke 6:36. Flee persecution. Matthew 10:23. Do not demand back what someone takes. Luke 6:30.

Suggested Readings

Counsel:

ADAMS, JAY E., THE CHRISTIAN COUNSELOR'S MANUAL—THE PRACTICE OF NOUTHETIC COUNSELING (Zondervan Pub. House 1973);

ALLEGRETTI, JOSEPH G., THE LAWYER'S CALLING—CHRISTIAN FAITH AND LEGAL PRACTICE (Paulist Press 1996);

KRUIS, JOHN G., QUICK SCRIPTURE REFERENCE FOR COUNSELING (2nd ed. Baker Books).

LEWIS, C.S., SURPRISED BY JOY (C.S. Lewis Pte. Ltd. 1955/HarperCollins 2002);

NEE, WATCHMAN, A BALANCED CHRISTIAN LIFE (Christian Fellowship Pubs. Inc. 1981);

NEE, WATCHMAN, SPIRITUAL AUTHORITY (Christian Fellowship Pubs. Inc. 1972);

NEE, WATCHMAN, THE RICHES OF WATCHMAN NEE (Barbour Pub., Inc. 1999);

PEALE, NORMAN VINCENT, THE POWER OF POSITIVE THINKING FOR YOUNG PEOPLE (Prentice-Hall, Inc. 1954);

SCHUTT, MICHAEL P., REDEEMING LAW—CHRISTIAN CALLING AND THE LEGAL PROFESSION (InterVarsity Press 2007).

Apologetics:

CARSON, D.A., THE GAGGING OF GOD: CHRISTIANITY CONFRONTS PLURALISM (Zondervan Pub. Co. 2002);

CHESTERTON, G.K., THE EVERLASTING MAN (Dodd Mead & Co. 1925/Ignatius 1993);

JOHNSON, TIMOTHY, FINDING GOD IN THE QUESTIONS: A PERSONAL JOURNEY (IVP Books 2004);

LEWIS C.S., MERE CHRISTIANITY (HarperSanFrancisco 2001);

LEWIS, C.S., THE CASE FOR CHRISTIANITY (The Macmillan Co. 1953);

LEWIS, C.S., THE SCREWTAPE LETTERS (C.S. Lewis Pte. Ltd. 1942/HarperCollins Pubs. 2000);

LEWIS, C.S., THE WEIGHT OF GLORY AND OTHER ADDRESSES (Macmillan Pub. Co. 1949/Simon & Schuster 1996);

OURSLER, FULTON, & APRIL OURSLER ARMSTRONG, THE GREATEST FAITH EVER KNOWN (Doubleday & Co. 1953);

SCHAEFFER, FRANCIS A., TRUE SPIRITUALITY (Tyndale House Pubs. 1971).

Theology:

AQUINAS, THOMAS, SUMMA THEOLOGICA, (Regnery Publishing 2001) (1265);

CAMPBELL, JOSEPH, THE HERO WITH A THOUSAND FACES (New World Library 3d ed. 2008);

FINNEY, CHARLES G., PRINCIPLES OF PRAYER (Bethany House Pubs. 1980);

FINNEY, CHARLES G., FINNEY'S SYSTEMATIC THEOLOGY (Bethany House Pubs. 1994);

LEWIS, C.S., THE FOUR LOVES (Harcourt, Brace 1960/1988);

LEWIS, C.S., THE GRAND MIRACLE AND OTHER ESSAYS ON THEOLOGY AND ETHICS (Ballantine Books 1970);

MOLTMANN, JURGEN, THEOLOGY OF HOPE (SCM Press 2010);

NEUSNER, JACOB, THE TALMUD—LAW, THEOLOGY, NARRATIVE (Univ. Press of America 2005);

PHILLIPS, ANTHONY, ESSAYS ON BIBLICAL LAW (Sheffield Academic Press 2002);

PETERSON, EUGENE H., THE MESSAGE (NavPress 1995);

STROBEL, LEE, THE CASE FOR FAITH: A JOURNALIST INVESTIGATES THE TOUGHEST OBJECTIONS TO CHRISTIANITY (Zondervan 2000);

Suggested Readings

STROBEL, LEE, THE CASE FOR CHRIST: A JOURNALIST'S PERSONAL INVESTIGATION OF THE EVIDENCE FOR JESUS (Zondervan 1998).

Relationship:

ALCORN, RANDY, HEAVEN (Tyndale House Pubs. Inc. 2004);

AUGUSTINE, THE CONFESSIONS OF ST. AUGUSTINE (E.M. Blaiklock, trans., Hodder & Stoughton 1983);

BAKER, WILLIAM M., THE TEN THEOPHANIES; OR, THE APPEARANCES OF OUR LORD TO MEN BEFORE HIS BIRTH IN BETHLEHEM (Anson D.F. Randoph & Co. 1883);

BARBOUR, THE BIBLE PROMISE BOOK (Barbour Pub. Inc. 1984);

BISHOP, JIM, THE DAY CHRIST DIED (Harper Bros. 1957);

BRIDGES, JERRY, THE PURSUIT OF HOLINESS (NavPress 1996);

KEMPIS, THOMAS Á, THE IMITATION OF CHRIST (Doubleday 1955/1989);

LEWIS, C.S., GEORGE MACDONALD—AN ANTHOLOGY—365 READINGS (C.S. Lewis Pte. Ltd. 1946/HarperCollins 2001);

LEWIS, C.S., THE GREAT DIVORCE (C.S. Lewis Pte. Ltd. 1946/HarperCollins Pubs. 2001);

NEE, WATCHMAN, THE SPIRITUAL MAN (Christian Fellowship Pubs., Inc. 1968);

SIMPSON, A.B., THE HOLY SPIRIT—POWER FROM ON HIGH (Christian Publications 1994);

SPURGEON, CHARLES, JOY IN CHRIST'S PRESENCE (Whitaker House 1997);

TOZER, THE PURSUIT OF MAN—THE DIVINE CONQUEST OF THE HUMAN HEART (Christian Pubs. 1950).

Journey:

BUNYAN, JOHN, THE PILGRIM'S PROGRESS (Ambassador Prods. Ltd. 1992);

LEWIS, C.S., OUT OF THE SILENT PLANET (Simon & Schuster 1996);

LEWIS, C.S., PERELANDRA (Simon & Schuster 1996);

LEWIS, C.S., THAT HIDEOUS STRENGTH (Scribner 1945/1996);

HURNARD, HANNAH, HINDS' FEET ON HIGH PLACES (Tyndale House Pubs. Inc. 1986);

MACDONALD, GEORGE, ROBERT FALCONER (George Routledge & Sons 1889);

MACDONALD, GORDON, A RESILIENT LIFE (Thomas Nelson, Inc. 2004);

PALMER, PARKER, TO KNOW AS WE ARE KNOWN—EDUCATION AS A SPIRITUAL JOURNEY (HarperColllins 1993);

PASCAL, BLAISE, PENSEES (Nabu Press 2010) (1669);

TERESA OF AVILA, THE WAY OF PERFECTION (Doubleday 1991).

Natural Law:

AMOS, GARY T., DEFENDING THE DECLARATION: HOW THE BIBLE AND CHRISTIANITY INFLUENCED THE WRITING OF THE DECLARATION OF INDEPENDENCE (Wolgemuth & Hyatt, Pubs., Inc. 1989);

BERMAN, HAROLD J., FAITH AND ORDER: THE RECONCILIATION OF LAW AND RELIGION (William B. Eerdmans Pub. Co. 1993);

BEYLEVELD, DERYCK, LAW AS A MORAL JUDGMENT (Sheffield Academic Press 1994);

BURLAMAQUI, JEAN-JACQUES, THE PRINCIPLES OF NATURAL AND POLITIC LAW (Liberty Fund Inc. 2006);

CHARLES, J. DARYL, RETRIEVING THE NATURAL LAW: A RETURN TO MORAL FIRST THINGS (Wm. B. Eerdmans Pub. Co. 2008);

Suggested Readings

DE VATTEL, EMMERICH, THE LAW OF NATIONS (Liberty Fund Inc. 2010);

FINKELSTEIN, JACOB J., THE OX THAT GORED (American Philosophical Society 1981);

FINNIS, JOHN, NATURAL LAW AND NATURAL RIGHTS (1980);

GEORGE, ROBERT P., IN DEFENSE OF NATURAL LAW (Oxford Univ. Press 1999);

GEORGE, ROBERT P., MAKING MEN MORAL: CIVIL LIBERTIES AND PUBLIC MORALITY (Oxford Univ. Press 1995);

GROTIUS, HUGO, THE RIGHTS OF WAR AND PEACE: INCLUDING THE LAW OF NATURE AND OF NATIONS (Cornell Univ. Library 2009);

HAYS, RICHARD B., THE MORAL VISION OF THE NEW TESTAMENT: COMMUNITY, CROSS, NEW CREATION, A CONTEMPORARY INTRODUCTION TO NEW TESTAMENT ETHICS (HarperOne 1996);

HEINECCUS, JOHANN, METHODICAL SYSTEM OF UNIVERSAL LAW WITH SUPPLEMENTS AND A DISCOURSE (Liberty Fund, Inc. 2008);

HIERS, RICHARD H., JUSTICE AND COMPASSION IN BIBLICAL LAW (T.T. Clark Intl. 2009);

PUFENDORF, SAMUEL J., ON THE DUTY OF MAN AND CITIZEN ACCORDING TO NATURAL LAW (Cambridge Univ. Press 1991);

STORY, JOSEPH, COMMENTARIES ON THE CONSTITUTION OF THE UNITED STATES (General Books LLC 2010);

VON PUFENDORF, SAMUEL, ON THE DUTY OF MAN AND CITIZEN ACCORDING TO NATURAL LAW (Oxford Univ. Press 1991) (1673);

WITTE, JOHN, JR., & FRANK S. ALEXANDER, THE TEACHINGS OF MODERN CHRISTIANITY ON LAW, POLITICS, AND HUMAN NATURE (Columbia Univ. Press 2005);

WOLTERSTORFF, NICHOLAS, JUSTICE—RIGHTS AND WRONGS (Princeton Univ. Press 2010).

Science and Philosophy:

BEHE, MICHAEL J., DARWIN'S BLACK BOX: THE BIOCHEMICAL CHALLENGE TO EVOLUTION (Free Press 2nd ed. 2006);

BERGER, PETER, GRACE DAVIE, & EFFIE FOKAS, RELIGIOUS AMERICA, SECULAR EUROPE? A THEME AND VARIATIONS (Ashgate Pub. 2008);

BERMAN, HAROLD J., LAW AND REVOLUTION, THE FORMATION OF THE WESTERN LEGAL TRADITION (Harvard Univ. Press 1983);

DAVIES, PAUL, THE MIND OF GOD—THE SCIENTIFIC BASIS FOR A RATIONAL WORLD (Simon & Schuster 1992);

KANT, IMMANUEL, GROUNDING FOR THE METAPHYSICS OF MORALS (James W. Ellington trans., Hackett Pub. Co. 3d ed. 1993) (1785);

KANT, IMMANUEL, THE PHILOSOPHY OF LAW: AN EXPOSITION OF THE FUNDAMENTAL PRINCIPLES OF JURISPRUDENCE AS THE SCIENCE OF RIGHT (W. Hastie trans., Lawbook Exch., Ltd. 2002) (1796);

PADGETT, ALAN G., SCIENCE AND THE STUDY OF GOD: A MUTUALITY MODEL FOR THEOLOGY AND SCIENCE (Wm. B. Eerdmans Pub. Co. 2003);

POLANYI, MICHAEL, THE TACIT DIMENSION (University of Chicago Press 1966);

POLANYI, MICHAEL, PERSONAL KNOWLEDGE: TOWARDS A POST-CRITICAL PHILOSOPHY (Univ. of Chicago Press 1974);

ROBINSON, MARILYNNE, THE DEATH OF ADAM: ESSAYS ON MODERN THOUGHT (Picador 2005).

Politics:

ARISTOTLE, NICOMACHEAN ETHICS (Oxford Univ. Press 1998) (350 B.C.);

CICERO, ON DUTIES (DE OFFICIIS) (Walter Miller trans., Harvard Univ. Press 1961) (44 B.C.);

DREISBACH, DANIEL, MARK DAVID HALL, & JEFFRY H. MORRISON, EDS., THE FORGOTTEN FOUNDERS ON RELIGION AND PUBLIC LIFE (Univ. of Notre Dame Press 2009);

SUGGESTED READINGS

HABERMAS, JURGEN, BETWEEN NATURALISM AND RELIGION (Polity Press 2008);

HELTZEL, PETER GOODWIN, JESUS AND JUSTICE: EVANGELICALS, RACE, AND AMERICAN POLITICS (Yale Univ. Press 2009);

LEDEWITZ, BRUCE, CHURCH, STATE, AND THE CRISIS IN AMERICAN SECULARISM (Indiana Univ. Press 2011);

MILLER, WILLIAM G., FAITH, REASON, AND CONSENT—LEGISLATING MORALITY IN EARLY AMERICAN STATES (LFB Scholarly Publishing 2008);

MUNOZ, VINCENT PHILLIP, GOD AND THE FOUNDERS: MADISON, WASHINGTON, AND JEFFERSON (Cambridge Univ. Press 2009);

PEARCEY, NANCY, TOTAL TRUTH—LIBERATING CHRISTIANITY FROM ITS CULTURAL CAPTIVITY (Crossway Books 2004);

WEIGEL, GEORGE, THE CUBE AND THE CATHEDRAL—EUROPE, AMERICA, AND POLITICS WITHOUT GOD (Basic Books 2005).

Management:

BEAUSAY, WILLIAM, II, THE PEOPLE SKILLS OF JESUS—ANCIENT WISDOM FOR MODERN BUSINESS (Thomas Nelson Inc. 1997);

BLOOM, STEPHEN, THE BELIEVER'S GUIDE TO LEGAL ISSUES (Living Ink Books 2008);

FOSTER, RICHARD J., FREEDOM OF SIMPLICITY (Harper & Row 1989);

MACARTHUR, JOHN, TWELVE ORDINARY MEN—HOW THE MASTER SHAPED HIS DISCIPLES FOR GREATNESS AND WHAT HE WANTS TO DO WITH YOU (Nelson Books 2002);

MANDINO, OG, THE GREATEST SALESMAN IN THE WORLD (Frederick Fell, Inc. 1968).

CPSIA information can be obtained
at www.ICGtesting.com
Printed in the USA
LVOW13s1203060317
526272LV00005B/975/P